MEETING JESUS AT UNI

The significance of student Christian groups for the spiritual development of young adults is widely acknowledged, and here Dr Edward Dutton explores the nature of their influence and the way in which this connects with other aspects of university life. A major strength of this work is its international perspective, drawing on ethnographic research from six different locations around the world. The combination of individual stories with discussion of wider methodological issues in the study of religion provides invaluable understandings of the nature of student Christian societies as well as offering social scientists new tools with which to reflect on a little understood aspect of university life.

John Drane, author of *The McDonaldization of the Church*

This comparative and international study touches the heart of religious identity as shaped by social class, life-contexts that hinder or foster maturity, and by the actual nature of each university. Pivoting around anthropologcal ideas of liminality in rites of passage it describes different kinds of uncertainty surrounding younger adults as they may move away from home, encounter religious groups and begin to develop a sense of life's meaning. It seeks to offer an Applied Anthropology that may feed back into evangelical groups and the way they believe they 'Meet Jesus at University.'

Professor Douglas Davies, Durham University, UK

Meeting Jesus at University is one of the rare books that will be influential both for the academic anthropological community and that of the practicing Christian. This book will also be an essential text for those who seek to develop Christianity in universities, giving them a better understanding of why particular types of approach will be more or less successful depending on the nature of the academic institution. I highly recommend this book as both an engaging and informative contribution.

Professor Seth D Kunin, Durham University, UK

Meeting Jesus at University

Rites of Passage and Student Evangelicals

EDWARD DUTTON

Routledge
Taylor & Francis Group
LONDON AND NEW YORK

First published 2008 by Ashgate Publishing

Published 2016 by Routledge
2 Park Square, Milton Park, Abingdon, Oxon OX14 4RN
605 Third Avenue, New York, NY 10017

First issued in paperback 2021

Routledge is an imprint of the Taylor & Francis Group, an informa business

Publisher's Note
The publisher has gone to great lengths to ensure the quality of this reprint but points out that some imperfections in the original copies may be apparent.

British Library Cataloguing in Publication Data
Dutton, Edward
Meeting Jesus at university : rites of passage and student evangelicals
1. Christian college students – Religious life – Great Britain 2. Evangelistic work – Great Britain 3. Identity (Psychology) – Religious aspects – Christianity
I. Title
378.1'98'08823

Library of Congress Cataloging-in-Publication Data
Dutton, Edward, 1980–
Meeting Jesus at University : rites of passage and student evangelicals / Edward Dutton.
p. cm.
Includes bibliographical references and index.
ISBN 978-0-7546-6520-5 (hardcover : alk. paper)
1. College students – Religious life. 2. Universities and colleges – Religion. 3. Evangelicalism. I. Title.

BV639.C6D88 2008
259'.24–dc22

2008009558

ISBN 13: 978-1-03-209957-6 (pbk)
ISBN 13: 978-0-7546-6520-5 (hbk)

For with wisdom comes much sorrow;
the more knowledge, the more grief.
(Ecclesiastes 1:18)

Contents

Preface

It is likely that almost everybody reading this book has been to university and some readers may even still be there. As I hope will become clear through the course of the book, there are many different kinds of university and a student's university experience can be very different – and indeed far more or less traumatic – depending on the kind of university that they attend. University is, to varying degrees, a Rite of Passage: a time when young people have their identities challenged, remoulded and even fundamentally changed as they become adults. When I began at university myself, I became aware fairly quickly of the potential for my university at least to bring about these kinds of changes and one of the most noticeable ways that it did this was through creating a situation where some students felt the need to join their own highly structured societies and in particular the Christian Union. The main purpose of this religiously conservative group was to preserve 'Christian' students as 'Christians' and to convert 'non-Christians' to Christianity – 'To Change and to Preserve' as Helander (1986) has so trenchantly put it. At the exact time when identity was being challenged, the Christian Union was there to offer a new identity to students left questioning who they really were. This book will examine the relationship between universities, the intensity to which they are a Rite of Passage and the evangelical student groups operating within them. The book is primarily aimed at Religious Studies scholars but I hope it will also allow any readers, no matter what their academic interest, who have been to university to further understand what they experienced while they were there and how and why their specific university experience may have modelled and changed them.

There are a number of people I would like to thank. This book is partly based on my doctoral thesis. I would like to thank Rabbi Prof. Seth Kunin who supervised the thesis at Aberdeen University and helped me to develop my ideas. Thanks are also due to Dr Jonathan Miles-Watson, a fellow Religious Studies doctoral student at Aberdeen University, for his advice on this study. In addition, I would also like to thank the Arts and Humanities Research Board for the funding that they provided and also my parents and my wife for their support. I am grateful to Rev'd Prof. Douglas Davies who first introduced me to Religious Studies when I was an undergraduate student of his and, indeed, inspired me to pursue research into student evangelical groups as well as subsequently giving me detailed criticism on the research. Prof. H.J. de Jonge appointed me a Guest Researcher in the Theology Department at Leiden University which allowed me to conduct my research there so I would also like to thank him.

There are relatively few scholars who have studied student evangelism and most of them helped me either through correspondence, conversation, sending me literature or all of these. In that regard I would like to thank Prof. Steve Bruce, Dr Alyssa Bryant, Prof. Simon Coleman, Rev'd Prof. Leslie Francis, Prof. Eila Helander, Dr Christy Moran, Prof. H.C. Stoffels and Dr John Turner. There is relatively little literature on student evangelism and I hope that this book makes a contribution to this under-studied but important area. A number of sections of this book have been published in various academic journals and I would like to thank the editors of *The Journal of Religion and Popular Culture*, *The Journal of Finnish Studies*, *Dutch Crossing* and *Acta Ethnographica Hungarica* for permission to reuse these sections as well as the anonymous peer-reviewers of these publications for their insightful criticisms and ideas.

I have found my fieldwork fascinating and I would like to thank all of the evangelical Christians with whom I worked during my research, many of whom have become friends, as well as those at Durham University who first got me so interested in student evangelism not least through their attempts to witness to me. There are numerous student evangelicals whom I would like to thank personally and space prevents me from doing so. But in particular thanks should go to Stanton, the Christian Union staff-worker in Aberdeen, who offered me many insights into my work from an evangelical perspective.

Finally, I would like to thank my friends on the corridor where I lived as a first year undergraduate at the College of St Hild and St Bede. It was an intense experience for many and it certainly played a significant part in my deciding to pursue the course of research that I have. I dedicate this book to them.

Edward Dutton
16 December 2007
Oulu, Finland

List of Abbreviations

AUCU	Aberdeen University Christian Union
CICCU	Cambridge Inter-Collegiate Christian Union
CSL	*Christelijk Studenten Leiden*
CU	Christian Union
DICCU	Durham Inter-Collegiate Christian Union
ELF	Evangelical Lutheran Church of Finland
Exec	Executive Committee
IFES	International Fellowship of Evangelical Students
Int.	Interview
IVCF	Inter-Varsity Christian Fellowship
OICCU	Oxford Inter-Collegiate Christian Union
OKO	*Oulun kristitut opiskelijat*
SCP	Social and Cultural Planning Office of the Netherlands
UCCF	University and Colleges Christian Fellowship

Chapter 1

The Corridor Where Jesus Lived

As soon as the new students arrived, the Christian Union set about introducing them to Jesus.

In my case, their evangelism began the second that my father parked in front of the small out-building of Durham University's College of St Hild and St Bede where I would be living for the next year. My parents and I were immediately approached by a very friendly third year called Peter who offered to help us unpack the car. He then went about assisting the other students on my corridor in unloading their parents' cars as well. It was October 1999 and we ranged in age from seventeen to nineteen, with most us leaving home for the first time.

About half an hour later, I was chatting to some of my new neighbours in the corridor when Peter approached me saying:

'Ok, Ed! It was really nice to meet you! I've left you an invitation to a party that we're having. The invitation's in your room. It'd be really great if you could come along!'

Durham University has a reputation for being a kind of 'mini' or 'wannabe' Oxford – a 'traditional' university where there are numerous students from privileged backgrounds with many students only there because they were rejected by Oxford or Cambridge.[1] So I imagined some kind of cocktail do. In fact, it was an invitation to the 'Hild Bede College Christian Union Chocolate Party'. I had never heard of the 'Christian Union' but as I was about to start a degree in Theology I was immediately interested. Only much later did I realise that the friendliness that I had just experienced was a form of 'witness evangelism' – living out the Gospel through everyday interaction.

The next few days were a blur of university ritual. That very afternoon we went to a drinks reception in the college's main hall and then to a semi-formal dinner for which we had to wear suits. This was followed by a 'Bop' (disco) that went on well into the night. Afterwards, almost everybody on our corridor ended up at an impromptu party in a particular student's room.

Even before the party, I had already met another 'Christian'. The student on my corridor from the prestigious 'public school'[2] Eton later informed me that he was

---

1 This point has been made by Margolis (22 September 1999) for example in a newspaper article on the Christian Union at Durham University and in the light-hearted booklet *A Bluffer's Guide to University* (Ainsworth 1999).

2 A 'public school' is a prestigious and usually single sex private school in Britain where pupils often board. In the USA, the same term is used to describe what in England would be called 'state schools' and specifically 'Comprehensives'. The English school system will be examined in more detail in Chapter 2.

reading for a degree in Arabic because God had told him to and he wanted to convert Muslims. At the impromptu party we somehow got talking about religion. Two female students claimed to be 'Christians' and it subsequently transpired that neither of them believed in Evolution. The fifteen room corridor was, it seemed, very geographically, socially and religiously mixed (with an independent evangelical, evangelical Anglicans, liberal Anglicans, two Roman Catholics, a Muslim international student and various atheists and agnostics). But despite these differences, there nevertheless seemed to be a strong sense of camaraderie – or what we will later call *communitas* – in those early days. There was a tangible feeling of togetherness.

By the end of the week, when it was time for the Chocolate Party, a kind of division had already developed on the corridor between those who were 'Christian' and everybody else. The three 'Christians' (who defined 'Christian' to mean only evangelicals) and another female student who was a liberal Anglican, had begun an early morning prayer meeting. The Arabic student had decorated his room almost exclusively with quotes from the Bible printed from his computer. At the college 'Freshers' Fair' (where student societies relating to hobbies, academic subjects and politics encourage you to join them) the Christian Union (CU) had a prominent stall and was leafleting various passing Freshers with information packs. Five people on my corridor joined 'DICCU' (the Durham Inter-Collegiate Christian Union) and, unlike with any other society (including political parties), they had to assent to certain stated views – the 'Declaration of Faith' – in order to do so. The Declaration implied that non-Christians would go to Hell and that Evolutionary Theory (as well as Catholicism) was incompatible with 'Christian' belief. Already, some of this group had told interested neighbours, when asked, that they would go to Hell if they did not become 'Christians' and that being a Christian was something you had to 'become' through 'giving yourself' to God. You were not a 'Christian' simply because you believed yourself to be one.

A number of us on the corridor eventually went to the Chocolate Party. There were various 'getting to know you' games and a lot of chocolate eating. Then the CU President introduced a third year student called Naomi and she arose to give her 'testimony'. Naomi said that her parents were Church of England and went to church regularly but that they 'weren't truly Christian'. When she had arrived at university, she had thought that she was a 'Christian' but, upon joining DICCU, realised that she was not a Christian and that she was going to 'go to Hell'. Then one day, on our corridor (where she had lived two years earlier), Naomi was having a shower when Jesus appeared to her in the room and invited her to 'follow Him'. Almost with tears in her eyes, she told us that she gave herself to Jesus that very day and finished by saying, 'I know that my place in Heaven is secure'. I stayed and talked to Naomi in depth, never having met anybody who had had such an experience in my life, and I listened to a speech by the CU President. A few days later, the CU President came to my room to ask me about my views on Christianity as did Peter – rather frequently – under the pretext of 'seeing how I was'.

Throughout the first term, there were university-wide Christian Union meetings at least twice a week as well as 'College CU' and 'prayer mornings'. Most CU members would go to church twice on Sundays – the majority to a particular church called Claypath United Reformed. Early the following term somebody else on my corridor – who was an atheist and not from a religious background at all – had a 'religious experience' where God appeared to him in his bedroom. Then in March there was a Christian Union 'Mission Week' where DICCU attempted to evangelise to the whole university. Around this time, one of the 'Christian' females on my corridor had a religious experience and realised that she had not become a Christian when she was fifteen, as she had previously said, but only now after this new experience of Jesus which had left her weeping on her bed about the possibility of going to Hell. A liberal Anglican student on the corridor also became a 'Christian' around this time and broke-up with her 'non-Christian' boyfriend partly as a consequence. DICCU members tended to be very strict in terms of lifestyle and especially sexual ethics. Dating 'non-Christians' also appeared to be unacceptable as did the heavy drinking culture which was common at the university.

Back in London, during the holidays, I found that my friends from school – most of whom were at former Polytechnics (which mainly offer vocational degrees) – had had no such experience of a highly organised, evangelical student group even though these groups existed on their campuses. However, there were – it seemed at least anecdotally – comparable groups at universities such as Oxford, Cambridge and Bristol. I began to wonder if there was something about the more established universities in England which meant that what would commonly be called 'fundamentalist' evangelical Christian groups (highly differentiated in belief and lifestyle) were more likely to develop than at other universities. On my own corridor there were minor aristocrats from Eton mixing with lower-middle-class students from northern English Comprehensives. For those students especially, going to this university marked a considerable change in lifestyle and, potentially, even social status. Evangelical Christians were forced to live with fervent atheists. People were forced to live and eat with people who they would be very unlikely to associate with outside of university. Most had never lived away from home (though some had been to boarding school and/or taken a Gap Year), all were a very long way from home, most had never previously had sexual relationships and few had been exposed to evangelical Christianity.

In a sense, the very structure of the university – in terms of accommodation but also in terms of various 'levelling' rituals such as 'formal dinners' – forced students together with people from very different backgrounds and with very different ideas, challenging their social position and bringing their world-view – and thus identity – into question. Perhaps as a consequence, cliques seemed to develop on the corridor which tended to overlap and were often based around social class or religious belief. Hence, there was a 'Christian' clique, a 'public school' clique (part of a broader university stereotype known as 'Rahs') and various others as well as those who were on the borders of these cliques. However, the 'Christian clique' was far more significant than 'Rahs' because it was not as loose. It was a localised part of a clearly defined, structured and highly counter-cultural university organisation which aimed to offer a new identity to the broader university.

Was this development necessary because the university was more transitional and thus more identity-challenging for many students than other universities? Did this challenge mean that students needed to retreat into little cliques of identity security where the world made sense? Indeed, did the fact that the university was identity challenging render the CU highly attractive to some outsiders – precisely because it offered a strong identity – leading, in some cases, to conversion (or re-conversion) and CU membership? Was that why, on my corridor alone, at least four students 'met with Jesus' over two years? Did the very structure of Durham University mean that students were more likely to meet Jesus there than at other universities and, indeed, more likely to meet Him due to a strongly differentiated and highly conservative student evangelical group?

Student Evangelism: An Under-researched Area

Even as a first year undergraduate, I thought that the possible connection between the degree to which a university was – in anthropological terms – a Rite of Passage (affecting status change and identity challenge) for students and the degree to which the university's main evangelical group was structured and differentiated was a fascinating question. It was important, if for no other reason, because highly evangelical groups – offering a strong identity – were possibly at their most fervent in environments where students' identities were the most challenged and thus where they were the most likely to be attracted to the new identity offered to them by the CU. Equally, I suspected – though I had not researched it – that university did indeed seem to parallel, in many respects, the kinds of traumatic Rites of Initiation that have been documented in various tribes where young men are taken away from the tribe ('separated'), inculcated with its ideas through violence and on return raised to the status of men (e.g. Bloch 1992, Ch. 1).

I was surprised to find that there was no specific research into this connection and relatively little in-depth, published social scientific research into student evangelism at all. Where it did exist, it tended to look at one CU in one university rather than compare different CUs and different university environments. Paul Bramadat (2000) has examined the Christian Union at McMaster University in Canada focusing on its evangelistic technique, Eila Helander (1986) has looked at the Christian Union in Trinidad in the 1980s while sociologist Steve Bruce (1978) has produced an article looking at 'Witness Evangelism' in an anonymous Scottish CU and a comparison (Bruce 1984) between the CU and the more liberal Student Christian Movement as broad, national organisations. Hammond and Hunter's (1984) article looks specifically at the world-view of American evangelical students and the means by which evangelical student groups maintain them as 'Christians' focusing on Campus Crusade for Christ and another student evangelical group called the Navigators. Drawing upon wide social survey, they find that evangelical student groups tend to be more fervent in their views at secular colleges than at Christian colleges, claiming that a 'fortress mentality' develops (233). Also Magolda and Ebben (2006) have presented an ethnography of an anonymous American student evangelical group while Moran (2007) and Moran *et al* (2007) have looked at the experiences of student evangelicals as part of a broader interest in education. Alyssa Bryant has examined the experiences of American undergraduate student evangelicals – again from an educationalist perspective – in an ethnographic article (Bryant 2005). I am not aware of any other published social scientific examinations of student evangelism and certainly there are no other published monographs on this subject. Francis (1992) and Francis *et al* (1999) have used Christian Union members to test a particular psychological method but have not conducted participant observation fieldwork with the groups.

There are also a small number of published historical discussions on student evangelism. Stoffels (1982) has written an article in Dutch on the history of the Dutch branches of evangelical student group 'the Navigators'. Goodhew's (2003) article examines the history of the Cambridge Inter-Collegiate Christian Union (CICCU) in the twentieth century and John Turner (2008) has produced a history of Campus Crusade for Christ in the USA. Otherwise, I am not aware of any other academic studies of student evangelism though there are a number of histories of the British Christian Union movement (e.g Barclay and Horn 2002, Barclay 1997 and Barclay 1977), many written from an insider evangelical perspective. Theologian Donald Coggan (1934) also provides a detailed history of the movement up until the 1930s written from a purely academic perspective.

Considering the salience of Christian Unions as organisations which offer identity in a time, for many, of identity crisis when they are most vulnerable to the attractions of a strong identity, I would submit that university evangelical groups are a field in which considerably more research is needed, especially from a social scientific perspective. However, there is also relatively little detailed research into university as a Rite of Passage. Psychoanalyst Anthony Stevens (1982) devotes a few pages to speculate about this idea drawing upon Turner (1969) and arguing that the tribal Rite of Passage separates boys from the power of the mother and that university parallels this. Morris (1969, Ch. 7) also argues this point in his zoological book *The Human Zoo.* Morris suggests that universities such as Oxford – like a tribal Rite of Passage – involve separation, inculcation with tribal knowledge through the trauma (reflected in high suicide rates) of exams, cliques and even failed relationships; the deliberate symbolic breaking-down of social boundaries and even intimidating tribal dress in the form of academic robes and so forth. Though this is fascinating, Morris does not go into considerable depth here drawing upon detailed fieldwork. Also, Fox (2004, 266–70) argues in her anthropological examination of 'the English' that university is a Rite of Passage in England. But, again, this is speculative in many places and is, anyway, a relatively short discussion.

As such, this book aims to make an original contribution to the field in two key ways. Firstly, it will examine six very different universities from six very different cultural environments and it will examine the degree to which they operate as modern Rites of Passage for students. In Victor Turner's (1969) terms, the book will look at the degree to which these universities are phases of transition – 'liminal' phases leading to status elevation – for students. It will also examine the extent to which they bring about *communitas* – a breakdown, within certain parameters, of the normal social structure existing outside of the Rite of Passage. The book will argue, drawing upon a combination of personal participant observation fieldwork and primary research, that, in general, Oxford University in England, Augustine Campus in Trinidad and many of the public, campus-based, residential American universities are highly liminal Rites of Passage which are structured in such a way as to precipitate *communitas.* By contrast, Aberdeen University in Scotland, Leiden University in the Netherlands and, in particular, Oulu University in Finland will be shown to be far less liminal. The book will then examine this broad array of universities in order to test whether the model of liminality that it proposes can be applied in different national and religious cultural environments. Each nation compared will be shown to have a somewhat different religious culture.

Secondly, the book will examine the most prominent student evangelical group at each university in order to understand the relationship between the degree to which the university is a liminal Rite of Passage and the degree to which the main student evangelical group is structured and differentiated. In so doing, it will aim to answer the questions posed above and understand whether or not there is something in the very structure of certain universities that encourages the formation of differentiated evangelical groups which attract non-Christians. As we have already seen, such an examination of student evangelical groups has not previously been conducted.

Communitas or Contestation?

This book also aims to make an original contribution in terms of our understanding of the nature of the Rite of Passage. This term will be discussed in more detail below but there are, in essence, two schools of thought amongst social anthropologists of religion with regard to the nature of the Rite of Passage or liminal phase. Turner's (1969) *Communitas* Model argues, drawing upon tribal initiations, that in a liminal phase – within the boundaries of the Rite of Passage set by the instructors – there develops *communitas*, a feeling of togetherness and bonding in which social distinctions break down. Eade and Sallnow (1991, 5) draw upon examinations of pilgrimage to dispute this. In the *Contestation Model* they argue that the pilgrimage, which Turner also claims exemplifies a liminal phase, involves a variety of reactions from pilgrims ranging from *communitas* to clear – even exaggerated – boundary-making procedures. Thus, it at best involves a kind of incomplete *communitas*. My fieldwork began as an attempt to apply Turner's model to an under-researched area in Religious Studies. However, I eventually concluded that neither his model nor Eade and Sallnow's rejection of it (a critique aimed at pilgrimage though potentially applicable to Rites of Initiation) appeared to fit what I was observing. This book will aim to reconcile these two positions by examining the issue in terms of level; to a certain degree in a structural manner. It will argue – drawing upon the examinations of university evangelical groups – that a Rite of Passage involves *communitas* but a concomitant reassertion of structure on another level because *communitas* is psychologically difficult (Turner 1982, 46). It will further be demonstrated that this reassertion leads to another level of structure and then another level of *communitas*. Structure and anti-structure thus breed each other anew on different levels. As such, the book will demonstrate, for example, that Oxford University is highly structured and this structure leads to a high level of *communitas*. This, in turn, is reflected in a highly structured and differentiated Christian Union. However, the Christian Union leads to a *communitas* of 'all being Christian' or 'all praying together' meaning that structure is further reasserted with, for example, students from higher social backgrounds tending to run the CU. By contrast, Leiden University will be shown to be relatively unstructured, leading to relatively little *communitas* and a relatively unstructured CU. Of course, it might be countered that these differences reflect differences in religious culture, church politics and national culture rather than liminality and these possibilities will be addressed and substantially rejected.

In this first chapter, before moving on to the examination of each university and corresponding student evangelical group, we will look at a number of methodological models which will be drawn upon in arguing the model of Rites of Passage outlined above. Firstly, we will discuss the notion of Rites of Passage within anthropology and we will argue in favour of the idea that universities – broadly at least – can be understood to be a modern Rite of Passage. Secondly, we will examine the issue of social class as this will be significant in understanding the social dynamics of Oxford University's Christian Union in particular. Thirdly, we will discuss the nature of evangelical Christianity and different forms of religious group as these relate to our discussion. Fourthly, we will look at, from a psychological perspective, the nature of dissociation and conversion experience as both will be significant in understanding the degree of which a university evangelical group or the university in which it operates is liminal and fosters *communitas*.

Rites of Passage

Turner draws upon Gennep (Gennep 1960) with the implicit view that life is divided up into a series of clear stages such as childhood, adulthood, old-age and so forth. When a person passes between one stage and the next – such as by going from being a child to being an adult – then a ritual is necessary to mark this passing. This, Gennep argues, is found across numerous societies. This ritual is called a Rite of Passage because a person is in the 'passage' between one clearly defined phase of life and another. This transitional rite is the central part of a ritual including, in some cases, various sub-rituals namely the 'Rite of Separation', when a neophyte is ritually separated, and the 'Rite of Incorporation', when the neophyte is ritually brought back into society.

Rites of Passage involve a 'passenger' passing through a gap between two clearly defined existential phases. Turner looks at the initiation ritual of teenage boys of the Ndembu tribe in Zambia to examine the Rite of Passage. Turner terms this period 'betwixt and between'; a 'liminal phase'. The word 'liminal' is drawn from the Latin 'limen', meaning 'corridor', a passage between one room and another. In this passage, the passenger (or 'neophyte' as Turner terms him) experiences a 'state of transition' which differs markedly from his previous pre-liminal or his future post-liminal experience. This passage tends to involve 'segregation, marginality and aggregation' (Turner 1969, 94). In this phase, the passenger lacks a specific place in 'cultural space'. He is made 'passive and humble' and, indeed, 'ground down to be refashioned anew'. Neophytes are deliberately traumatised and must undergo physically and mentally arduous tasks. As a consequence, the fellow-passengers tend to experience a strong sense of togetherness in which social distinctions and structure become less relevant. Turner terms this feeling *communitas* (95). For Turner '*Communitas* is where structure is not' (126). He earlier defines *communitas* less starkly, admitting that it can involve 'rudimentary structure' (96). However, *communitas* develops within the broader structure of the Rite of Passage. Turner makes clear that 'neophytes' must 'obey their instructors ... and accept arbitrary punishment without complaint' (95).

Turner also distinguishes between the 'liminal' and the 'liminoid'. The distinction between these two is quite nuanced. The 'liminoid' tends to be noted in industrial societies. In such complex societies, people's work lives are segmented into different groups that might have little actual contact. Thus, the city or office-worker is likely to have no contact with the farm labourer even though they are members of the same albeit complex society. These workers are controlled, more so than in tribal societies, by structured time and rhythm. They must get to work at a certain time, leave at a certain time, even catch a specific train every single morning. The liminoid is understood, by Turner, to be a break from such rigidity in the form of leisure time for example. To suddenly decide to go to a boxing match after work one day is liminoid. Thus, the liminoid is a ritual that is a break with societal structure. By contrast, the 'liminal' is a ritual that is part of societal structure, as in the pubescent rituals of the Ndembu (Turner 1992, 54–56). Liminality is perceived to be less likely in a fragmented, industrial society. However, Turner admits that the liminoid can be found in tribal societies and that the liminal can be found in industrial societies in the form of Church and even academic rituals. He further notes the way in which 'today's liminoid is tomorrow's liminal', (Turner 1992, 58) citing the way in which pilgrimage gradually became part of the structure of Medieval Christianity, having previously been liminoid.

Turner distinguishes between different types of *communitas*. Firstly, there is *existential-spontaneous communitas*. He gives the example of hippie groups as conforming to this type. It is sudden and almost entirely unstructured. Second is *Normative Communitas*. Here, the original *existential-spontaneous communitas* has been organised into a social system which attempts to maintain the *communitas*. Finally there is *Ideological Communitas*, in which a utopian group is formed around the original *communitas* (Turner 1969, 132). In tribal societies, however, these liminal rituals can be divided into two kinds according to Turner. Firstly, there are 'life-crisis rituals'. These tend to occur at times of physical or social development – an example might be a funeral or the process of giving birth. These can, themselves, be subdivided into 'status elevation rituals' such as marriage and 'status reversal rituals' as in the case of the 'humbled chief'. I would, however, point out that these two kinds of ritual tend to be very different in result. The former tends to be permanent while the latter is only temporary and, perhaps, provides some kind of emotional release for the community before the original situation is restored.[3] Turner argues that pilgrimage is a status raising ritual (Turner 1992). The other type of ritual highlighted by Turner is the 'Ritual of Affliction'. This is performed on individuals who are perceived to have been possessed. It is, effectively, a ritual of exorcism which, through the removal of the spirit, affects status change. Exorcisms can, of course, still be seen in many contemporary Pentecostal groups. Both, however, are characterised by a ritual allowing a person to separate from the group, between one realm and another.

[3] An example of such a ritual might be the Roman ritual of Saturnalia in which the masters served their slaves and gave them gifts once a year (Morris 1992, 30).

Criticisms of Turner's *Communitas* Model

Turner's view that a liminal phase will involve *communitas* has been criticised by Eade and Sallnow on empirical grounds. Turner cites the pilgrimage as being a liminal phase. They claim that, certainly in the context of a pilgrimage, there often appears to be evidence of boundary-making procedures and strong animosities between pilgrims (Eade and Sallnow 1991). Eade later argues that the pilgrimage involves *communitas* which is only partially realised. The pilgrimage shrine stimulates a drive to consensus in some but a drive to factionalism in others due to the 'universalism proclaimed by the shrine' (Eade 2000, xii). For Eade, therefore, Turner's model is problematic because it presents a universal model – or 'archetype' as it has been termed (Bowman 1985, 3) – which fails to take into account the varying nature of pilgrimage between and within cultures. Eade and Sallnow, in essence, find that pilgrimage is far more complicated than Turner suggests.

Eade and Sallnow have presented a thought-provoking critique but I think that there is even further room for refinement and that such refinement may allow us to reconcile the two models. Firstly, if we examine a Rite of Passage comparatively in terms of different levels of structure and liminality – rather than simply implying, as Turner does, that *communitas* is some kind of absolute – then we can allow Turner's model to take cultural issues into account because we can see how the degree of *communitas* brought about by a pilgrimage varies between cultures or even subcultures. In this sense, Turner's model can be salvaged in a nuanced form whereby the *communitas* and factionalism are interrelated within the same broader model as we will see. I think this also develops Eade and Sallnow because it presents a model than can be applied and thus attempts to structure and understand the Rite of Passage as well as accepting that it may be highly complex.

Secondly, pilgrimage is somewhat different from the Rites of Initiation that Turner assesses. Many pilgrimages might be regarded as much less clearly status-raising by comparison. Moreover, a pilgrimage is not always structured in the same manner as a tribal initiation which, in Turner's ethnography, seems to effectively force *communitas* as we will observe that some universities do. Turner's in-depth assessment of the Ndembu of Zambia portrays a highly structured initiation ritual in which Ndembu boys are taken away into the forest and inculcated with the knowledge of the tribe through, in effect, trauma brought on by violence and ritual. If my model is correct, we would expect this to lead to a high level of *communitas* at least on one level. Eade and Sallnow are criticising Turner's *Communitas* model by drawing upon examinations of pilgrimage. There has been much discussion of pilgrimage as a liminal phase (such as Coleman and Eade 2004) but it appears that pilgrimage is not always as highly structured as Ndembu initiation. In these cases, we would expect the level of *communitas* to be far lower and indeed 'partially realised' or at least not considerable and it might therefore result in some reassertion of structure but this might not be considerable. Indeed, differences between the pilgrims would be observable because a high level of *communitas* had not been developed in the first place because the whole ritual is not heavily structured. However, we might expect the exaggerated 'boundary-making procedures' between pilgrims that Eade and Sallnow refer to in a context where, at least to some extent, social structure has been brought into question and some form of *communitas* has developed. Obviously this would vary according to the place of pilgrimage within society, the transitional nature of the pilgrimage for the individual and so forth and this model allows these differences to be taken into account in a way that Turner's does not.

As such, I think that Eade and Sallnow's *contestation* critique can be met and reconciled with Turner's *communitas* model if, as will be argued in this book, we examine the Rite of Passage in terms of levels of structure. I also think that Eade and Sallnow's observation of factionalism can be further refined by examining the dynamics of such factions within the context of the Rite of Passage. Turner has assessed a highly structured ritual and reached the *communitas* model before applying it to pilgrimage. Eade and Sallnow have employed, in general I think, a somewhat less structured ritual to observe a lack of *communitas* which is 'partially realised' as well as 'boundary-making procedures' which we would still expect if there was some *communitas.* The two can be reconciled into a broader model by comparing like rituals – in this case initiation rituals – where the level of structure varies. Thus, this book will argue that the more structured the initiation ritual is in a society, the more it will create *communitas.* But in turn the higher the *communitas* the stronger the structural counter-reaction – or boundary-making procedures – will be. Each structure then breeds *communitas* anew. This structural model thus helps to explain the very different conclusions reached by Turner and Eade and Sallnow in understanding different Rites of Passage. In an early review of Turner's *The Ritual Process,* Schwartz (1972) asked whether the 'pseudo-oppositions' observed by Turner amongst Ndembu neophytes were really 'pseudo'. I would argue that they may not be but they would still be congruous with a broader intense *communitas* and, indeed, a product of it.

University as a Rite of Passage

I think that there is a strong case for arguing that university at its broadest is a kind of Rite of Initiation though, as will be argued below, the degree to which this Rite of Initiation is liminal can be seen to vary substantially leading to very different university experiences and very different evangelical student groups. In general, however, I think that there is a reasonable case for agreeing with Morris (1969, 239) that the entire education system – including school – has developed into a kind of highly extended Rite of Passage, though obviously the degree of liminality varies. If we focus on England, to give just one example, school appears to parallel tribal initiations, though in a much diluted form. Pupils go to school during the day and are separated from their families until they come home in late afternoon. In some more prestigious private schools, they board at school during term time. While in school, there are various structural methods of creating *communitas* between pupils. For example, in England most pupils wear a standard school uniform and often a standard Physical Education (PE) kit. Morris observes that the aim of lessons is to inculcate students with the accepted norms – in terms of behaviour and knowledge – of society. There is also an element of trauma involved in this process. Traditionally, Morris notes, this was through corporal punishment, often in a highly ritualised form in certain schools and especially some public schools (105).[4] Since 1998, in the UK, this has been banned in all schools (BBC 25 March 1998) but Morris observes that there are other ways of deliberately traumatising or instilling fear in pupils such as intense – and ultimately life-changing – examinations as well as the public tests of physical stamina involved in Physical Education. Indeed, though school is highly extended it marks the transition from childhood to very young adulthood, meaning that there is a further liminal dimension. American schools, typically at least, would seem to parallel this as well. Though most do not involve school uniform, there are other rituals such as saluting the flag, reciting the Pledge of Allegiance and the ritual of school graduation. As in England, school involves tests of stamina not least through public examinations such as SATs (Scholastic Aptitude Tests) which have a significant effect upon the kind of university, if any, that an American student can attend. Indeed, some schools in some American states still retain corporal punishment.

University, to a certain extent at least, might be regarded as an extension of this Rite of Initiation required for those who it is assumed will go on to take a more specialised role in running what Morris calls the 'super-tribe' of a modern nation – those who have, to varying degrees, excelled at school. Morris points out that in a small tribe of a few hundred every member is required. Every male will contribute – through hunting – to running the tribe and thus everybody needs to be fully initiated. Morris suggests that as society becomes more complex and social classes develop those at the top – and therefore those likely to assist in running a far more complex society – require even further initiation and from this develops the university system. In Europe, university was originally mainly for the training of those who would work in the church – the ultimate guardians of the mysteries of the super-tribe. It has broadened as more and more professions – teaching at first as education was substantially controlled by the church – have required a university degree. (Of course other social classes had similar rites such as those involved in joining a guild for example.) Therefore, university, like school, involves inculcation with the norms and knowledge of society but at a more in-depth level. Its liminality is, perhaps, heightened as it occurs at a time when students are looked upon as being, essentially, in a liminal space moving between child and adult (Kingsbury 1974, Fisher 1994). Universities vary substantially in relation to the extent to which they are liminal but many might be seen as more liminal than many schools. In England, for example, many universities involve living away from home for the first time. They involve many university levelling rituals, as we have already seen, such as living with people from very different social backgrounds. Students may not even have met such people at school as many wealthy English people tend to send their children to private schools rendering education segregated by more than mere geography (e.g Lynn 2006, 188). Equally, as Morris points out, university has a highly traumatic dimension exposing students to the trauma of intense exams, intense relationships and their failure and a general questioning of identity and world-view. And, as with school, it involves a submission to the rituals of university and Morris notes that the 'bizarre' robes of graduation have clear parallels with shocking clothes used for

[4] See Gibson (1978) for a more in-depth discussion of this issue.

effect in tribal ritual (Morris 1969, 239). We will go into far more depth below, but I think there is a strong case – at its broadest – for understanding university as a Rite of Initiation in modern society.

Evangelical Christianity

As discussed, this book will argue that student evangelical groups parallel – in their internal degree of structure and *communitas* – these factors in the university of which they are a part. Thus, it will be shown that Oxford University's CU is highly differentiated, but also involves high *communitas*, while Aberdeen University's CU is far less so meaning that certain universities, in a sense, help to foster highly structured 'Christian' student groups whose aim is to provide a new identity at the very time when a student's identity is most under challenge. It will be useful, therefore, to examine these groups at a broad level in terms of belief and practice as well as how we might distinguish between them.

How, precisely, we should define an 'evangelical group' is a matter of some debate. Bebbington, for example, defines an evangelical group as one which is Protestant, highly Biblically inspired, one to which conversion is important and one which is active in attempting to convert others to Christianity (Bebbington 1989, 2–17). Therefore, a distinction has to be drawn between a conservative Christian group which is not evangelical – such as the Exclusive Brethren – and those for whom conversion and evangelism are, at least in theory, central issues such as many evangelicals within the Church of England. However, Armstrong (2001) and many others such as Bruce (2002) and Barr (1981) tend to conflate the term 'evangelical' with 'fundamentalist'. Armstrong argues that fundamentalist Christians tend to be highly conservative in both belief and lifestyle. Drawing upon a traditionalist reading of the Bible, they will tend to oppose such notions as premarital sex, homosexuality and evolutionary theory amongst others. Equally, traditional notions such as Hell for non-believers and the activity of both God and the Devil in the world are firmly adhered to. Obviously, there are differences in emphasis, belief and stringency amongst different groups that might be termed 'fundamentalist' but for Armstrong Christian fundamentalism, at its broadest, involves a retreat from the contemporary culture into a strongly differentiated counter-culture which usually aims to evangelise. I entirely appreciate that this summary of evangelicalism is doubtless simplistic. It overlooks disputes within evangelicalism, such as the appropriateness of Charismatic worship and so forth. There is also a movement known as 'Post-Evangelicalism' which, though evangelical, is more 'liberal', particularly with regard to lifestyle (see Tomlinson, 1998 or Drane 2006). But, as a general summary, I think it is useful. Some readers might also take issue with the term 'fundamentalist' because it has been so widely employed outside of its original purely Protestant context and it might be seen to have become a kind of epithet for evangelical Christians. I am, though, merely quoting the term in this context. I would submit that all six groups that I will examine are 'evangelical' to varying degrees. Conversion is central to all groups assessed to varying degrees. However, there is an interesting typological difference between the groups which seems to parallel the differences in the structures of the universities.

Bryan Wilson has presented a sect-typology in which he highlights a 'conversionist' type amongst religious groups (Wilson 1970, 66). As with any typology, this suffers from the difficulty of dealing with 'ideal types' and drawing boundaries between them. Following Wilson's typology, however, we can distinguish between two kinds of student evangelical group. As we will see below, the student evangelical groups at the more liminal universities tend to be very clearly 'conversionist' in Wilson's terms. OICCU for example is highly conversion oriented both in theory and practice. By contrast, OKO at Oulu University in Finland (which we will examine in Chapter 7) would at best be described as 'mildly conversionist' – its apparent purpose being to maintain as 'Christians' those who already are rather than necessarily to convert new members. Indeed, it might even be understood to be 'introversionist' and merely maintaining as Christians those who already are despite claiming to be evangelical. It will be demonstrated that the student evangelical groups in the more liminal universities tend to be conversionist whereas those in the less liminal universities tend to be more concerned with maintaining those who are already 'Christian' though the more conversionist groups also do this. The latter kind would, I think, be congruous with a university environment where identity is not exposed to substantial challenge meaning that the evangelical groups are less differentiated, less structured, less central to identity for their members, less strict in their definition of 'Christian' and in their other views and thus less inclined to evangelise to those whom they perceive to be 'non-Christian'. Consequently, the groups act as a gathering point for those who already are Christian and do not provide a new identity for non-Christians as their identity is less exposed to question. It has been suggested (e.g. Bloch 1992, 93) that conversion experience often leads to a conversionist orientation and it might be argued that less liminal universities result in fewer conversion experiences – as these reflect a transition in identity – and thus, more broadly, evangelical groups that are less concerned with making converts. But this is speculative. Certainly it will be demonstrated below that evangelical groups at highly liminal universities appear to be more conversionist.

Conversion and Ritual

Before moving on, it would be useful at this point to define a number of concepts which will be employed in our analysis of the relationship between university liminality and student evangelical groups. I will begin by defining 'conversion experience' and this will be employed as evidence of transition and liminality and a group emphasis on it will be understood to be evidence of differentiation from the broader student community and thus a high level of structure. Equally, discussing conversion – through public testimony in meetings – will be understood to evidence *communitas* due to the emotional catharsis and consequent social bonding that such a sharing of self might be understood to involve, a point made for example by Nuttall (1996).

William Sargant contends that conversion is strongly related to 'dissociation' – where a person experiences a heightened state of emotion in which they can be highly susceptible to stimuli or apparently dead to it (Sargant 1997, 37). Such situations can especially be caused by distress (85) and, in his work on the subject, William James finds a connection between great distress and subsequent conversion (James 1952, 149). Equally, Lewis Rambo highlights the tendency for there to be some kind of 'crisis' in a person's life before conversion (Rambo 1993, 17). Rambo submits that conversion 'is very rarely over night' (1) and further highlights a number of conversion types which include the dramatic, Pauline-type conversion experience where people hear or see God and others where people simply describe a vague feeling of the world making sense and certainty that they should be a Christian. Rambo also argues that having converted, converts reconstruct themselves autobiographically in relation to the conversion with the conversion as a central existential and identity turning-point (137). This point has also been made by Stromberg (1993) and Furseth (1999). Thus, conversion appears to be related to distress. Distress would be expected to increase due to the uncertainty of a liminal phase and, as such, the number of conversions would be expected to increase as the liminality does. Indeed, Conn (1986, 26) points out that conversion tends to occur at times of existential change and Fisher (1994, 41) notes that this is precisely what occurs at many universities with many left asking such existential questions as, 'Will I ever find a partner?' or 'Will I ever be happy?' She observes, indeed, that many British universities have the effect of questioning a student's sense of self often leading to relatively high incidences of depression. Moreover, if an evangelical group becomes highly significant to a student's identity and the student feels that they are still an outsider then conversion may be understood as a crucial cementing of identity in certain groups and even a play for social status in the group. Hence, an examination of conversion levels – which involve moving from an old state of identity to a new one via a religious experience – will be a useful indicator of broader degrees of liminality.

Ritual activity might also assist in creating *communitas*. Andrew Newberg and Eugene D'Aquila, drawing upon detailed physiological research, suggest that the rhythms and repetitions of ritual activity allow the body to reach a state of 'physical bliss' such that the limits of the self 'soften' and a person becomes 'One with something greater' (Newberg *et al* 2002, 106). This would seem to be in line with Durkheim's conception of 'collective effervescence' (Durkheim 1995), whereby the group is brought together through the focus of ritual, which is comparable in many respects to Turner's *existential spontaneous communitas* outlined above. An assessment of such ritual areas as prayer, hymns and even public-speaking as a part of ritual will allow us to discern the levels of structure and *communitas* in a group. It is perhaps beyond the boundaries of this discussion to look into sociologist Max Weber's notion of 'charisma' (Weber 1991, 246). Weber notes that the 'charismatic' is a person who is able to make a group experiencing crisis 'feel warm' through inspiring oratory, for example. It might be suggested that many students at more liminal universities are indeed undergoing a crisis of identity and we would expect to see some evidence of Weberian 'charisma' – perhaps in a very diluted form – at evangelical student meetings and, indeed, such speeches would create *communitas*, as Sargant (88) points out, by dissociating the audience such that they collectively feel strong emotions. This is a point which Turner implies is central to *communitas*. Equally, a number of social scientists such as Douglas (1996, 76) and Galanter (1999, 72) have found that the more tightly structured a group is, the more ritual it will tend to engage in to insulate it from outsiders. As such, it will tend to have more meetings, for example, which members will attend more regularly because the group is more significant to identity. These findings will be borne in mind in the following analysis. Moreover, Douglas (1996, 33) observes that highly structured groups will tend not only to have high levels of ritual but also their own in-group language or 'restricted code'. In analysing prayers and other such spoken material, this concept will be employed and it will be noted that the more liminal the university is, the more evidence of restricted code there is in the main university evangelical group. In terms of language usage, swearing will be used as another significant marker both of social class, social class pretensions and differentiation and structure. Theoretical and cultural issues surrounding swearing will, however, be discussed in greater depth in our assessment of Oxford University in Chapter 2.

Social Class

Finally, before moving onto looking at the evangelical groups themselves, I would like to look at the issue of social class. I examine this issue here because I think it requires some theoretical discussion; however it will be mainly employed in understanding the Christian Union at Oxford University. According to various experts in this field, social class remains a significant issue of identity in England (e.g. Fox 2004, McDonagh 1997) even if it may not be so important, overtly at least, in other cultures that will be assessed. It will be argued below that the extent to which Oxford University is a liminal phase would be likely to vary according to a number of factors such as whether or not a student has gone on a 'Gap Year' – a year out between school and university which often involves living or working abroad – but also according to a student's social class because if a student is not from a high social class then the experience of Oxford University might be even more transitional. An understanding of class is also important as if the level theory propounded is correct it might be suggested that the Christian Union breaks down boundaries – because all are 'Christian' – and social class could be one way that they could reassert themselves, at least if social class, and symbolic evidence of it, is significant to identity and social differentiation outside of the university context.

Frank McDonagh has argued that class boundaries have blurred somewhat in recent decades, with greater emphasis on the individual (McDonagh 1997, 179). But, even he admits that class prejudices still exist, especially in Britain. Jørgen Sevaldsen and Ole Vadmand claim that Britain is dominated by class (Sevaldsen and Vadmand 1993, 32). The main definition of class upon which I will draw is psychologist Michael Argyle's. The fact that the perception or identity of class has become less important does not subtract from the fact that there are, in Britain, marked social groups with different lifestyles. Using this reasoning, Argyle categorises the upper class as the aristocracy and leaders in commerce and other areas. He then distinguishes between a 'middle-class' of higher professionals and lower professionals. Higher professionals would include lawyers, doctors and members of other such professions, many, though not necessarily all of whom, would be relatively well-paid and highly educated. Lower professionals would be people such as school teachers, nurses and civil engineers. Then there is a lower-middle-class of 'white collar workers' (Argyle 1994, 15–16). All of these people may regard themselves simply as 'middle class' but there remain, he suggests, significant social differences between them. Beneath these classes are a working-class engaging in physical labour (such as builders) and an under-class comprised of the long term unemployed, criminals and marginalised immigrant groups.

Kate Fox presents another model of class which is significant because it relates to class perceptions and how people perceive their own class and class differences, specifically in Britain; though she focuses on England. She argues that in England, more than in many other countries, class is generally conveyed and inferred by virtue of certain symbolic factors with regard to how a person lives. These would include the minutiae of what words a person uses, their accent, the way in which they communicate, the way that they talk about money, their hobbies and so forth. Also the kind of school attended is significant as a symbol of class background rather than merely of wealth. These observations are important because they demonstrate that people perceive a person's social class according to various symbolic factors and that these factors can become a part of class self-perception. Thus, in understanding how social structure reasserts itself, these factors – whether observable or 'known' as a result of gossip and so forth – are important. Accent and school, amongst others, are symbolically significant and, if Fox is right, they could be legitimately used as an indicator – though not necessarily a perfect one – of social class in England. They are important because they are perceived by English people to indicate social class even if the sociological 'reality' might be somewhat more complex. Fox emphasises that a person's job does not really always indicate social class in England and that, for many of her subjects, a doctor with a working-class background will always be a 'working-class doctor' who, ultimately, is not of high social status. Indeed, it might be argued that a job such as a doctor becomes less respected – moving down the social scale – as increasing numbers of women and possibly people from lower social backgrounds pursue that job, a point that has been made in relation to the rise in female doctors by Black (Heath, 21 August 2004). Moreover, jobs like teaching or even the priesthood are difficult to place because a teacher at a private school might be from an upper-class background whereas another, at a Comprehensive, might be from a working-class background (Fox 2004, 81). So if accepted social structure reasserts itself in the manner mooted in the CUs, we would expect people with the facets Fox outlines to be in positions of power. Fox does provide some kind of methodology with regard to certain phrases and accent intonations that indicate class and even class pretension. But appreciating the complexity of the matter, I will use both Fox's and Argyle's methodologies. However, the emphasis will not be on Fox because I think there is a rather subjective dimension to judging accents which is not perhaps conducive to detailed analysis. A number of other theoretical discussions – such as the nature of swearing for example as evidence of differentiation – will be drawn upon but these will be discussed within each analysis.

Fieldwork Issues

In the following chapters, the level model of liminality that has already been outlined will be applied to six different university evangelical groups. Some of these groups are substantial in size and in these instances the groups' real names will be employed. In the case of the groups at Leiden University and Oulu University the names will be changed to avoid any identification of individuals. The group at Leiden University will be termed Christian Students Leiden (CSL) after what would have been the Dutch translation *Christelijk Studenten Leiden.* The group at Oulu University will be termed Oulu Christian Students (OKO) after the Finnish *Oulun kristitut opiskelijat.* Any evangelical Christian referred to by name in this book has had their name changed and some small details – such as personal information in prayers – have been altered or omitted in certain areas in order to further protect individual identities.

The following analysis will draw upon my participant observation fieldwork with Oxford Inter-Collegiate Christian Union (OICCU) at Oxford University, Aberdeen University Christian Union (AUCU) at Aberdeen University, CSL at Leiden University in the Netherlands and OKO at Oulu University in Finland. With the exception of CSL, all of these groups are affiliated to broader national groups which are in turn affiliated to the International Federation of Evangelical Students (IFES) and they ascribe to its doctrinal basis.[5] CSL is affiliated to another evangelical group based in the USA. In the first three cases a sample of twenty-five were surveyed and this was balanced according to gender. Drawing upon this, a further twenty-five were interviewed with various variations such as extent of meeting attendance, religious views and so forth to create a representative sample. (This information was discerned through a preliminary interview.) It is perhaps beyond the scope of this book to go in detail with regard to how data was accrued in this regard and how it was analysed but I followed traditional, accepted anthropological methods in conducting participant observation. I spent two university terms (or one 'semester') with each group and drew upon both survey – to create a sample – and then open-ended interview based around a series of central questions. In addition, I obviously attended many meetings and made copious notes eventually looking for patterns under certain headings such as 'Attitudes to Prayer' or 'Conversion'.[6] The book will also employ the terms 'religion' and 'culture'. I am aware of the debate in contemporary social anthropology over whether or not these terms – and especially 'culture' – are meaningful. Again, it is beyond the scope of this book to deal with this at any length. I will be employing these categories as they are generally understood by contemporary speakers of English. I appreciate that there has been considerable debate over such concepts – and the anthropological method more broadly. This discussion is based on certain assumptions as stated but I will nevertheless examine this debate in more depth in Chapter 8.

---

5 See Lowman (1983), for example, for an examination of this group.

6 See, for example, Fetterson (1988) for a discussion of fieldwork method.

Primary Research and Sources

The book will further draw upon primary research into the Inter-Varsity Christian Fellowship (IVCF) at the Trinidad Campus (St Augustine) of the University of the West Indies which was conducted in the late 1970s and early 1980s by Finnish sociologist Eila Helander as well as an interview that I conducted with her about her research. It will also draw upon primary research (and some survey research) in relation to student evangelical groups at American universities. I appreciate that this latter dimension is less than ideal and these examples are meant merely as a means of further substantiating the conclusions drawing upon my own participant observation fieldwork. With these latter examples the theory can still be tested but only employing the available information present in primary research or other non-fieldwork-based sources. However, I think that these comparisons add to the discussion because they take the field outside of Europe and add further credence to the theory being propounded. Obviously in order to compare six cultures and six evangelical groups within a reasonable sized book some areas have been explored in less depth than they might be. This may frustrate any expert on the history of the Finnish Lutheran Church or on American Protestantism. But I hope that this expert appreciates that such brevity in certain areas has been necessary in order to compare a sufficiently wide sample of groups.

Outline

The research will demonstrate the model of liminality discussed above. As such, Oxford University, St Augustine Campus, Trinidad and a number of American campus universities will all shown to be highly liminal for students to varying degrees. The universities will be demonstrated to be highly structured and transitional in such a way as to create a high level of *communitas* as part of a highly structured Rite of Passage. The university evangelical groups will then be shown to be highly structured themselves as our model of liminality would predict. Equally, those same groups will show evidence of *communitas* on another level. By contrast, at the less liminal universities, it will be demonstrated that the university is not especially structured and nor is it – to varying degrees – especially transitional. As such, the level of *communitas* will be shown to be low while, again to varying degrees, the student evangelical groups in these contexts will be demonstrated to be somewhat more loosely structured with OKO at Oulu University, seemingly the least liminal example, having the weakest structure of all. The final chapter will summarise both the methodological and ethnographic findings and examine their consequences for understanding the liminal phase, for the anthropology of religion, anthropology more broadly, research into higher education and for student evangelism itself.

The ethnography will begin with the more highly structured universities and first and foremost with Oxford University and its main evangelical group the Oxford Inter-Collegiate Christian Union (OICCU).[7]

[7] Parts of this chapter have been published in Dutton (2008b).

Chapter 2

Re-converting at Oxford

Oxford University and OICCU

Oxford, known as 'the city of dreaming spires' is around an hour from London and has a population of just over 130,000. Established in the 1200s, Oxford University is England's oldest university. It is highly prestigious and competition for places is widely acknowledged to be intense. Along with Cambridge University, 'Oxbridge' are generally perceived as the two most academically rigorous universities in the country and they were England's only universities until the establishment of Durham University in 1832. Unlike most other English universities Oxford employs a college system. A student's degree is therefore awarded by the particular Oxford college which they attend. (This means that students have academic tutors within the college in which they live but also attend university-wide lectures relating to their subject. Students apply to an individual college.) Perhaps it suffices to say that many eminent English people – from Prime Ministers to Poet Laureates – have been to Oxford University. But in addition to its academic rigour, Oxford also boasts a considerable social side for undergraduates such as the Oxford Union (a well known debating society) and a relatively active evangelical Christian Union.

I spent two terms studying both OICCU and Oxford University in the Summer term of 2003 and the Spring term of 2004. As a participant observer, I was also able to attend many OICCU meetings though I was not permitted to attend their weekly 'College Group' (relating to the CU in every Oxford college) and was restricted in my ability to attend their 'informal' Saturday worship meeting 'Powerhouse'. Interestingly, I was invited to attend a 'College CU Meeting' by junior members but this was vetoed by the broader OICCU 'Executive Committee' ('Exec') as it was felt that my presence as an observer would somehow be intrusive on a small group. However, before beginning our discussion both of Oxford University and of OICCU it would be useful to conduct a brief examination of the religious background in England and also the nature of the university system in England, especially in relation to the issue of liminality.

England's Religious Background

Like many mainly Protestant European countries, England has an established national church: the Church of England. In theory every baptised English person is a member of the Church of England because England is divided into numerous parishes and there is no part of England that is not part of a parish. Membership of the parish involves simply living in the parish. On the most recent census (2001)

72 per cent of English people claimed to be 'Christian' with most being 'Church of England'. However, many sociologists such as Bruce (2002, 65) and Brown (2001) have argued that the Church of England is undergoing a sharp decline and that English people have relatively low involvement with institutional religion compared to some other mainly Protestant countries.

Essentially, Bruce argues that England is not an especially 'religious' country in the sense of its involvement with church institutions. Since the 1950s, Church of England baptisms and marriages have declined considerably and now only around 20 per cent of English babies are baptised. Marriage in church has also declined and confirmation has declined even more sharply than the other rituals. However, the Church of England remains, in Bruce's view, the 'default' provider of funeral services. Equally, regular church attendance has also declined considerably. According to recent statistics (Brierley 2006) under 7 per cent of English people attend church services on Sundays in a culture where regular church attendance has traditionally been normative. Sunday church attendance has likewise undergone a sharp decline since the 1950s and, indeed, since 1900 though there was a small rise in the wake of World War II. In sociological terms, the tendency is also that those who are from more middle-class (or upper-class) backgrounds are far more likely to be involved in the Church of England than those who are from working class backgrounds (e.g. Bruce 1995, 44). Thus, it has been widely noted that institutionalised religion is declining in England and, indeed, doing so more markedly than in some other cultures which we will examine.

However, in terms of national religious culture it is perhaps uncontroversial to claim that the Church of England, as the established national church, is the most influential organisation. It would obviously be an injustice to an ancient and complex organisation such as the Church of England to attempt to summarise it in a few paragraphs but it is, I think, nevertheless necessary to be equipped with some background to OICCU's religious culture. The Church of England is divided into two main parties – though there would be many shades in between. These are the Anglo-Catholics (informally known as 'High Church') and the Evangelicals ('Low Church') and even Theological Colleges, for the training of Anglican priests, tend to reflect one of the two parties or 'traditions'. It would be useful to summarise both traditions though OICCU, of course, is clearly influenced by the latter. Anglo-Catholicism could be seen to trace its origins back to the English Reformation and the similar divide between those who were Puritan-leaning and those who remained more influenced by Catholic ideas and rituals. During the reign of Queen Elizabeth I (1558–1603), the Church of England was attempting to negotiate a 'middle way' between Protestant and Catholic heritage (Shepherd 1987, 287). The Anglo-Catholic Movement came to considerable prominence in the early nineteenth century with the rise of the 'Oxford Movement' amongst clerics at Oxford University. Members advocated the 'Branch Theory' – that the Church of England was a branch of a broader church which included the Roman Catholic Church and the Orthodox churches. Moreover, members emphasised the importance of ritual, especially the Eucharist and the use of vestments. Thus, in very basic summary, Anglo-Catholicism emphasises and employs various Catholic dimensions, especially in terms of ritual practice. There are conservatives within this movement who, for example, oppose the ordination of women priests because it puts the Church of England out of step with both Rome and the Eastern churches. But typically Anglo-Catholic theology tends to be more liberal with an emphasis on the Social Gospel; applying Christian principles to social issues.

The other main tradition is Evangelicalism and we have already discussed the kinds of beliefs held by many evangelicals in the previous chapter. The emphasis in the 'Low Church', with its foundations to a great extent in Puritanism, tends to be less towards formal ritual and more inclined towards free worship and an emphasis on the Bible and therefore preaching. This movement is increasingly influential within the Church of England with more and more parishes identifying as evangelical (e.g. Randall 2005). Bruce (2002, 168) notes that there is a history of religious revivalism in England which has led, at various points, to the forming of the Methodist Church, which broke away from the more Puritanical wing of the Church of England in the eighteenth century as well as various other free churches connected to this such as the Pentecostals and the Baptists. More recently, there is a growing movement within English Evangelicalism which has been termed the 'Charismatic Movement' which Bruce (2002, 168) and Bebbington (1989, Ch. 1) note began to develop in the Church of England in the 1960s. Charismatic services will also tend to emphasise worship and 'the Word'. However, the worship can be highly emotional and often include 'gifts of the spirit' or 'charismata' whereby worshippers believe that they are possessed by the Holy Spirit. This has various manifestations such as 'glossolalia' (speaking-in-tongues) and even healing (see for example Percy 1996 or Davies 1984). Often, such churches also emphasise the importance of 'conversion experience' in order to become a Christian and will often, as we have discussed, define the term 'Christian' in a narrower sense, propounding a rather conservative interpretation of many Christian ideas. The Charismatic Movement also includes many of what are called House Churches (see Walker 1998) which are independent of any denomination. Also, Bruce (2002, 172) notes that the most recent large-scale Charismatic revival to hit the Church of England was the 1994 'Toronto Blessing' phenomenon.[1] This stemmed from a 'Vineyard Church' in Canada (Toronto Airport Vineyard) of which there are also various branches in England. As such, we might suggest that English established Protestantism, to a greater extent than other cultures that we will assess, has a Catholic influence. But it also contains an increasingly strong evangelical and in particular Charismatic evangelical influence. Significantly, the Anglican theological tradition has generally been towards Arminianism – the belief that people must come to God through their own free will – rather than the Calvinist belief in a divinely ordained elect that is theoretically held by many Reformed churches in various forms (e.g. Douglas 1974).

---

[1] In 1994, the 'Toronto Blessing' phenomenon swept through many Anglican and other churches in England. It involved people collapsing, supposedly under the power of the Holy Spirit (see Bruce 2002, 172).

English Universities, Schools and Liminality

Though the numbers studying for separate Masters degrees are increasing, English students generally study for a three year Bachelors degree. Until 1992, there was a separation within English Higher Education between 'universities' (which mainly offered degrees in academic subjects) and 'polytechnics' (which mainly offered degrees in vocational subjects). As of 1992, all were termed 'universities' but there is generally a perception that English universities vary in the standard of research and teaching – and certainly vary in terms of prestige – considerably. Thus, Oxford and Cambridge are generally regarded as the most prestigious institutions followed by various others that, I would suggest, mix being established and being rated highly in terms of research with attracting a significant portion of students from private schools. These include London, Durham, Bristol and Nottingham and many students who fail to get into Oxbridge attend these kinds of universities. Many students I spoke to at both Durham and Oxford were aware of and agreed with this kind of hierarchy. Thereafter, there are various 'Redbrick' universities (established at the beginning of the twentieth century) or those established in the 1960s which, whether rightly or not, are often regarded as somewhat less prestigious but still 'respectable' such as Leeds, Reading and Leicester. Thereafter, there are the many former polytechnics. Obviously, the main issue in constructing this kind of hierarchy is the prestige that the university has and this may only be partially because of the perceived quality of research conducted there. Since 1998, English undergraduates have had to pay tuition fees (£1000 per year during my research). However, prestigious universities such as Oxford subsequently successfully lobbied to be allowed to charge considerably higher tuition fees ('top-up fees' of £3000) than many former polytechnics, for example, on the grounds that a degree from such an institution is perceived to be worth more (as it carries more prestige) than a degree from another university. Indeed, a former British government minister dismissed certain polytechnics as offering 'Mickey Mouse degrees' (BBC 14 January 2003) that were not really worthwhile studying. English students – some of whom may go to university in other parts of the UK – are accepted into university according to the results that they achieve in their school leaving exams (A-Levels) though many of the more prestigious universities (and especially with the more popular subjects) will also interview students and sometimes make them sit separate examinations.

The English schooling system is divided into the public and private sector. Over 90 per cent of children attend 'state schools'. These are publicly funded and free. However, it should be noted that there are substantial differences in standard between Comprehensive Schools, where admission is according to proximity to the school. Equally, in certain areas there are state-funded Grammar Schools which children attend if they pass their 'Eleven-Plus' exam, though relatively few of these schools remain. In the private sector, parents pay school fees and private schools (most of which are single sex) are generally perceived to achieve better academic results and render it more likely that a child will attend a prestigious university (Fox 2004, 367) though, of course, there are differences in standards between these. At most private schools, which are entered by passing an exam, students tend to live at home. The most prestigious private schools are known as 'Public Schools'. These schools, again generally single sex at least in the lower school, often involve pupils boarding at school during term time. As we have noted, Fox (2004, 79) points out that attendance at private (and especially public) school is perceived as an important symbolic indicator of high social class in England.

Clearly, there are many differences between English universities and the degree to which they are transitional for undergraduates might be seen to vary accordingly. It will be argued below that Oxford University is particularly liminal for many of its students however this would not necessarily be the case with all universities. For example, at a typical former polytechnic such as Kingston University there will be very few students from private schools meaning that there is little social *communitas*, many students will live at home which would be likely to reduce the liminality for them and even those who are not from the area will often be from relatively close at hand. Moreover, unlike at Oxford University, a degree of this kind is perhaps relatively unlikely to lead to a significant rise in social status at least for many of the students. It should be noted that English degrees are classified either 1st Class, 2:1, 2:2, 3rd or Pass and many employers will be interested in the degree classification and may even stipulate a required classification. However, as we have already discussed, there is at least a case for claiming that many English universities are liminal if only because there is a tendency for English students to move away from home and sometimes far away from home, at least with regard to the more prestigious institutions (e.g. Kingsbury 1974, 115–17).

The Student Union at British Universities

All English – and indeed British more broadly – universities tend to be relatively structured in the sense that there is, at each university, a Student Union. The officers are elected by the student body and there is effectively a kind of student parliament at many universities. In general, the ‘Student Union’ runs a heavily subsidised student bar, offers help for second and third years in finding accommodation, runs a student shop and offers services such as free contraception and even free counselling. The Student Union has a reputation for being politically left-leaning and many Student Unions include positions such as ‘Women’s Officer’ and ‘LGBT (Lesbian, Gay, Bisexual and Transgender) Officer’. Indeed some Student Unions have an ‘Ethnic Minorities Officer’. At many universities the Student Union – or at Oxford the Student Union in addition to the College Exec – organise a raft of activities for first years during Freshers week – many based around drinking – so that they can meet and socialise.

The Student Unions are also ultimately in charge of Student Societies and only those affiliated to the Student Union have the right to a free stall at Freshers Fair and the right to use the Student Union’s facilities. Groups which are not in line with the union’s policies – that all groups must be democratic and open to all and cannot be racist and so forth – can be disaffiliated. At a number of universities the Christian Union has been thrown out of the Student Union for a variety of reasons such as that it discriminates against non-Christians through its ‘Declaration of Faith’ or even that it discriminates against transsexual and inter-gender students by using the words ‘man’ and ‘woman’ in its constitution (see Dutton 2006a).

OICCU and Social Background

During my research, I surveyed twenty-five OICCU members. Of this number ten had attended private schools (three of which had attended public schools, where they boarded) while the other fifteen had attended state schools, in all but three cases these were Comprehensives. As such, state-school students would appear to be over-represented in OICCU as 50 per cent of Oxford students were from state schools during my research (Oxford University Statistics). The same surveys indicated that the overwhelming majority were from backgrounds that Argyle would term 'professional'. However, following Argyle, there was a distinction between 'higher professionals' and 'lower professionals' and, to a great extent, this distinction was paralleled in terms of whether the student had attended state or private school. In making this point, it is important not to engage in class stereotyping with regard to who attends state and private schools. It is perfectly conceivable, for example, that a person from a working-class background could attend a private school by means of a scholarship. Equally, there are, of course, differences in standard amongst state and private schools. However, I would submit that, in general, the standard, and academic results at private schools are considered to be superior and that these schools, to a greater extent than state schools, direct their pupils towards the more respected universities such as Oxford. Thus, even if there were a student from private school whose parents were simply wealthy or *nouveau riche*, they would still be directed towards universities of this kind and be educated amongst students who would, in general, be from higher professional backgrounds or above meaning that being from such a school could render Oxford less transitional.

But having said that, a distinction, following Argyle's model, could be found. Of the ten OICCU sample members who had attended independent schools, all of the parental professions were at least 'higher professional'. They included three barristers, two architects, a vet and a hospital consultant. Amongst those from state schools there were a very large number of students whose parents' main profession was 'school teacher', one of the main examples cited by Argyle of a 'lower professional'. Two cited 'Civil Engineer' as the main parental profession. There were a very small number, indeed, that might not fit into this class such as one whose father was a 'bookseller'. There were a small number of state-school pupils whose parents were, it might be argued, 'higher professionals'. There was one whose father was an architect and one whose father was a solicitor but, I would submit, a social difference between those at state and private school can be noted from these results.

However, following Fox, there were differences in accent with regard to school attendees. In general, those from state schools used what Fox terms the 'new RP'. That is say, 'received pronunciation' with a hint of regional accent on certain words. Many of those from private schools spoke in a noticeably 'posher' accent, which would be associated with the upper-middle class and higher. Amongst this group, a minority spoke in the clipped tones that Fox associates with the upper class and in all cases they had attended public schools. There were, of course, a few exceptions to this rule. And some public school pupils attempted, I would argue, to play down their accent by addressing me as 'mate' for example, a term of friendliness associated with the working-class especially in London. Particularly amongst women, there were some from state schools who seemed to affect an almost stereo-typical 'posh' accent which Fox indicates is normally an indicator of being higher-professional, in Argyle's terms, and trying to seem higher. But I appreciate that Fox's method is rather subjective and, while using this analysis, I think it needs to be substantiated with Argyle's more concrete profession-based method. This is important because this method, on its own, might also lead to over-simplified conclusions.

Of twenty-five members, eleven had been raised in the Church of England, five in various independent evangelical and Charismatic churches, four in the Baptist church, two in the Brethren (which is largely evangelical), one as a Methodist and one in the Presbyterian Church of Northern Ireland. The overwhelming majority of students were also English with twenty-one self-identifying as such. The remainder were from other parts of the UK.

Oxford University as a Rite of Passage

There is a strong case for arguing that the Oxford University is a particularly intense Rite of Passage and that it would likely be especially so for students who have attended state schools and are thus from backgrounds where attendance at such a university would, to varying degrees, be far from normative and also socially status raising. Equally, it would be likely to be more liminal for those who had not boarded at school – which would again include all state-school pupils – and those who had not taken a Gap Year, which appeared to be the least popular amongst those from state schools. Of my sample, none of those from state schools had taken a Gap Year while it was considerably more popular amongst those from private schools. This is congruous, to a great extent, with other research from that time though the Gap Year has become far more popular in recent years (see for example Jones 2004).[2] But let us examine the liminality of Oxford.

In many ways, according to those students I interviewed, Oxford University seems to be highly liminal. At Oxford, a student is a child in a number of senses. According to my interviewees, most students were financially reliant on their parents due to tuition fees and the absence of a student grant. A student generally lives in college for the whole three year degree. In this context, students are catered for (at certain regulated times) and cleaned for by the college, they are looked after by college authorities with a pastoral and academic tutor, a college master and chaplain and even symbolic punishments for transgressions. Also, depending on the college, they may be required to follow certain rules with regard to attendance at compulsory 'formal dinners', for example, where students must wear formal dress and academic robes. Thus, there is submission to arbitrary – and *communitas* fostering – rules rather like at many schools or in a tribal Rite of Initiation (e.g. Morris 1969, 239). However, in many other senses, students are adults. Students are effectively left to

[2] It might be suggested that this change is congruous with Orans's (1965) 'Rank Concession Syndrome Model' whereby those at the perceived top of society are imitated. This may also partially explain the prestige universities with large numbers of privately educated students hold.

organise themselves – but there is a student structure to facilitate this known as the Student Union – and also the 'College Exec' or 'Junior Common Room'. At the university level, students have their own elected government (the Student Union) which has its own newspaper, *Oxford Student*. There are other student newspapers (e.g *Cherwell*) as well as various societies including political parties. However, some of the aspects of adulthood are regulated in a way that they would not be in the real world. For example, Oxford University Student Union provided free condoms to students who required them. Thus, there is an ambiguity with regard to this kind of status.

Clearly, Oxford is transitional in terms of identity from childhood to adulthood. However, I would suggest that it is more transitional for many from state schools because it may betoken a further rise in social status in relation to their family and social background where attendance at such a university might not be entirely expected. There has been considerable research on how university can change a student's relations with their parents (e.g. Berman and Sperling 1991). Anthony Stevens (1982 149) argues, from a psychological perspective, the main point of a Rite of Initiation is to break the boy's bond with his mother. Moreover, unlike at many other universities Oxford is transitional by bringing together people from different backgrounds. Only 7 per cent of British students attend private school but these students compose 50 per cent of the students at Oxford University. As such, students of different backgrounds are bound to meet rendering the experience even more psychologically transitional. This said, the experience of Oxford would still be liminal to some extent for those from public school backgrounds. Oxford attracts members of the upper class who hail from and have been schooled all around the country. Such undergraduates would have been unlikely to have had intimate contact with pupils from state schools, adding a further transitional aspect to the experience. Also, historically, the purpose of Oxford was a transformative one. It took young gentry from around the country in order to prepare them for certain professions such as the Law and the Church (Allen 1988, 35). Hence, university can be seen to remodel members of the upper class. It is still liminal for them even if it is likely to be more liminal for those from state schools. Even though Oxford might be perceived as less liminal for those from public schools there would still exist, we might suggest, an atmosphere of liminality, which they would be influenced by, simply because Oxford is so liminal for so many of its students. Moreover, all would experience the symbolic *communitas* of university ritual and the trauma of intense examinations and relationship breakdown.

Oxford University is highly structured and structured in such a way as to foster *communitas* through bonding and trauma. Every first year Oxford student has passed a number of rigorous academic interviews in order to be offered a place so this in itself is likely to aid bonding. The college system at Oxford brings people together from very different social and geographical backgrounds and it is perfectly possible that the daughter of a carpenter would end-up living on a corridor with the son of a Lord, as indeed occurred in my research. No Oxford student that I interviewed lived at home in term time or was from Oxford, none regularly went home at weekends and many did not 'go home' during term time at all. This would be likely to create liminality and *communitas* as would the initial Matriculation ritual when beginning university, which does not occur at many universities. This ritual would seem to mark 'Oxford' out in a kind of formal Rite of Separation. The college system would mean that students from different backgrounds would not only have to live together but also dine together and, indeed, dine together at the college's various 'formals' at which social distinction would further be broken down through the use of formal clothes and academic gowns. As with any university, lectures and tutorials might seem to create *communitas* but at Oxford there are further traumatic dimensions such as one-on-two tutorials where a student must read out their essay to another student and the tutor in order to have it critiqued there and then. Oxford students must write on average one and a half essays per week. This, as we will see below, is in contrast to a few essays a term at some other universities. Obviously, this is likely to be very stressful and foster bonds amongst students. There are many other rituals – such as a room ballot if you wish to live in college in the second or third year – which might also foster a sense of college community and shared submission to authority. Interestingly, examinations must be taken in formal dress and academic gown which would be likely to further create *communitas.* When students graduate from Oxford, there are further *communitas* fostering rituals. A student's 'Finals' are taken in their third year over a week and their entire degree depends upon them. There are no 'modules' or 'credits' and certainly no 'retakes' in the final year. Many students reported to me just how stressful this week of exams is and there were various anecdotes about students killing themselves. The 'Finals' are often followed by, in the words of one student, 'riotous' partying. Finally, there is the Graduation ceremony – the Rite of Incorporation – which is in Latin. The presence of both of these rites encircling the extended Rite of Passage would seem to further demonstrate its liminality and the degree of status-raising involved.

The *communitas* is, I think, further evidenced by the strong sense of 'Oxford University' identity. In a sense, Oxford University is very much separate from the Oxford city itself in what is known as 'the Town and Gown'. Students to whom I spoke generally had no friends who were not Oxford University students and did not generally socialise with 'locals' or, for that matter, students at 'Oxford Brookes University', the city's former polytechnic. Indeed, they would avoid certain pubs because they were perceived as 'local' domains. Much of students' social life appeared to be provided by their college – at which there was a bar that sold cheap alcohol – and then by the Student Union which, likewise, had cheap bars as did the Union Society. The Student Union included every possible kind of club meaning that students could be entertained – provided with theatre, films, two newspapers, sports clubs and so forth – all produced by other students. This I think would be likely to compound a sense of 'Oxford student' *communitas* in contrast to outsiders and especially 'locals'. This would also, I think, further evidence liminality whereby students are, in a sense, being 'exaggerated adults'. They are playing adult roles – such as editing a newspaper or being a politician – which they may well be less likely to do in the outside world. This exaggeration might reflect the fact that they are liminal in identity and thus exaggerate the perceived 'higher' status which would be in line with research into ethnic groups in this regard (see Eidheim 1966 and Dutton 2005b).

'Rahs' and 'Brainwashing'

However, we would expect structure to reassert itself on another level if our model of *communitas* is accurate and there is certainly evidence for this. Notably, many Oxford students to whom I spoke had naturally gravitated, as university progressed, towards people with relatively similar backgrounds to their own, certainly with regard to their closest friends. Indeed, there was a perceived divide at Oxford between 'Rahs' and everybody else. The former were those from public schools (and some private schools) who socialised together, spoke in a certain way, dressed in a certain way, went to certain restaurants and generally were perceived to conform to a certain social stereotype. These students would also gravitate towards certain student societies – such as the Scottish Dancing Society for example. However, it should be stressed that this term was a kind of tongue-in-cheek insult and students would not generally self-identify as 'Rahs' or, for that matter, 'Ethno-Rahs' – 'Rahs' that wore hippie or 'ethnic' clothing – according to those to whom I spoke. Students were, in a sense, pre-divided according to their college and the subject that they studied. Indeed, there was a certain amount of college rivalry with ribald rhymes about those from other colleges and the like though it should be stressed that this was very good humoured and might be regarded as 'pseudo-oppositions' rather than actual oppositions. Other than social class, the other divide that appeared to reassert itself formally was in relation to religion. There were two evangelical student groups at Oxford: OICCU and the far smaller 'Fusion'. [3]

My research, however, was with OICCU and the group appeared to arouse strong emotions amongst many students to whom I spoke that were not involved in it. When I first got to Oxford I asked directions to a particular church from a female student and we got talking. I asked her if she had heard of OICCU to which she spat back, 'Oh! Are you gonna try and brainwash me! That's what you did to my friend!' A male friend of hers approached and, once we had established that I was not in OICCU, he began to explain to me why he 'despised' OICCU. I would suggest that OICCU, in this context, reasserts structure – in a highly pronounced way – by dividing Oxford between 'Christian' and 'non-Christian' and this evidences strong boundaries. Indeed, the hostile response of certain 'non-Christian' students towards OICCU might assist in explaining the leadership's suspicions of me and the degree to which they restricted my fieldwork. I was an outsider. In a group with very strong boundaries that may have even felt persecuted to a degree, I was 'other'. Of the groups that I participated in as an observer, OICCU was the only group where any members directly asked me whether or not I was a 'Christian' and wanted me to explain my views about the nature of life and so forth to them. One member in particular turned my interview with him into an attempt to persuade me to become

[3] There is perhaps not sufficient space to look at the history of OICCU or the CUs in the UK here. OICCU was established in 1879 and finally broke with the increasingly liberal and Social Gospel-oriented Student Christian Movement (SCM) in 1927 to be part of Inter-Varsity Fellowship which was renamed UCCF in 1974 (Fielder 1988, 38) and which was more openly 'evangelical'. Those interested in Christian Union history might consult Barclay and Horn (2002) or Fielder (1988) though both are from an insider evangelical perspective.

an evangelical Christian which began when I asked him if he believed in the literal truth of the resurrection. 'What do *you* believe about that?' he responded and when I hesitated to give a firm answer he informed me of the eschatological importance of giving a firm answer to this question and proceeded from there. Though this kind of reaction was only found amongst a minority it may still be seen as indicative of relatively strong boundaries. But let us then examine this structural dimension.

OICCU and Belief

OICCU is, in many respects, a highly structured group and this is clearest in the fact that it has a kind of Rite of Initiation. In order to join, whether at the university 'Freshers' Fair' or at the college 'Freshers' Fair' you must sign the group's 'Declaration of Faith'. OICCU is part of a broader British organisation called the 'Universities and Colleges Christian Fellowship' (UCCF). It is they that help to fund OICCU and provide a paid, full-time 'staff worker' to help direct the group. The 'Declaration of Faith' or 'Doctrinal Basis' is the same with every British Christian Union and is from UCCF. The Declaration implies, at least, a conservative form of evangelical Christianity. Thus it implies a belief in Hell for non-believers and Biblical inerrancy meaning that it strongly implies a belief in creationism and the Bible as a model for contemporary ethics.

Religious and ethical belief is perhaps the most obvious structural issue. All those whom I interviewed from OICCU claimed to believe in Hell and to believe that non-Christians would go to Hell. All of those to whom I spoke claimed to believe in the Devil as an actual force in the world. Twenty four out of twenty five in OICCU rejected Evolutionary Theory and all believed in the reality of doctrines such as the resurrection. The numbers who had undergone a conversion experience were very high; higher, as we will see, than in other groups. In OICCU only one person from the sample claimed to have never had a conversion experience. I would submit that these kinds of beliefs – and experiences – render OICCU highly differentiated. I also noted conformity in terms of social belief. In OICCU, all thought it was acceptable for Christians to drink but none to become drunk. Only one felt it was acceptable for Christians to smoke, only one felt it was acceptable to date a 'non-Christian' and none felt it acceptable to take drugs of any kind in a university context where drug experimentation was not uncommon. All felt premarital sex was unacceptable and that homosexuality was unacceptable. The issue of swearing will be discussed below but members, in general, were not prepared to swear, at least not conventionally.

Conversion Experience at Oxford

Interestingly, relatively high numbers in OICCU 'became Christians' or underwent a conversion experience while at Oxford University. Of my sample, 20 per cent of OICCU claimed to be from non-Christian backgrounds while 24 per cent had become Christian while at university. This would seem to demonstrate that the degree of transition in identity is considerably higher at Oxford than in some other universities to which it will be compared. This is evidenced by a high level of conversion experience which, as we have discussed, would be congruous with distress caused by questioning of identity. It would also reflect liminality in as much as so many students appeared to have remodelled or reconsidered their previous sense of identity by becoming 'Christians'. As such, it would seem to demonstrate a vital change in students' relationships with their parents because, in some cases, they have broken with their parents' belief system in order to become evangelical Christians but in some cases this issue was nuanced. Members from 'non-Christian backgrounds' had, in fact, been baptised and in some cases their parents attended Anglican churches weekly. It is thus evidence of the liminality of Oxford that these students retrospectively concluded that their parents were not real 'Christians' and they had, in fact, not been raised as Christian. Indeed a minority of the converts had been raised as evangelical Christians and had regarded themselves as 'Christian' until they became involved in OICCU, realised that they were not 'Christian' and underwent a conversion sometimes even 'realising' that what they previously understood to be their conversion, when they were a teenager for example, was either not really a conversion or that they had 'back-slided' from it since. This would all seem to testify to the liminality of Oxford University.

Moreover, students from state schools were over-represented amongst those who became Christians while at Oxford. All but one of those who had converted at Oxford had been to state schools and none of them had been on Gap Years. Thus, this could be understood to be further evidence of the liminality and consequent psychological difficulties caused by the Oxford experience. In essence, those for whom Oxford University might be perceived as more liminal – because they had not previously lived away from home and the university was more status raising and so forth – seemed more likely to undergo conversion at university. Obviously, it should be remembered that there are many factors which may explain why one person has a conversion and another does not and it is important not be reductionist in this regard. However, conversion – as an identity change generally brought on by distress – would be congruous with a highly liminal phase and it would appear that Oxford would be the most liminal for those, broadly, from state schools that have not been on Gap Years, which was the majority of state-school pupils at that time.

However, the salience of conversion might also indicate the degree of structure in OICCU itself. A number of OICCU members to whom I spoke who appeared to be on the borders of the organisation indicated, for example, that, 'Those people who get onto the Exec ... they're usually established 'Christians'. Their families are Christian and they are and that's that'. Certainly, I found that those in senior positions had generally not become 'Christians' while at Oxford and were from 'Christian' backgrounds or perceived to be such by other members. As such, conversion could be understood as a kind of Rite of Initiation for those who are not perceived as being truly 'Christian' due, perhaps, to various 'non-Christian' aspects of their character. The conversion – and sometimes the subsequent public 'testimony' at an OICCU meeting – heralds their initiation into the centre of both OICCU and Christian life more broadly. This would further indicate a group with very strong boundaries and structure. As with many tribes, to be initiated involves an emotionally intense ritual. Of course, it might be suggested that once a person who is not a Christian has many friends in a religious organisation there would be a certain degree of psychological pressure which would bring about a conversion experience (e.g Galanter 1999, 88). 'Conversion' might also be seen as motivated by a desire for status within the group and would therefore be more necessary for those whose status was lower because they were not accepted as 'Christians' or perhaps because their background was not 'Christian'.

OICCU Involvement

OICCU's members appeared to be very highly committed in the sense that, in my experience, the same people would be observed to be at the '7:14' worship evening every week and, equally, similar people would be observed at their speaker meeting on Fridays where members were encouraged to bring along non-Christian friends for a free lunch and to hear an invited evangelical speaker. Moreover, the group had around two-hundred members of which about three quarters would attend 7:14 so it was possible to construct a sample with such a relatively large and constant group.[4]

OICCU met relatively frequently compared to some other groups that we will assess. During my research, there were five OICCU meetings every week. Mid-week there was 7:14, the main meeting in St Aldate's Church where members would sing often lively hymns and there would be a sermon by an evangelical speaker. After this, members would return to their colleges for 'College CU' which I was not permitted to attend. On Fridays there was, as I have said, a free lunch and evangelical speaker in the hall of another Oxford church. In my experience, around thirty would attend this and these were often the more active members. Then on Saturdays there was 'Powerhouse'. This meeting was very informal and in Charismatic style and involved hymn singing and spontaneous prayer followed by group prayer. Some members would attend this but not other meetings. Also, a small minority ran a weekly course which was aimed at introducing non-Christians to Christianity. Moreover, throughout each term, there were various 'outreach events' organised by College CUs such as cheese and wine evenings at which there might be an evangelical speaker. These might occur as frequently as once every few weeks. On May Day morning there are special celebrations in Oxford. Traditionally, there is a kind of informal student party by the River Cherwell with some students traditionally diving in. According to my interviewees, OICCU students would go to this and distribute Biblical tracts and coffee to the sometimes inebriated students. Following Douglas (1996), OICCU is high in terms of ritual which we would expect from a highly structured organisation. Galanter (1999, Ch. 1) points out, likewise, that what he calls 'charismatic groups' tend to meet frequently to reassure themselves of their counter-cultural identity.

Then, once a year OICCU would organise a 'Mission' the aim of which was to evangelise or 'witness' to the whole university. This would involve an entire week of evangelical events including a daily meeting with free lunch provided where a noted evangelical speaker would, each day, examine a different theological issue such as 'Why Does God Allow Suffering?' During this period, many OICCU

4 It was named after II Chronicles 7:14: 'If my people, who are called by my name, will humble themselves and pray and seek my face and turn from their wicked ways, then I will hear from Heaven and forgive their sin and will heal their land.'

members would be observed to wear special 'Mission Week Hoodies'. The Mission would always have a particular name – such as 'Saved?' – and a related logo and Bible quote. The 'hoodies' would prominently display these and, according to many students to whom I spoke, members would interview other students about their beliefs, positioned in busy areas such as the library or their college dining hall.[5] This would all seem to imply that OICCU has strong insider/outsider boundaries, is highly differentiated and, indeed, is highly significant to the identity of many of its members as reflected in the frequency of their attendance at OICCU meetings and the relative frequency of these meetings. The evangelism itself might also be seen to imply a tightly structured group with a strong group identity and Bruce (1978) notes that evangelism and 'witness' are often used as a means of monitoring group behaviour in Christian Unions. Galanter (1999, Ch. 1) makes the same point about proselytising in charismatic groups more broadly.

OICCU Clothes and Gender

OICCU members were also differentiated from other students with regard to the way that many of them dressed. It was noticeable, for example, that almost no female members partook in the fashion of wearing a crop-top with hipsters thus exposing the midriff which was fashionable when I was conducting my research. Nor, indeed, did female members tend to wear low-cut tops for example. A great deal has been written on the significance of clothes as a means of expressing identity (e.g. Lurie 1992, Hebdige 1979, Arthur 1999) and all find that the more differentiated a group is and the more intent on *communitas* it is, the more it will control the clothes that its members wear. Some OICCU females to whom I spoke gave jokey responses when I raised this issue saying things like, 'Well ... if only I had the figure to wear that!' while one woman joked, 'I wouldn't want people to think I was a slut!' However the general consensus appeared to be that such clothing had 'negative associations', was 'provocative', 'unhelpful', 'too sexual' and 'not good witness'. This last word is very significant. OICCU's stated aim was to evangelise to the university and preserve as Christians those who already were. It was felt that such clothes would be 'unhelpful' to this aim because of the negative connotations associated, apparently, with those who wear them. Male members agreed that such clothing was 'not appropriate' as it was 'unhelpful' and might even make concentration on such issues as prayer difficult. This may well have also reflected a broader differentiating issue of attitudes to women.[6] Normally, the CU President was a man and this had almost always been the case. The general attitude appeared to be that because he was in a position of ultimate leadership then he should be male.

Male clothing was not such a conspicuous issue but certainly I tended to find very few men who dressed in an individualist manner or had long, unkempt hair for example. Moreover, members also differentiated themselves through specific

[5] Rambo (1993), for example, points out conversion can often begin through bonding with an individual member. It might be argued that this kind of evangelism is an attempt to persuade Non-Christians to share aspects of self with the group thus bonding them with it.

[6] See Dutton (2005a) for a more in-depth discussion.

'Christian' dress. This would most clearly be observed through the wearing of crosses but also the wearing of shirts that indicated attendance at specific Christian festivals, which might be seen as a play for status within the group. Also, some members would wear Christian wrist-bands with acronyms such as 'WWJD' ('What Would Jesus Do?') or 'FROG' ('Fully Reliant on God'). One male member commented to me that these were useful for evangelism because people would ask what they meant which created an opportunity to witness.

The OICCU Exec

Even the Executive Committee of OICCU is differentiated from that of other student societies. Most student societies have a Chairman, a Secretary and Treasurer. OICCU is far more structured with an entire committee of 'secretaries' including those for 'Prayer', 'Outreach' and 'Colleges'. In all other student societies, anybody can join but OICCU restricts membership to those prepared to sign its 'Doctrinal Basis'. Other societies elect their 'Exec' members one by one. OICCU is a theocracy in which the outgoing Exec will meet and pray about who should be on the new 'Exec'. From an emic perspective, God will inspire them with an Exec which will be put to the membership to either elect or reject *en masse.* According to members to whom I spoke this election is a formality with the Exec always passed as presented.

Also, unlike in other student societies, there are further levels of structure beneath the Exec. Thus, each Secretary chairs a committee relating to their area. For example, each 'College CU' has a chairman and all of these together with the relevant secretary make-up the CU committee. OICCU also has a permanent 'staff-worker', trained by UCCF, whose job is to assist in the direction of the organisation. Thus, OICCU is highly internally structured and even this form of structure differentiates it considerably from other student organisations.

Christian Language

We have already noted Douglas's observation that tightly structured groups will tend to have their own language or what is known as a 'restricted code'. This was clearest in OICCU in relation to swearing.[7] Twenty-four from a sample of twenty-five claimed that they would not use conventional swearwords such as 'fuck' and 'cunt' and even milder terms such as 'shit' and 'piss'. Some of the female members went even further claiming that they would not let 'fuck' pass their lips if quoting it and would instead say 'the f-word'. A significant minority of group members mentioned the issue of witness and bodily cleanness with regard to not swearing conventionally. In relation to conventional swearing a number of justifications were given. Most gave non-religious explanations in the first instance. These included: 'It's disgusting', 'It's lazy', '... because it's rude', 'it's offensive'. However many members also agreed that to use conventional swearing was simply 'bad witness'. It was felt that most people found words such as 'fuck' and 'cunt' offensive at least to

[7] For more detail, see Dutton (2007a).

a degree and associated negative ideas with those who used such words. People who used words like that were 'undesirables' or 'riff raff' as one OICCU member put it. Both of these terms, in British English at least, refer to a person being, essentially, working class. These views seem to reflect the middle-class perception, as McEnery (2006, 48) points out, where swearing is associated with being working class. As one OICCU member put it:

> I think it's just lazy to swear like that. I don't know, maybe I do occasionally but I shouldn't ... Because it's rude ... it's offensive. I think a lot of OICCU members would be offended by it as well as many non-Christians. And, in all honesty, it's just plain bad witness. I can't say it's particularly helpful, in all honesty.

Moreover, a small number of members cited a specific Biblical passage in I Corinthians which they felt implied that they should not swear because they had to reflect the purity of God and so be purer than non-believers.[8] Leach (1964, 28) observes that swearing generally relates to the 'taboo', especially bodily excretions, sex and the mixing of people with animals (as in 'bitch'). He therefore suggests, along with various other scholars in this area, that swearing is a matter of impurity. It might be suggested that Christians, by not swearing, are implying that they are somehow purer than non-Christians. As might be expected all members were opposed to what might be called 'profanity' or 'blasphemous swearing'. However, interestingly, members were prepared to use various examples of disguised swearing such as 'flip' and, indeed, the word 'pants' as a replacement for 'shit' or 'crap'. It might be countered that this simply reflects the fact that most members are from professional middle-class backgrounds as McEnery (2006, 48) notes that the middle-class use strong swear-words the least. However, I think it is more than that because many Oxford students of similar backgrounds were perfectly happy to swear and there were upper-class students in OICCU who were equally unhappy to use strong swearwords. I would therefore suggest that this is another matter of differentiation. But it might be suggested that as some swearing is kind of allowed – through the use of words such as 'pants' – students can keep part of their pre-Christian identity meaning that OICCU maintains an aspect of cultural heritage which both Stark (1996) and Reiss (2000) argue is important in successful religious groups.[9]

Equally, as has been noted, the frequent use of the term 'non-Christian' would also seem to imply a strong sense of differentiation. Members would pray with lines such as, 'Father in Heaven ... I really pray that you really just help Non-Christians in Oxford to come to know you Lord'. Obviously, this term would imply a group with strong boundaries. Moreover, there were a number of other terms employed by OICCU both in prayer and conversation which might seem rather idiosyncratic to outsiders. These included 'witness' and 'bad witness'. 'Witnessing' meant, effectively, 'to evangelise to people' and often it further implied doing so through one's behaviour. 'Minister' appeared to mean something quite similar to 'witness'

8 'Do not you know that your body is a temple of the Holy Spirit, who is in you, whom you have received from God? You are not your own' (I Corinthians 6:19).

9 For a more in-depth examination of swearing as a means of evangelism in British Christian Unions see Dutton (2007a).

– to be 'Christians' for the broader community. (This is significant as, in England, 'minister' is generally used to refer to a junior member of the government rather than to a priest, as is the case in Scotland. The word 'vicar' is used, colloquially, to refer to anyone who is ordained in the Church of England.) There was also the word 'back-slide' which referred to somebody who had become a Christian and had then stopped being a Christian normally as evidenced in supposedly 'non-Christian' behaviour. As such, a female student who has been, for example, snogging (tongue kissing) men she does not know very well in nightclubs might generally be perceived as not being truly a 'Christian'. If she is within the CU, members might say in response to the question of her Christianity, 'Well, only God can know whether she's a Christian'. She then becomes a Christian, through a conversion experience and ceases this behaviour. A year later she is doing it again and she has therefore 'back-slided'. We have already observed the use of the word 'unhelpful' in our discussion of swearing. OICCU, as we would expect of any tightly structured organisation, had many group acronyms such as SLOBs (Study Leader's Own Bible Study).

Communitas and Structural Reassertion: The Exec

Clearly there is evidence that OICCU is a strongly differentiated organisation in terms of religious belief, lifestyle, university activity, attitudes to women, language usage and even clothing. All of this is likely to foster a strong sense in-group *communitas* as all are 'Christians' and, as such, we would expect structure to reassert itself. This can be perceived – on the level of the group's structure – in a number of ways.

Firstly, as has already been noted, OICCU is hierarchal and this is evidenced by the relatively large Exec and its various subcommittees. However, there is a sense in which this Exec reasserts structure in a broader environment in which all are 'Christian' by more than simply being a hierarchy. A number of members to whom I spoke were convinced that those in the most senior positions were always 'established Christians'. Senior Exec members had generally not become 'Christian' while at Oxford. Secondly, gender division was reasserted. Though some Exec members were female, the President was, according to members, essentially always a man. Thirdly, there was evidence that social class differences were also reasserted within the Exec. Despite the fact that the majority of OICCU members were from state schools, the most senior positions in the Exec – including the President – were held, and had also been held the previous year, by people who expressed the symbols of English social class highlighted by Fox (2004, 75) by virtue of having been to public or private school, speaking in a posh accent and even, to some extent, wearing the kind of clothes associated with Oxford's 'Rah' stereotype. Fourthly, there was a sense in which a further religious division seemed to assert itself. OICCU's 7:14 meeting tended to be relatively conservative in style with, in effect, formal introductions and formal public prayer conducted in St Aldate's Church. By contrast, 'Powerhouse' was run by a certain female Exec member who was also involved in another Charismatic group called 'Speak' which had some contacts with another such group in Oxford called 'Fusion' (see Dutton 2006b). In this meeting there were no chairs and members simply sat or even lay on the floor. A considerable part of it was given over to worship and spontaneous prayer. This prayer, in my observation, became very emotional and there was evidence of 'the gift of prophecy' with students saying things like, 'I think that what God is really telling us to do is ...' and certainly audible glossolalia, the 'gift of the spirit' whereby Christians believe they are inspired to speak a seemingly 'spiritual language'.[10] The president was at this meeting but he was not running it. In a sense Powerhouse was a separate, loosely controlled group on the borders of OICCU but certainly under its auspices. When I spoke to former Exec members about this they agreed that there had, some years earlier, been a kind of split within OICCU between 'conservative evangelicals' and Charismatics. The result was that Charismatics were moving away from OICCU and towards Fusion. The Exec had decided that, as one put it, 'We'd maybe start to emphasise our differences rather than just what holds us together' and, as such, Powerhouse was developed. Obviously, Powerhouse itself created *communitas* through spontaneous prayer, lively worship music and even charismata and thus we might expect a reassertion of structure and this did indeed occur within the ritual. Having examined OICCU's structure I think it would be helpful to examine ritual as a separate category.

Ritual and *Communitas:* 7:14

OICCU's main meeting, like OICCU itself, was on a certain level structured, to the extent of being choreographed rather like an evangelical Anglican service. The Wednesday night meeting, in the Evangelical-Anglican St Aldates Church, would begin with the President conducting a relatively formal opening prayer before making introductory remarks often of a relatively humorous nature. There would then be the singing of a number of 'worship' songs after which the President would invite a different member each week to read a Bible passage. The President would then invite the speaker – who would always be male – to the front and pray for him before he preached. The speaker would usually be an evangelical vicar or from an evangelical church outside the Church of England. For example, during my research speakers included Rev'd John Stott, a leading evangelical Anglican. After the speech, the President would invite another member to the front to conduct a prayer. In my experience, this was always in a much more informal style as the President deliberately selected somebody likely involved in OICCU's Charismatic wing, perhaps for political reasons. The President would then give a series of notices and ask members to 'Talk to someone you don't know before you leave'.

As such, the meeting itself might be seen as relatively highly structured but it was a structure which brought about *communitas* and the first example can be observed in the worship music which was controlled by the band – which included electric guitars and drums – and thus the group more broadly. Unlike in other groups, OICCU's band was playing quietly in the background as people entered, creating a calming effect. Then the first song would always be a very fast-paced, exciting hymn such as '*Over All the Earth*'. The second hymn would normally be considerably

[10] A further 'gift' involves the ability to interpret this language.

slower, the third hymn very fast and then often the hymn singing would culminate in a hymn that was both fast and slow and highly complex such as, '*The Spirit of the Sovereign Lord is Upon You*'.[11] Thus, the order and style of the hymns appeared to deliberately dissociate the singers by bringing about a kind of emotional oscillation (see Reed 1978) and building up to an ultimate climax. Creating a climax in this manner, where one moves between different emotions while gradually reaching the climax, is a well-known technique for dissociating an audience in rhetoric (e.g. Percy 1996 or Nash 1989) and it appeared to work in this case. Indeed, unlike in AUCU for example, the band continued playing between songs such that the emotional climax was not lost. It was generally during the final song that I would observe evidence of considerable dissociation such as members shouting out, 'Oh yes! Jesus!', closing their eyes and holding their hands out, crying and even, in a small number of cases, speaking-in-tongues.

But it should be stressed that it was a minority that engaged in this kind of charismatic activity and this is important sociologically and in terms of our model of liminality. Broadly, whatever the religious response, we might suggest that the structure of the 7:14 meeting creates *communitas* because all are singing and worshipping together. We would therefore expect social division to reassert itself within the worship and this, indeed, was noted. A large minority would engage in Charismatic activity and the majority would become highly emotional. However, those in positions of authority did not appear to react in this manner. As such, there appeared to be a social difference in how OICCU members responded to precisely the same emotional-religious stimuli with those at the top of the group generally appearing to maintain control to a greater extent. This would be congruous with Douglas (1996, 76) Purity Rule whereby those closer to the centre of power are required to retain greater control over their bodies.[12] As such, the refusal of certain senior members or formerly senior members to involve themselves in such emotional worship could be interpreted as an expression both of OICCU and even of broader social class status. By contrast, the Charismatic activity engaged in by many of the students who appeared to be on the borders of OICCU – and involved in Powerhouse – might be understood as a play status. It was an assertion that though they do not have power within the group, they are, in a sense, more legitimate because the Holy Spirit works through them. Many anthropologists such as Lewis (1989, 91) have observed accordingly that spirit possession is more common amongst those on the borders of the group and especially women who are disempowered in certain tribal contexts. It might be countered that students are simply reflecting their religious backgrounds but this is surely question-begging. Why would they be doing this in a very obvious way in a situation where symbolic *communitas* has been created? I would suggest that a reasonable answer is that it is a reaction to this very *communitas* and an assertion of or play for status. Also, if the issue is only 'background' it forces us to ask why so many state-school students from conventional Anglican ('non-Christian' in OICCU's terminology) backgrounds are 'Charismatic' in the context of OICCU.

11 For further discussion of Christian music see Ward (2003).

12 However, it might be argued that those at the centre of power (such as God) are able, in effect, to 'break the rules' in terms of taboo and general behaviour (see Dutton 2007a).

Though the majority of OICCU (around two thirds) claimed to be 'Charismatic' this did not appear to be reflected amongst those running the organisation. I therefore do not find this counter entirely persuasive.

Powerhouse

Equally, group prayer would be likely to create *communitas* and I will focus in this regard on the prayer conducted in Powerhouse. After the hymn-singing there was a long silence followed by spontaneous prayer and prophecy. For example, Sarah's prayer ran:

> I really just pray ... Father God ... I really just pray ... that you come to us today. That you let us know you ... Father God ... that you let us feel you ... and you let everyone in Oxford just feel you (...) We don't deserve you, Lord. We love you.

So informal was this that it did not even end with the conventional 'Amen'. After this, members divided into small prayer groups to pray about various topics. At this point a clear difference in prayer style could be observed and I would submit this is a matter of liminality as to claim it is matter of 'culture' raises the question of why a person would deliberately assert difference in such a context. In general the prayers were comparable to Sarah's apart from the fact that they were focused on a specific topic and ended in 'Amen'. For example:

> Father God ... I really pray for Unda's trip to Belarus ... I really pray that you she can just ... like ... make them see Lord. I really pray that people don't ... like ... become disheartened Lord ...

We might note from this prayer the issues of evangelising abroad in the holidays as a play status and the way that the person praying attempts to seem authentic by using highly informal language as in 'like' as a kind of sentence breaker to show that they are so sincere they are lost for words. However, Ben's prayer was different. The language was far more formal:

> Lord I pray you provide Tony with the strength to organise the Christian Rugby Ball so that it fully glorifies you, Lord. (…) I pray that as many non-Christians as possible attend and enjoy themselves. (…) I pray this in your precious name.

This student had been to public school and also conformed to the social class stereotype outlined above. Thus, this might be regarded as a reassertion of social status in the context of *communitas* brought about by prayer and indeed the earlier spontaneous prayer. The few students who prayed in this manner during Powerhouse kept quiet during the earlier spontaneous prayer. As such, I think what we can see is evidence of the structural model of liminality outlined. OICCU is highly structured and brings about *communitas* just as Oxford University does. Aspects of the meetings also bring about *communitas* and in both contexts structure reasserts itself in various ways relating to, especially, social differences within OICCU and Oxford University more broadly.

Charisma

There are two other highly significant ways in which OICCU deliberately created *communitas* and, as I have argued, this would, following the model being presented, be congruous with OICCU's high level of structure. The first is the use of speakers who were able to stir up the emotions of their audience – speakers who were 'charismatic' or at least partially so in the Weberian sense of the term. Such speakers, as Weber notes, would be accepted in a group that is in crisis and, as we have seen, a highly liminal phase is a kind of crisis of identity for many of those passing through it.

There were, I would argue, charismatic dimensions to many of OICCU's invited speakers. Many of the OICCU speakers were 'famous' amongst evangelical Christians according to OICCU members to whom I spoke. Certainly, many OICCU speakers were able to arouse both considerable mirth and other less pleasant emotions and as we have seen this ability to encapsulate human experience and take the audience on an emotional journey is often the sign of a charismatic speaker. For reasons of space, it is difficult to convey this without a lengthy aside involving a detailed analysis of specific sermons, many of which lasted for around an hour in themselves. But I think that the following quote from the beginning of a sermon by a missionary encapsulates what I mean. In order not to identify this person I have altered the wording slightly.

> Well I think you'd probably expect me to start with a joke. But I didn't get much sleep last night so I didn't get round to thinking of one. So I'll skip the joke. I'll skip telling you my beliefs. I'll skip playing on your emotions and start with a fact. Both fundamentalist and nominalist Muslims will stand side by side in Hell ... Islam is a blockade to Christ's presence.

The bluntness of this speaker was not representative but what was representative was the emotional nature of his speech and his ability to move convincingly between different emotions with ease. As discussed, it is this kind of oratory that creates dissociation and thus *communitas.* Many scholars such as Gilhus (1997, 2) and Berger (1997, 6) have looked at the place of laughter in various religions and all agree that it is a loss of control. Mary Douglas (quoted in Berger 1997, 72) even claims that it is a break with structure, something very close to Turner's understanding of *communitas.* Presumably, the shared experience of negative emotions would also foster *communitas* as would being taken on an emotional journey as has been suggested is the case of catharsis (Nuttall 1996). Indeed, we might argue that the speech itself – by virtue of its ability to take the audience on an emotional journey – is highly structured and it is this structure which assists in the development of *communitas.* This would unlikely be the case in a casual, conversational presentation.

Testimony

A very small number of OICCU meetings which I attended – two during my entire fieldwork – involved members, somewhere near the beginning of the meeting, standing-up and giving their 'testimony'. This involved recounting their conversion (or re-conversion) to Christianity and how it occurred while at Oxford and due, to some extent, to their involvement in OICCU. I found that when members gave their testimony it involved not merely a discussion of the immediate circumstances surrounding their conversion but a broader discussion of their entire life inasmuch as it culminated in that conversion and substantially altered thereafter. Hence the testimony was essentially members sharing their biography with the group but presenting this biography such that their conversion to Christianity at Oxford was of central importance to it.

Before looking at examples of what I mean it might be worth pausing to further examine precisely what we mean when we discuss biography. Hudson, in exploring the identity dynamics of language, argues that each human is individually distinguished by their own personal experience and hence their biographies (Hudson 1996, 11). Thus, the uniqueness of a person's biography is perhaps that one tenet which ensures that they are able to foster a unique sense of self. 'Testimony', however, encourages members to contextualise themselves within the parameters of joining a certain community and, moreover, to render the joining of that community central to the biographical statement itself. This community was usually the CU and also the broader 'Christian' community of 'the saved'. But, in a sense, almost all OICCU members had similar biographies in as much as their conversion was the turning point in life. As such, a group emphasis on 'testimony' might further indicate a high level of structure. I will look at one of the two testimonies here as both were very similar. The first testimony was given in front of OICCU at their Wednesday night meeting '7:14'.

> I'd always believed in God but I didn't have a relationship with Him. I didn't really know Him. So when I arrived in Oxford I wasn't Christian. I knew some CU members from college but I thought they were all crazy frankly. My parents aren't really Christians. They took me to church a few times at Christmas and occasionally read me the Bible as a child but (...) Then that summer *(between 1st year and 2nd year)* I went to America, to a talk by a Christian and it just got me really interested. So when I came back to Oxford at the beginning of this year I went to the ID Course *(an evangelising course run by OICCU)* and I was asking all kinds of hard questions ... And eventually I prayed and I sort of became a Christian and attended College Group but I didn't really feel that I understood it properly and for the first two terms of this year and I just like slipped away. I forgot about God but He never forgot about me. And ... erm ... I just felt more and more unhappy without Him ... I felt more and more like I didn't make sense without Him there and then I realised that maybe that was Him telling me something. So I prayed, I prayed harder than I've ever prayed, and I just dedicated myself to God ... Oh! It's good to be back!

I would suggest that this testimony creates *communitas* in a number of ways. We are taken on an emotional journey where Steve empties himself before his audience, admits that he has been a bad Christian and builds to an emotional climax where he breaks with his relatively composed language style to exclaim, 'Oh! It's good to be back!' It is 'good' to have returned to the Christian community and to be at the heart of OICCU. Presumably this is also highly emotional because of the part OICCU has played in saving him from Hell and his relationship with his parents is somewhat emotive as he implies that he believes that they will go to Hell. Thus again we see the way that OICCU's highly structured meetings are designed, as with Oxford University and many tribal initiations, to foster *communitas* amongst the group. Indeed, Noakes (1984, 160) points out that even witnessing dissociation can itself dissociate which further demonstrates the power, in *communitas* terms, of this kind of catharsis. OICCU itself has already reacted to that broader university or college-wide *communitas* by establishing a highly differentiated community. As noted, within this then psychologically difficult *communitas*, such as in meetings, further boundary-making procedures are not infrequently observed.

Oxford Church Politics and the Charismatic Movement

It may be countered that Charismatic behaviour, conversion and even meeting structure in OICCU do not necessarily relate to liminality but are a matter of OICCU imitating the kind of behaviour that they observe in the Charismatic Christian churches that many of them attend on Sundays or are influenced by. OICCU is substantially Charismatic in its worship style. As such, if the nature of the local churches is a salient influence, we would expect the majority of OICCU members to attend a church, on Sundays, that was at least to some extent Charismatic and even for the rector to be Charismatic. Indeed, OICCU was heavily influenced in its recent history by Canon Michael Green, a former senior OICCU member who went on to be the Rector of the Charismatic church St Aldates. My surveys appear to indicate something somewhat different. Of the twenty-five OICCU members surveyed, only eight attended Charismatic churches. Of this eight, three attended 'Oxford Community Church'. The Fusion group, which has already been discussed, operates from this church. Five attended St Aldates. This church is Church of England and the rector was Rev'd Simon Ponsonby. It is evangelical and Charismatic. The majority of those whom I surveyed, including many students who specifically claimed to be Charismatic, attended St Ebbes, which is also Church of England. This is generally recognised as being far more traditional in its style than St Aldates, although some members commented to me that some OICCU members sometimes try to make the morning service 'a little more lively'. The rector was the Rev'd Vaughan Roberts. This rector is evangelical, though not a Charismatic, and has publicly expressed his reservations with regard to the Charismatic Movement (Baker October 1999). This would seem to imply that OICCU are influencing a generally non-Charismatic church rather than the other way around.

But, anyway this alternative explanation is question-begging and this can be demonstrated with the following example. A hypothetical Charismatic church is highly structured and is fostering *communitas* amongst its congregation through such activity. This raises the question of why they would do that. Presumably the answer is to cement a tightly structured group with a strong identity which in turn raises the question of why people would want to be in such a group which leads us back, I would suggest to Armstrong's (2001) understanding of 'fundamentalist groups' as well as Galanter's (1999) assessment of 'charismatic groups'. Such groups become attractive in particular to people undergoing identity crisis of some kind due to considerable change; people who feel that their identity – or a significant aspect of it – is under threat. Indeed, Bruce (2002, 35) notes that throughout recent British history religious revivals and the rise of Charismatic-style religious groups can be connected to times of rapid transition – in a sense times of intense liminality – in the areas in which they occur. This, I have argued, is precisely what Oxford University brings about for many students and especially state-school students and in particular those who have not been through the liminal phase of the Gap Year, something which seemed to be far more popular amongst students from private schools. It therefore strikes me as no coincidence that in university terms state-school pupils are over-represented amongst OICCU and amongst those who had conversion experiences while at Oxford. OICCU members may be influenced by the Charismatic Movement in England but, if Bruce is correct, this form of worship would not be sustained without a sense of crisis and this is what Oxford University – and thus OICCU – manage to provide to many students each year.

I am not suggesting that highly structured evangelical groups will always become 'Charismatic' in their worship. However, what I am suggesting is that their very structures will in themselves lead to in-group *communitas* and because this lack of structure is psychologically difficult, as Turner implies, this will likely lead to the development of further levels of structure which will then themselves lead to *communitas.* And as I will show, if the structure is weaker then the *communitas* is likely to be weaker as well. The *communitas* may take the form of charismatic worship but it would only be likely to develop in this way in highly transitional circumstances, the kind of circumstances conducive to a Charismatic revival. These, to some extent at least, are the circumstances which Oxford University provides.

Conclusion

Oxford University is highly structured and intense. It is also highly transitional in terms of status and identity and is likely to be especially keenly felt by students for whom attendance at such a university is especially status-raising and who have not previously lived away from home. Though this generalises to some extent, the evidence indicates that in England these are more likely to be state-school pupils. Due to the way that Oxford separates and traumatises its students and breaks down social boundaries through living arrangements and symbolic rituals it creates a strong sense of *communitas.* As this is psychologically difficult, we see structure reasserting itself in the form of OICCU. This is a highly differentiated group in terms of language, clothes, religious belief, lifestyle ethics and even its social organisation and system of election. However, it fosters a kind of 'Us' v 'Them' 'Christian' *communitas.* We then note structure reasserting itself again, for example in the social and religious composition of the group's Exec and in the Powerhouse subgroup amongst other areas. Indeed, even *communitas*-creating meetings appear to involve a reassertion of social structure during certain forms of worship.

As stated, the counter that this does not relate to *communitas* and that the students are simply reflecting the influence of the Charismatic Movement in England or at the Oxford church that they attend on Sundays is less than convincing. I would submit that an analysis of Oxford University and OICCU provides a strong case for the model of liminality being proposed.

Chapter 3

'The course Caribbean nations take will partly depend on us'

Eila Helander's Fieldwork with IVCF at St Augustine Campus (University of the West Indies) in Trinidad

Eila Helander conducted a study of the group IVCF (Inter-Varsity Christian Fellowship) at St Augustine Campus in Trinidad. This Caribbean island is part of the state of Trinidad and Tobago and is just north of Venezuela. In the town of St Augustine there was at the time and remains one of the three main campuses of the University of the West Indies where it was possible to study a broad range of subjects including sciences, social sciences and the humanities. The other two campuses are in Jamaica and Barbados. The Christian group itself was affiliated to IFES. In historical terms the period of her research was from 1962 to 1983 because she conducted studies both of former students and of current students in the group. However, in terms of participant observation she spent two periods in the Caribbean firstly from 1977 to 1979 and then again from 1981 to 1983. As such she was able to produce a highly detailed and meticulous thesis which is, therefore, of particular use as a primary source in attempting to apply the level theory of liminality to a further evangelical student group and university. Though the thesis was indeed very detailed in terms of data it was not primarily concentrating on the issue of liminality – though this issue was discussed – and I was therefore able to supplement the information provided in the thesis by conducting a telephone interview with Eila Helander.

Before moving on, however, it would be germane to at least look at the potential difficulties with employing a primary source of this kind. It raises the basic anthropological problem, from my perspective, that I did not conduct the fieldwork myself. Reading Helander's thesis raised a number of questions but fortunately I was able to speak to her and discuss these issues in depth. To a certain extent, therefore, this difficulty was surmounted. But it should be remembered that in drawing upon Helander's thesis we are drawing upon what is essentially an historical primary source. It might be argued that there may be mistakes in the fieldwork and any analysis drawing upon them would simply perpetuate these. I can only counter that the fieldwork seems to be very thorough indeed. The fieldwork has been substantial, the fieldwork methodology is laid out in considerable depth and it is a doctoral thesis published exactly as submitted rather than a commercial book where this methodological aspect might be cut down somewhat. Helander also appends all of the information that a critical eye would require – such as her surveys – which allows the critic to assess the quality of the fieldwork to an even greater extent. In this regard I am confident about drawing upon Helander's thesis as an historical source. Though this is a fallacious appeal to authority, her thesis was passed by Helsinki University which is a highly internationally respected institution which might give us greater cause for confidence than we might have had it been passed by a very different institution. With any historical sources we might raise questions about the personal motivations of the writer when these relate to the subject in question. Helander states in the thesis that she is a 'Christian' and from an evangelical background in Finland. She does not state that she was in accord with the views of IVCF, however, and she is evidently examining these as an outsider as she writes, 'It was taken for granted that I subscribed to the basic evangelical doctrinal views' (Helander 1986, 59). Helander now claims to be a 'liberal Christian' (Int. 2007). She is also a cultural outsider in Trinidad by virtue of being Finnish and she notes that the Caribbean evangelical tradition is rather different from her own experiences of it. I would therefore not be concerned that Helander – a Christian (albeit influenced by evangelicalism) – would be biased in favour of her fellow 'Christians' in IVCF. For these reasons I think it is possible to draw upon Helander's thesis – and indeed assess her data in line with the level model of liminality – without too many concerns and this is what I propose to do.

Religious and Cultural Background in Trinidad

Before moving on to the assessment it would be germane to examine both the religious and cultural background in Trinidad and Helander examines these issues in depth in her thesis. I think the most useful course would therefore be to paraphrase what she has discussed.

According to statistics from 1980, 60 per cent of the population of Trinidad were Christian of which 14.7 per cent were Anglican, a decline of 4 per cent in the ten years since 1970 (92). This reflects the fact that Trinidad was part of the British Empire until 1962 when it was granted independence. It subsequently became a republic in 1976. In the ten years between 1970 and 1980, free Protestant congregations had grown somewhat and this was particularly the case with Baptists and the Pentecostals, who had not been part of the statistics in 1970. In addition to Anglicans a further 14 per cent were in various Protestant groups the largest of which was the Presbyterians (3.8 per cent) and then the Pentecostals (3.5 per cent). As Helander points out, the Pentecostal churches tend to be relatively strict in terms of 'purity' of lifestyle, highly evangelical, conversion oriented and they lay emphasis on spiritual gifts, such as speaking-in-tongues and a Charismatic form of worship (Helander, 164). In addition, 33 per cent of the population were Roman Catholic reflecting the fact that Trinidad had been run by Spain prior to being run by Britain. More than 24 per cent of those in Trinidad were Hindu and 6 per cent were Muslim which reflected Britain's policy of bringing in labour from around the Empire after the abolition of the Slave Trade. There is also a small Chinese minority in Trinidad for the same reasons.

As such, in religious terms Trinidad appears to be very mixed. However, the majority are Christian. That said, Helander observes that in understanding Caribbean Christian groups during this period it is vitally important to account for the influence of the Black Power Movement which was 'sweeping the Caribbean' in the 1970s. This political empowerment movement argued that Christianity was a 'white religion' (93) which upheld 'colonial cultural values in the country' (94). The group promoted the idea, beginning in the 1960s, that 'black is beautiful', black culture should be revived and colonial culture such as that of the USA should be rejected (230). As such, the group promoted 'Shango' and the 'Shouters' as authentic Trinidadian religion, both being voodoo-style movements. The movement also prepared the ground for Rastafarianism in the 1980s. Helander later observes that traditional pre-Christian beliefs were still held to some extent amongst many people in Trinidad. One IVCF member told Helander that he had been ill as a baby and that his mother had taken him to see the 'obeah' – a kind of Voodoo 'shaman' who could be possessed by the 'obeah' spirit. Many IVCF members regarded this spirit as a manifestation of Satan (206).[1]

Cultural Background

Helander observes that much of Trinidadian culture at an institutional level is influenced by the British system as we will see below in terms of education. As already discussed, since the 1960s a kind black cultural renaissance had been developing in Trinidad with the rise of the Black Power Movement. There were attempts to revive traditional African beliefs – as the majority of the population are of African descent – and also traditional cultural practices such as 'Calypso' (234). In terms of Trinidad's racial composition Helander notes that 40.8 per cent were black, 40.7 per cent were East Indian, 0.9 per cent were white and 16.3 per cent were classified as 'mixed' (82).

Helander also observes that social stratification in Trinidad, during the periods of her fieldwork, was based around education. It had been based around race and this process has been seen to develop in many other nations where one race is colonised by another and those with mixed heritage tend to become of a higher social class with the colonisers at the top (e.g. Rasmussen 1986 finds this in Greenland). Helander observes that social stratification in Trinidad in the 1950s was substantially noticeable in terms of race. As such the overwhelming majority of what she terms 'the upper class' were white people – though they were a very small minority of those living in Trinidad. Also within this class were a minority of coloured people – of mixed black and white descent – and a very small minority of Chinese. The middle class was substantially coloured with a large minority of black people and a small minority of Chinese and Indians. The working class was mainly black (37). However, she points out that this would have changed considerably by the 1970s though there is no detailed analysis of this. She claims that by this time, for reasons that we will later discuss, education had become the main means of social stratification within Trinidadian society.

[1] For a discussion of shamanism see Lewis (1989).

The Education System in Trinidad

The education system in Trinidad had changed rapidly in a few decades prior to Helander's fieldwork. She notes that under colonialism there was no university in the West Indies and as such only the elite could afford Higher Education, usually in Britain or America (97). However, even secondary education was restricted to those who could pay for it and consequently to the whites and a minority of affluent coloured people. To be educated at secondary level students had to pass the 'College Exhibition Exam' (which they had to pass previous exams even to take) and even then they had to pay school fees. As such only the very brightest children from less affluent backgrounds received any secondary education (95). Free state education was introduced in 1961 and this was contingent on passing a new exam called the 'Common Entrance Examination'. All but three of the students and graduates in IVCF that Helander studied had received this free form of education, the remainder having attended the remaining private schools. In 1971, this developed into a division between junior secondary schools and academic secondary schools (97).

The University of the West Indies was established in 1962 and St Augustine Campus – where Helander conducted her fieldwork – was incorporated into this. As with England, students took a three-year Bachelors degree and admission to the university, as with many British universities, was determined by the marks that they received in the school leaving exams known as A-Levels. Interestingly, Helander observes that evangelical or 'born again' groups were extremely active in many Trinidadian secondary schools (118) which may also help to explain the very high numbers of students who were not necessarily from religious backgrounds but underwent conversion experiences at secondary school (Int. 2007). However, as we will see, she also observes conversion while at university. As there was, during Helander's fieldwork at least, only one university in Trinidad there is no need to examine the issue of liminality at universities more broadly. We can move straight on to St Augustine Campus as a branch of the University of the West Indies. But prior to doing this it would be useful to examine the social and religious background of IVCF in Trinidad during Helander's fieldwork.

IVCF Social and Religious Background

The social background of IVCF during Helander's fieldwork was quite diverse reflecting, perhaps, the relatively egalitarian educational policies that had only relatively recently been introduced. Of a sample of twenty three students, one was upper class, thirteen were middle class and thirteen were working class according to the model that Helander had previously outlined (106). Though Helander does not provide any statistics for this, it is likely that the upper class may be somewhat under represented within IVCF though it must be remembered that Charismatic and Pentecostal groups were then popular in Trinidad and that the groups were active at schools. These revivalist churches have traditionally been more popular in Trinidad amongst the middle class and the working class and thus have less prestige than the Anglican Church, leading to parental criticism of converts for lowering the family's prestige (122). Helander includes within the upper-class bracket the children of professionals such as doctors which Argyle would term 'higher professionals'. 'Class II' is then lower professionals, such as school teachers, and the lower-middle class while 'Class III' is the working class. These findings might also indicate that such a form of structure is more attractive to working-class students for whom the university experience would be especially transitional and status-raising and we will discuss this possibility below. Helander notes that most of the students that she surveyed were not only the first in their families to attend university but were in many cases the first to attend secondary school (106).

The religious background of IVCF members is provided in detail. Of a sample of forty two students, eleven had what Helander terms an 'evangelical' background (meaning Baptist, Pentecostal, and so forth), twenty-five had changed their religious affiliation at some point and six were Anglican, Presbyterian or Catholic 'though paying frequent visits to an evangelical church' (120–21). Those who had changed religion had moved from Roman Catholicism, Anglicanism, Presbyterianism or Hinduism to the evangelical churches discussed. It has been observed that, historically at least, race was a defining issue in understanding social dynamics in Trinidad and Helander provides interviews where correspondents imply that people play for status in Trinidad by imitating 'the white man' (184). However, Helander observed that IVCF were a 'mixed group' including Chinese, Asians, Coloureds and Black people (Int. 2007). Having looked at the social and religious dynamics of IVCF let us then turn to the degree of liminality at St Augustine College.

St Augustine Campus and Liminality

Helander implies that for Trinidadian students – who make up two thirds of the student body – attendance at St Augustine Campus was particularly socially significant especially if, as with many IVCF members, they were not from particularly educated backgrounds. Firstly, those that had been to the college would have been a tiny elite in Trinidad in the early 1980s as only 1.6 per cent of the population had been to university, though this percentage was rising (102). Consequently, at the time attending St Augustine Campus would have been highly significant in the raising or maintaining of social status in Trinidad, hence the comment from an IVCF member quoted in the title of this chapter. The future leaders of the Caribbean were being educated at the college and IVCF had a perfect opportunity to influence them with their brand of evangelical Christianity. Helander summarises that 'Education has been one of the most important means for upward social mobility for members of the middle and lower classes in the Caribbean' (103). Consequently, attendance at St Augustine would be very significant within Trinidad in terms of its potential for raising status. This is especially pronounced amongst IVCF as Helander observes that most were the first in their families to attend secondary school let alone university. However, in terms of the potential for status raising within the Trinidad of the time we might even venture to suggest that the university is comparable to somewhere like Oxford, or another prestigious university, within contemporary England.

In many respects, Helander's description of life at St Augustine Campus would imply that it is highly liminal but perhaps not to the extent of Oxford University. Firstly, she observes that it is a very small university with only around 2000 students (98). This kind of intimate size – where students are aware that they may well be the future of the country in many respects – might be seen as a form of structure that assists in the development of *communitas*. Unlike at Oxford University, however, Helander does not recall that there was a ritual of Matriculation (and thus a Rite of Separation) at the college (Int. 2007). However, there is a graduation ceremony paralleling the British model. Following Douglas, this might be seen to imply a highly liminal Rite of Passage. In that sense, as with a university such as Aberdeen, the school leaving exams are the only enacting ritual required to gain entrance into the university. But unlike Aberdeen, the student population of St Augustine is broad. As it is the only university in Trinidad it attracts people from all social backgrounds and has, as we will see, the facilities in place to ensure that they mix together apart from simply through lectures. As discussed, during the 1980s, there were a number of private schools in Trinidad for the elite and the university would inevitably mix these students with the rest who had attended ordinary secondary schools by passing the newer examination. Moreover, as a part of the University of the West Indies, Helander notes that one third of St Augustine students are not from Trinidad. They are mainly from other parts of the Caribbean and this would, consequently, be likely to produce cultural mixing as well and might render the university experience particularly liminal from those outside Trinidad.

One dimension which, in a sense, renders the university slightly less liminal for many students from Trinidad is the fact that, for quite a few, it is not their first highly status-raising Rite of Passage. If they are the first in their family to have attended secondary school then this schooling – following the British system – would also have been highly significant. However, St Augustine Campus would also involve living away from home. Helander recalls that St Augustine was a campus university in its entirety when it was first established. By 1980, the university had expanded to such an extent that only 16 per cent of students lived in the catered Halls of Residence with the rest having to find accommodation in the surrounding town. Those that did live in the Halls of Residence would, of course, have been more likely to meet and bond with people from different social, religious and national backgrounds during their time there through living and eating arrangements for example. Helander points out that she was not aware of traditions such as formal meals as we have seen at Oxford University (Int. 2007). However, she notes that around two thirds of the students she studied had lived on campus at some point during their degree and all of the students that were from somewhere other than Trinidad lived on campus. This would, again, mean that they would be likely to meet and bond with the students from Trinidad and beyond – another structure that would be likely to assist in fostering *communitas* amongst students. Interestingly, Helander observed in interview that whereas many of the students did not live on campus, 'all the IVCF students lived on campus'. This is a fascinating observation and we will later return to it.

Student Identity

We would expect *communitas* to create a strong sense of student identity of the kind that we have observed at Oxford University and Helander does provide some evidence for this being the case at St Augustine College. She observes, for example, that during the 1970s there had been a great deal of political unrest amongst campaigning students on campus and that the campus had actually been closed for various periods of time in the 1970s to stop the unrest from spreading (108). This kind of strong political activism might be seen to indicate a sense of student self-awareness as a separate societal group who will one day be influential in the running of society. University students criticised the established system and were regarded as a kind of threat to it (108). Certainly, I would suggest that the campus conditions of St Augustine College would assist in creating a strong sense of student *communitas* – and student consciousness – which might not necessarily be fostered otherwise and as such I think that these observations are not insignificant.

Moreover, as with the British universities which we have discussed, there was and remains a Student Guild at St Augustine Campus which appears to be comparable to a British Student Union. Operating like a Trade Union, it has elected officers, organises social events, provides pastoral assistance for students and generally assists their interests including organising an orientation week at the beginning of the year and so forth. This would also imply a relatively high level of structure which would lead to a sense of student *communitas* at least to some extent. This might also be seen to reflect and further create a strong sense of student identity. In academic terms, the university did not have the same intense levelling rituals that were observed at Oxford University. Examinations were not all in the third year, there was the possibility of re-takes and it was not necessary to wear any manner of formal clothing in order to sit examinations. Consequently the element of deliberate trauma, in this regard at least, might be seen to be lower as would the consequent *communitas.*

Structural Reassertion

Following this level of liminality and consequent *communitas* we might expect to see some structural reassertion within the *communitas* created by St Augustine and certainly within the campus itself. Helander observes that there is at least some evidence for this. Structure was clearly reasserted in religious terms, reflecting the religious divisions in Trinidad which it might be suggested St Augustine's liminality might bring into question. As such there was IVCF (as a evangelical Protestant society), a Catholic Chaplaincy society, an Islamic Society and the 'Society for the Promotion of Indian Culture' (SPIC, a kind of Hindu Society) and Helander points out that all of these had 'regular' meetings which would imply that they were significant in preserving or creating a new identity for the students involved with them at least to a degree (157). Currently there are also a number of student groups at St Augustine which might be seen to reflect a reassertion of regional identity such as 'VINSA' (St Vincent and the Grenadines Association). The presence of such a group on campus would be congruous with the theory under discussion if we understand

St Augustine as being a relatively liminal environment and the environment as being more liminal, in many respects, for foreigners.

Helander does not record the attitudes of other students towards what was a highly evangelical and fervent student group. However she does make one significant point which further parallels my own experiences with OICCU, which I have suggested operate in a highly liminal environment. She observes that IVCF were very interested in whether or not she was a 'Christian' and she recalls a conversation where a member, talking to her about what she might expect during her fieldwork, said, 'You're a Christian, right?' to which she said 'Yes' to which the student responded, 'So there should be nothing to worry about' (59). Some years later when she returned to St Augustine and was being funded by the World Council of Churches she was aware that this provoked 'discussion' about her 'doctrinal allegiance' (61). In interview, Helander felt that there would have been 'big problems' successfully conducting her fieldwork if the students had suspected that she was not a 'Christian' and that it would have been very difficult indeed if she had been an open atheist because 'they would have targeted me for conversion'. Helander summed-up by saying that had she not been a Christian (at least in IVCF's view) when conducting her fieldwork then, 'It would've spoiled the whole thing' (Int. 2007). Though this is speculation to a certain extent, it would at least appear to imply a group with strong boundaries against outsiders which is what we would expect in these relatively liminal circumstances.

IVCF Belief and Initiation

In terms of both their religious and ethical beliefs, Helander portrays IVCF as being highly differentiated from the broader student population even if accounting for the fact that Trinidad in the early 1980s may have been more conservative than some of the other cultures under assessment. But before looking at this, further evidence of IVCF's tight structure can be seen in a kind of initiation ritual which was absent even in OICCU as far as I am aware. In order to join a member had to 'Sign the Constitution' but, unlike in OICCU, this appeared to be a kind of ritual. Indeed, it had to be repeated every year in order for a student to continue to be a member (136). Interestingly, Helander also observes that though a person had to be an IVCF member to be on the Exec the group was more interested – in terms of 'Rank and File' members – in anybody who had had a conversion experience and been born again (136). Helander interprets this as possible evidence of malleable boundaries. But I think it might equally be seen as evidence of very strong boundaries. To be truly accepted as a member and certainly to be a senior member it is insufficient to simply sign the constitution. One must have had a conversion experience – a direct experience of God.

Obviously, Helander's research into belief does not parallel precisely the method that I have followed but I think that the results can still be reasonably compared. The Doctrinal Basis of the IVCF is roughly the same as that of OICCU's. Helander makes it clear (166) that members believed in 'the infallibility of scripture' at every level. Hence it is strongly implied that like students in OICCU they would strongly believe in Christian doctrines in their traditional form and would be likely to reject modern critical methods and Evolutionary Theory. There was a firm belief, for example, that non-Christians would go to Hell. As such, the religious beliefs would appear to at least compare to those of OICCU. Helander also points out that the lifestyle of IVCF members was likewise highly differentiated. As with OICCU, members would not have pre-marital sex, they would not drink a great deal and many would not drink at all, they would engage in fasting (which I was not aware of in any of the groups that I studied), they would socialise and have relationships almost exclusively with other group members and so forth (150). Indeed, she finds that when a few members did have, for example, non-Christian boyfriends this was highly problematic for many group members with one saying 'you cannot associate darkness with light' (238). Helander summarises that, 'Evangelicals in Trinidad, university students and graduates being no exception, hold the strong opinion that Christians should not establish dating relationships with non-Christians (i.e. 'the unsaved') or get married to them' (237). This is certainly a stronger view than was held by many in AUCU as we will see. I was aware of a number of members – some relatively senior – who had 'non-Christian' boyfriends. As such, in terms of both belief and lifestyle ethics IVCF can be regarded as highly differentiated within their St Augustine Campus environment.

'*To Change and to Preserve*' at St Augustine

If St Augustine is understood to be a relatively liminal campus and IVCF a tightly structured evangelical group then we would expect to find conversion experiences – which would betoken a change in the identity of a student – occurring at St Augustine and we would also expect students for whom university would be likely to be the most liminal to be over-represented in the group. Though the situation is not as stark as it has been shown to be in the case of Oxford University, Helander does provide some information which substantiates these ideas.

Helander observes that of those she interviewed 'quite a few' underwent conversion experiences and became Christians either towards the end of school or after they came to St Augustine. In the majority of cases the conversion occurred at school and of her sample of fifty-two IVCF students five converted while they were at St Augustine (142). This is marginally more than my own findings with regard to Aberdeen University as will be discussed. However, in this regard, Helander stresses that IVCF were also highly active in secondary schools in Trinidad (118). Obviously the experience of school is liminal – even if somewhat less so than that of university – and especially likely to be so for many of the students in her sample who were the first people in their families to have ever gone to secondary school. In these circumstances the presence of such a group – which is not generally a presence in British state schools for example – would be significant. It would render university less liminal in that non-Christian students would already have been exposed to IVCF and secondary school would in itself have been a so much more significant Rite of Passage in terms of changing a student's relationship with their parents and changing a student's identity. But even accounting for this, five students out of a sample of fifty two spaced over a few years in a group that was somewhat smaller than AUCU might be seen as noteworthy and congruous with the degree of liminality and structure in the group and in St Augustine Campus.

Helander does not assess this but we might also expect St Augustine to be more liminal for people who are not from Trinidad. We might expect people from other parts of the West Indies to be over-represented in IVCF considering that they make up only a third of the students and we might expect this to be increased by the fact that all of the students from outside of Trinidad live on the campus. This is precisely what Helander finds. In the 1960s, when the university was somewhat smaller, IVCF was dominated by Jamaicans and men and it had around twenty members (125). Since that point the group started to evangelise in schools in Trinidad which has ultimately boosted the membership (132). Helander further implies that in 1975 many of the foreign students in IVCF had converted after they arrived at university (153) which is precisely what we would expect because of the greater liminality caused by being abroad, living on campus and possibly not having been exposed to IVCF, or anything like it at school, as had occurred with many in IVCF.

Equally, Helander observes that even though the majority of IVCF members were from Trinidad during her fieldwork they were all amongst the small minority of students from Trinidad who lived on campus (Int. 2007). Thus, those who were the members of IVCF – including those who had undergone conversion experiences – were, as with Oxford University to a certain extent, the very people for whom university would be likely to be the most liminal. They lived within the structure of campus, many were the first in the families to attend school or university and in many cases they may have been foreigners. It is therefore unsurprising that they would be attracted to a highly structured evangelical group either to preserve the evangelical religiosity that they had been raised with or found at school or because some other form of identity was open to question and IVCF provided a new, tightly structured identity in these circumstances of *communitas*. In that sense, ICVF is comparable to OICCU. Here, as we have seen, almost all students live in college, which is highly structured and *communitas* fostering, for at least a year and usually far more, and students from state schools who have not taken Gap Years are over-represented in the highly structured OICCU either because it preserves their identity or provides them with a new one. However, Helander emphasises that 75 per cent of IVCF members had been exposed to such groups at school and she does not indicate that this only includes members from Trinidad.

Helander herself implies that the very structure of St Augustine might be significant, in certain cases, to non-Christians getting involved in IVCF though she does not expand on this. She claims that, 'For some students the actual social setting of university students can function as a catalyst to their joining IVCF'. The degree course is 'well scheduled' and 'prescribed' though students are 'constantly put in situations' where they are left to 'articulate their passage' though this can vary according to various social and personal factors (146). Helander equally notes the opposite phenomenon and cites a number of IVCF members who claimed that they felt that they would have lost their Christian faith at university were it not for IVCF. 'I needed IVCF to keep me balanced on campus' said one. '... had I been at university without that kind of Christian support (...) I think I might have floundered as a Christian', said another (146).

IVCF Involvement

If it is accurate that IVCF is a highly structured group then we would it expect it to be highly significant to the identity of its members and we would anticipate that levels of group participation and ritual would be high. Helander's thesis provides solid evidence for this proposition.

IVCF, during Helander's fieldwork, had a weekly Bible meeting and also various frequent social events (132). Helander writes that joining the group was never simply left to the initiative of the student. The group made special efforts to tell students about their existence and their functions. Known Christian students newly arrived from school were written to by IVCF. Also the group made a 'special effort' to target new students during the Orientation Week for first years, manning a book stall on campus with information about IVCF every day of that week. In addition, during Orientation Week – and throughout the academic year – there were IVCF 'informal socials' to welcome the new students to the campus in the first instance and thus establish contact with them.

As with OICCU and AUCU, IVCF ran an annual Mission. Helander describes an entire week of outreach events including 'open air meetings, banners, and special IVCF T-Shirts ...' to tell students about the campaign (145). Indeed, during the mid-1970s IVCF had effectively set up their own church which met at one of the student halls. Helander observes that if the President was from Trinidad the emphasis would tend to be that IVCF should not be a substitute for church and members should attend a local church. If the President was foreign then there tended to be a movement towards an IVCF as a church, though this is also in the context of a rise in the Charismatic Movement in the 1970s and an attempt to return to a certain interpretation of New Testament practice (155). However this would all appear to imply that IVCF met frequently and was highly active as we would expect of a tightly structured group that is highly significant to the identity structure of its members. And we have already observed that members mostly socialised with other members meaning that even social meetings might be seen as effectively group meetings to a certain degree.

IVCF, Clothes and Gender

We might also expect IVCF members to be distinctive, at least to a certain degree, with regard to the kinds of clothes that they would wear in comparison to those worn by 'non-Christian' students. As with OICCU, and to a lesser AUCU, Helander observes the use of T-Shirts during Mission Week. I would argue that it is significant that also everybody present at OICCU Mission Week events who I knew to be in OICCU wore these. However, very few people present at AUCU events who I knew to be in AUCU wore them. AUCU members therefore rendered themselves less differentiated in terms of clothing than was the case with OICCU.

With regard to clothing in IVCF, Helander does not go into any great detail over this issue in the thesis itself. In interview, however, she recalled that there was 'nothing obvious ... nothing that singled them out' in relation to the clothes worn by IVCF members. Then she further observed that the women in particular perhaps dressed in a more 'modest' manner than non-IVCF females at St Augustine. They wore trousers and sleeveless tops but they were more 'modest'. It is this very subtle 'modesty' that we have already noted with regard to a particular revealing fashion of around 2001–2005 (e.g. Barbieri 2004) of wearing crop-tops with hipsters which appears to have gone out of fashion at the time of writing. Helander also recalled that IVCF members would involve themselves in activities such as the Carnival and Calypso in Trinidad, reflecting the broader student culture, which was influenced by the Black Power Movement (230), in much the same manner as OICCU would with evangelical wine and cheese parties and as AUCU would with its 'Ceilidhs' as we will see. However, female IVCF members would shun the kind of revealing costumes that would generally be worn by young women at such events (Int. 2007). As such, from the limited evidence that we have both from Helander's thesis and from the interview I conducted with her, I think it is possible to argue that IVCF was differentiated in terms of clothing – at least with regard to women – and was differentiated to at least the same extent as AUCU and possibly to a slightly greater extent as would be expected in such liminal circumstances.

Attitudes to women in IVCF certainly appear to be more differentiated than AUCU and more in line with OICCU. However, it should be remembered that Helander points out that Trinidad appeared to be a particularly macho, male culture and she had personal experience of this during her fieldwork, something which made her pay greater attention to gender roles in Trinidad (62). Also it should be remembered that her fieldwork was conducted in the early 1980s and attitudes to gender roles may have been slightly more conservative for this reason. For example, IVCF's constitution dictated that the President should normally be a man and should only really be a woman if no suitable male candidate can be found (137). Helander also found that members held to the sex roles for men and women as outlined in the Bible. This was interpreted to mean that the husband should ultimately be responsible and should ultimately have the final say. A woman should submit herself to his leadership (240–41). Men are therefore trained to stand at the forefront of the group while women have less prominent positions (245). Helander finds that this view of womanhood was in many ways quite differentiated in the Caribbean. Many of the students she studied were from families where the mother was the dominant figure and one even refers to the Caribbean as being traditionally 'matriarchal' (244). As such it would appear that IVCF are also strongly differentiated in terms of their attitudes to gender roles.

The IVCF Exec

The IVCF Exec was also highly structured and comparable to OICCU in this respect. As already discussed, the President was, effectively, constitutionally male which would differentiate IVCF from other societies. Equally, the Exec had a larger number of officers than was the norm in student societies as was the case in OICCU (137). Significantly, Helander points out that each of the Exec members chaired a subcommittee on their particular area such as evangelism or prayer. Indeed she observed that most IVCF members were or had been at some point part of a particular sub-committee (140). These committees would also nurture the 'special talents' of those who could make a particular contribution to IVCF but were not perceived to be Exec material. Helander also discusses the ability of the Exec to ultimately throw out unsuitable members which would also imply a high degree of control. Moreover, the Exec was not elected, as with most other student groups, but was, as with other CUs, a theocracy in which God would supposedly inspire the out-going Exec with the names of who should be on the in-coming Exec. As such, the structure of the government of IVCF is highly differentiated from most student organisations and is in itself highly complicated and structured. As discussed, we would expect this to be the case in a group that fosters a high level of *communitas* and is highly significant to preserving or re-shaping students' identity.

Christian Language

Helander does not concentrate on the linguistic dimension in her analysis. However from a combination of a close reading of the quotes that she includes in her thesis and from interview with her it is possible to argue that IVCF reflect a high level of structure by virtue of having, to a certain degree at least, their own evangelical Christian restricted code. This is, in many respects, highly comparable to the code observed in OICCU or AUCU though there do appear to be some differences.

Obviously the word 'Christian' is employed in a very exclusive manner to mean those who are 'born again' Christians and this is evidenced in the assumptions made about Helander after she informed group members that she was a Christian in whatever sense of the word she meant it at the time. Equally, she observes the use of the word 'non-Christian' (239) as a designation for almost any student who is outside IVCF. This would again imply a group with strong boundaries. Helander records a number of other 'Christian' terms, many of them exactly the same as those found in OICCU or AUCU. Most obviously Helander records the frequent use of the term 'witness' (as a verb) (216) which we have already discussed in relation to OICCU. Helander also recalls a member discussing how she had a 'non-Christian boyfriend' and, as a consequence, other members 'thought I was backsliding' (238). She also points out the frequency of certain terms that I have not found in my own research such as students claiming that they are being 'used by God' (206) and that they are in the process of 'winning souls' (216). Helander recalled in interview that members would 'punctuate' their speech with phrases such as 'praise the Lord' and 'Amen'. As such, as with OICCU there is clear evidence of a highly restricted code in IVCF.

Helander does not look, in her thesis, at the issue of swearing amongst IVCF members and this was therefore something which I raised with her in interview. She recalled that members 'did not swear', something which they justified with recourse to Christian 'purity' in general. This form of differentiation would be as we would expect.

Structural Reassertion in IVCF

Clearly the IVCF that Helander portrays is a highly structured and differentiated group which would be likely to foster a high level of in-group *communitas.* As this can be psychologically difficult we would expect some form of structural reassertion and this indeed is what we observe drawing upon Helander's fieldwork.

Structural reassertion is not as pronounced in IVCF as it appears to be in OICCU but nevertheless it can still be discerned to a certain extent. Most obviously we observe that there was structural reassertion with regard to gender roles on the Exec. Thus, the person who was running the IVCF was, in effect, constitutionally male. There was also evidence of structural reassertion with regard to the form of Christianity practised by those who were on the Exec. Helander points out that they had to be 'mature Christians'. This would be likely to mean that they had been Christians for a very long time rather than converting at secondary school or even at St Augustine. In effect, therefore, the Exec, unlike the ordinary membership, had to be from solid 'Christian' families (139). Moreover we have already discussed the importance of the senior members having been, at some point, 'born again'. They needed to have had some kind of direct experience of God. This might, once more, be seen as a way in which 'Christian' structure reasserted itself in IVCF within the *communitas* which the group brought about.

In interview, however, Helander remarked that she did not recall there being any clear sociological difference between those who were on the Exec and the ordinary members. Indeed, she also notes that in racial terms the Exec tended to be representative of the racial dynamics of the group as a whole. But certainly some reassertion of religious structure can be seen and this will not be observed in AUCU for example and nor will it be in CSL. Equally she notes that prior to her research the group had tended to be dominated by foreigners and in particular Jamaicans. This could, therefore, be understood as a kind of a nationalist form of structural reassertion. The group creates *communitas* but the majority are Jamaicans meaning that the group is run by Jamaicans. Helander does not look, in her thesis, at specific meetings and to attempt to understand the dynamics of such meetings from interview evidence would, I think, be difficult.

Church Politics in St Augustine

Helander points out that the Charismatic Movement was highly significant in Trinidad in the 1970s. It might be argued that IVCF are simply reflecting the Charismatic Movement which was prevalent at the time and to which many students had been exposed – in the form of IVCF – while still at secondary school. However, in this chapter we have not even examined the salience of Charismatic worship or speaking style in the group, though we have looked at the significance of conversion experience which is salient to this movement. IVCF cannot simply be seen to be following their local churches and one piece of evidence for that is the deliberate split from local churches and the formation of their own church in the 1970s. Secondly this does not answer the question of why these Charismatic students would feel it necessary to create their own student organisation. Why not simply attend a certain church – as most of IVCF did – and meet other students through this? Why become involved in such a highly structured student organisation outside of the church context? As I have argued, I think a reasonable answer is that the church is part of a distinctly different realm – in many respects – from the Rite of Passage that they are within and, therefore, it is important to form groups within this highly liminal, identity-challenging and anti-structure creating university context. Moreover, if IVCF is nothing to do with liminality then why, we might ask, was it dominated by the very people for whom we would expect university to be the most liminal?

Conclusion

There are of course difficulties in attempting to apply a theory to a primary source and to interview, which is in effect armchair anthropology, though it does actually involve fieldwork. But, as I have argued, as long as we are careful in this regard and relatively confident in the nature of the source then I think that many of these difficulties can be overcome.

Eila Helander's fieldwork adds further credence to the level model of liminality which is under discussion here. We see in St Augustine Campus a Rite of Passage which is highly liminal for many of its students and in particular for students who are not from educated backgrounds or are from abroad and who live on campus. The university fosters a strong level of *communitas* for such students and is highly transitional. We observe, therefore, structural reassertion in particular in relation to religious identity and this can be observed in SPIC but also in IVCF. As we would expect in these circumstances IVCF is highly structured and differentiated in terms of belief, lifestyle ethics, attitudes to women, the nature of the Exec and, to a lesser extent, the way that members dress. It evidences a high degree of ritual – implying that it is highly significant to student identity – and Helander also presents evidence of restricted code which is in line with a tightly structured group. Indeed, we see a modest number of conversions while at St Augustine amongst group members, though the high degree of liminality caused by secondary school in Trinidad must also be taken into account in this regard. Helander finds that the very people for whom St Augustine would be the most liminal – first generation university students, those living on campus and, to a lesser extent, foreigners (who all live on campus) – are dominant within IVCF.

Consequently there is high group *communitas* and some evidence of structural reassertion, as we would expect. This is seen most clearly in reassertion in terms of gender division but also with regard to a person's perceived Christianity. Helander also provides some inference for the possibility that there was, on some occasions, a kind of nationalist division within the group as well with students from outside Trinidad tending towards forming their own church. Thus, I think that an analysis of detailed fieldwork helps to further our case.

Chapter 4

'Trial by Fire' at Universities in the USA

Student Evangelical Groups at American Universities

Surprisingly, there do not appear to be any published social anthropological monographs on student evangelical groups operating at universities in the USA. However, I think it is important to examine the student evangelical groups at American universities in their university context and see if, from the data that can be drawn upon, the model of liminality under discussion here would be workable. One significant reason for my drawing upon the USA is not only simply to broaden the scope of the enquiry but also because the university system in the USA – unlike in a country such as Finland for example – is extremely broad in terms of the degree of liminality and there is some social scientific research which has compared universities with different levels of liminality and examined the kinds of student evangelical groups that appear to operate in these contexts.

Research on American Evangelical Students

Before beginning the analysis it would useful to provide an overview of precisely what has been written about student evangelical groups at universities in the USA. The published research comprises of a sociological article published in a Religious Studies journal and a few ethnographic articles written by American educationalists. These are useful, and can be drawn upon, but they are not purely sociological – like Helander's thesis – and therefore do not have the same kind of focus or level of empirical detail.

As we have already noted, Philip Hammond and James Davison Hunter (1984) conducted a detailed sociological examination of student evangelicals at a variety of American higher education institutions in the early 1980s. Employing the survey method, their research involved over 2000 evangelical students spread over Wheaton College in Illinois, Gordon College in Massachusetts, Westmont College in California, Bethel College in Minnesota, Houghton College in New York, Seattle-Pacific University in Washington State, Taylor University in Indiana, Messiah College in Pennsylvania and George Fox College in Oregon. With the assistance of other sociologists, Hammond and Hunter drew up a sample from each college stratified in terms of social class. They then sent out detailed questionnaires to the evangelical students which included members of Campus Crusade for Christ and the Inter-Varsity Christian Fellowship. The highest response rate was 74 per cent from Westmont and the lowest was 63 per cent from Gordon (Hammond and Hunter 1984, 223). A further institution was drawn upon at this stage for comparative purposes

– the University of California at Santa Barbara. The institutions examined ranged from public, research intensive universities and private liberal arts colleges through to evangelical Christian 'Bible Colleges'. Some of these Christian colleges allowed members who were not necessarily evangelicals to attend while others were strict in ensuring that any potential student must be an evangelical Christian. Hammond and Hunter's research produced some very interesting results and it will be demonstrated below that these results appear to be broadly in line with the model of liminality that I have already outlined. Indeed, one of the key aims of Hammond and Hunter's surveys was to discover the nature of the relationship between the kind of university attended – in relation to the degree to which it challenged a student's world-view – and the kind of student evangelical group or student evangelical which this tended to produce (222).

Christy Moran (2007) and Moran *et al* (2007) have also produced some very useful research on evangelical students as part of a broader attempt to further our understanding of the nature of student life in the USA. Moran draws upon fieldwork at the University of Kansas in order to understand the sense of differentiation amongst student evangelicals as she argues that this university is in the 'American Bible Belt', an area where evangelical Christianity might actually be understood to be highly influential in a number of respects. These articles are not systematic ethnographic analyses of student evangelicals but the articles do allow us to draw some inference about the nature of these groups at a university of a certain kind. This chapter will also draw upon a detailed ethnographic analysis by Peter Magolda and Kelsey Ebben (2006). They conducted fieldwork in 2004–2005 with a group which they term 'Students Serving Christ'. They do not provide the name of the university at which they conducted their fieldwork. It is a Mid-Western, medium sized, public, campus-based university but we are not told which one it is. Also, Alyssa Bryant (2005) has examined a group which she gives the pseudonym 'Sharing the Faith Fellowship' operating at the anonymous 'West University' in 2003. Her research will also be looked at and it will be supplemented with a further interview conducted with her. All of the research on American student evangelical groups that I will be drawing upon has kept anonymous the name of the Christian group and usually the name of the university in which it operates as well. However, it should be said that the largest student evangelical group on American campuses is 'Campus Crusade for Christ'. This was founded in 1951 at the University of California (Los Angeles) by evangelist Bill Bright (see Turner 2008). Other significant groups include the 'Inter-Varsity Christian Fellowship', which is affiliated to the International Federation of Evangelical Students and which operates on around five hundred campuses in the USA.

There are some difficulties drawing upon this kind of research but, nevertheless, I think that it can be useful if brought together. Magolda and Ebben provide us with a considerable amount of data and information on an American evangelical group at a Mid-Western university. Though they do not tell us which university it is, we can draw a certain degree of inference about its nature by virtue of its size, location, public status and the fact that it is a campus university. In understanding liminality, this will be the main ethnography that will be drawn upon in this chapter. Moran's work is useful because it also relates to evangelical students at public, campus universities and therefore further assists us in understanding the relationship between this kind of structure and the student evangelical groups. Bryant's work is germane for similar reasons and as it is focused on a particular group in its specific campus university context and goes into some depth it is therefore helpful in terms of ethnographic data though obviously, as an article, there are limitations of space in relation to the extent of this depth. Finally, Hammond and Hunter's research is helpful because it examines student evangelical groups at a broad array of higher education institutions which would be structurally very different. As such, taken together I think that this relatively limited amount of research can be drawn upon to allow us to understand the dynamics of liminality at American universities and at the more liminal universities in particular. However, the research available is limited in a number of senses. It does not allow us to examine the internal social class dynamics (or even racial dynamics as this might be perceived as a symbolic class issue to a certain extent in the USA) of the groups, an issue that I was able to examine drawing upon Eila Helander's research into IVCF in Trinidad. Indeed, in general, the level of detail in these articles is obviously considerably less than is provided in Helander's research. Equally, the religious dynamics of 'Students Serving Christ' has not been presented. However, I think it would be useful in terms of background to conduct just a brief overview of the religious culture in the USA.

Religious Background in the USA

Attempting to summarise the religious culture in the USA exposes any writer to considerable criticism. Obviously the USA is a very large and culturally diverse nation within which religious differences are considerable. Indeed, religious culture can be seen to vary within different parts of the USA and between different states. But let us just briefly examine this religious background before moving on to the issue of American education.

Firstly, in comparison to the European cultures examined in this book, the USA can be broadly perceived as a relatively religious culture but I should stress that this is at a very broad level and there would certainly be areas of the USA that would be far more 'religious' – in the sense of religious belief and church involvement – than others. Polls on American belief in God imply that the level of atheism in the USA is very low with some polls claiming that only 8 per cent of Americans do not believe in God and other polls putting this as low as 1 per cent. For example a Harris Poll in 1998 found that 94 per cent of Americans believed in God (Harris Interactive 2007). By contrast, just under 70 per cent of British people believe in God and only half that Jesus was the son of God (Brierley 2006). Sunday worship is also considerably higher in America than in other cultures with a history of regular Sunday worship such as England. Forty-one per cent of Americans attend church weekly compared to only 7 per cent of people living in England. However, Bruce argues that these self-reported levels of church attendance appear to be somewhat inflated (Bruce 2002, 206). Armstrong (2001) points out that certainly since the 1980s what she terms 'fundamentalism' in the USA has risen considerably in terms of political importance and power. She argues that the Moral Majority – a group which aimed to increase evangelical influence in the USA – and evangelical groups in general have risen to highly prominent positions in American society and have been able to exert considerable influence over the Republican Party in particular. This influence has led to serious debate over issues such as whether or not Intelligent Design Theory should be taught alongside Evolution as an alternative scientific theory in school science classes and equally discussions over whether or not abortion should be re-criminalised in the USA. Indeed the American President at the time of writing – George W. Bush – is a Republican and is himself a 'born-again' Christian. Ronald Reagan, another Republican who was President from 1981 to 1989, was also a born-again Christian and a member of a Pentecostal denomination.

Unlike in England or Finland there is no state church in the USA and nor is there even a *de facto* state church in the USA as Protestantism is divided into numerous denominations and independent churches. Separation of church and state is perceived, in theory at least, to be a crucial dimension to American identity despite the apparent influence of organised religion in American life. According to information collated in 2001, the largest single denomination in the USA is Roman Catholicism with almost 26 per cent of Americans adhering to it. Over half of the American population is Protestant and they are distributed between numerous Protestant denominations. Seventeen per cent categorise themselves as Baptist, 7 per cent as Methodist and another 7 per cent as simply 'Christian', which may imply membership of independent evangelical churches where, as we have seen, the word 'Christian' is used in an exclusive sense. In addition, 5 per cent recorded themselves as 'Lutheran', around 3 per cent as Presbyterian and 2.4 per cent as 'Protestant' which might also conceivably indicate membership of independent evangelical churches. Pentecostal or Charismatic churches were adhered to by 2.2 per cent, just under 2 per cent were Episcopalian (Anglican) and other smaller churches included the Mormons, the Assemblies of God and the Congregationalists. The survey also indicated considerable religious variation between states. For example, the most highly religious areas appeared to be southern states such as Louisiana and Mississippi as well as North Dakota while the least religious states appeared to be areas such as Washington and Vermont. In terms of denominational distribution, states in the Deep South tended to have an above average population of Baptists, states in the middle of the country tended to have an above average population of Methodists, some north eastern states had an above average population of Pentecostals while others had an above average population of Catholics. Naturally, religious identity in the USA is at least partly influenced by the religiosity of the immigrants that settled in the area. Thus New York – with influence from Italian and Irish immigration – has a substantial population of Roman Catholics and, indeed, a number of the founders of US states or settlements in the country's early history were Puritans, a group that we have already discussed in our section on the Anglican church.

Clearly, the religious situation in the USA is very diverse but I would argue that it is not unreasonable to claim that there is at least a Puritan and Non-Conformist Protestant influence on American culture as it was people from such backgrounds who were highly influential in founding the Republic. Equally, there is a notable Baptist influence in the USA and this is especially prominent in the Southern States whereas the Northern States tend to be somewhat more oriented towards Methodism and Lutheranism reflecting the different kinds of immigrants that settled there originally. As we have already discussed there is evidence for claiming that the broader evangelical influence on American culture is relatively strong and perhaps stronger than it was in the middle of the twentieth century at least in terms of political influence. The 2001 survey also notes that certain more established congregations – such as Baptists, Methodists, Catholics, Presbyterians and Lutherans – appear to be slowly declining in numbers while independent evangelical and Charismatic churches and the Pentecostal churches are growing and in some cases growing considerably (Graduate Centre 2007). Obviously the religious background to the USA is profoundly complicated and diverse and merely an overview can be offered here without a substantial aside. However, I think it is important to gain such an overview before continuing.

Secondary Education in the USA

In many respects I would argue that secondary education is the USA is highly liminal. However it should be stressed that the level of diversity is substantial which obviously makes it difficult to generalise. There are many private schools in the USA which are generally attended by the relatively wealthy and many of these may or may not be attached to a certain denomination. Hammond and Hunter (1984) point out that there has been a growth since the 1950s in evangelical secondary schools. These are normally private institutions which allow an insulated, Christian education for students. However, most students attend 'public schools' which is what state schools are termed in the USA. Again, there is likely to be considerable variation in standard and style according to the area in which a particular public school is situated. But significantly, religion is kept out of public schools. This is in contrast to the situation in England, for example, where some kind of weekly act of worship is mandatory at state secondary schools. This does not occur at American public schools. In addition, having children 'home schooled' is also something that is permitted in the USA. It has been estimated that up to 20 per cent of American children are home schooled and it is a growing trend (Bauman 2001). This is in contrast to a country such as Finland where home schooling is simply illegal. Sending your child to school is a legal obligation and there is not the facility for a parent to educate the child at home – if the parent is a qualified teacher – or employ a private tutor. We might therefore expect certain American universities to be especially liminal for students who have never actually attended school.

But for the majority who partake in America's free public schools, I would argue that there are a number of ways in which the experience is relatively liminal. American public schools do not tend to involve school uniform and uniform might be seen to create *communitas.* However there are other school rituals through which what has been termed a kind of American Civil Religion is inculcated into the students (Bellah 1967). Most obviously there is the saluting of the flag and the joint reciting of the nation's 'Pledge of Allegiance' every school day. Indeed, the American flag is supposed to be displayed in every classroom and outside every school. I would argue that this daily ritual – relating as it does to a kind of Civil Religion – would be likely to create *communitas* amongst students and would thus be indicative of a relatively high level of surrounding structure. In order to enter various institutions of higher education, American students must sit intensive examinations – known as SATs (Scholastic Aptitude Tests) – the results of which directly influence the kind of university which they can attend and this might be perceived to create group trauma and *communitas* as a consequence. Moreover, there are various other leaving rituals which might be seen to both foster *communitas* and cause distress. At many schools, there is the tradition of the 'High School Prom' – a kind of student Ball which is traditionally attended by either couples or those who have decided to be couples for the purposes of the Ball. This might be interpreted as a kind of play for adult status as well as something traumatic, especially for less confident students, a point that has been made by Best (2000). In addition, there is a school graduation ceremony at many schools. This has developed into something of Rite of Passage for many American students and involves wearing an academic-type gown and mortarboard and so forth. Thus, I think there are many ways in which the school experience is liminal. It also brings together people from different backgrounds. However the degree of this might vary according to the position in which the school is situated.

Higher Education in the USA and Greek Societies

Higher Education in the USA is also very diverse and the degree of liminality would be likely to vary considerably though students generally begin aged eighteen and graduate at around twenty-two, younger than in some countries. The most respected institutions, which are highly competitive to gain entry to, are America's Ivy League Universities such as Harvard, Yale and Princeton. Such institutions would be likely to attract students from all over the country. With their extremely high tuition fees they would be likely to attract large numbers of wealthy students but as these universities also offer many scholarships – for which competition is again intense – such universities would be further likely to foster *communitas* through the mixing of students from diverse social backgrounds. There is a tradition, at most institutions, that students share bedrooms which would be likely to foster *communitas* and possibly even an element of trauma for some. It should also be noted that, as with British universities, American degrees tend to be classified and employers will tend to interested in these classifications either of the entire degree – thus a student might 'graduate *magna cum laude*' – or of individual modules. Also, unlike in Britain, American students are required to study a relatively broad array of subjects. They will have a 'major' subject and then 'minors' outside of their subject. In Britain students must generally concentrate on one specific subject though there are variations to this.

Indeed, there has been detailed study into the development of highly structured student fraternities – Greek Societies – in this context. It is difficult to apply the information to any given university as there appears to be such a strong tradition amongst American fieldworkers of disguising the names of groups being studied. However, Leeman (1972) directly compares initiation into these Greek Societies to tribal initiations. The societies have often traumatic Rites of Separation and

Incorporation. This includes the practice of 'hazing' whereby potential members may be forced to engage in various less than pleasant activities such as stealing, eating vomit-inducing food, being locked in a cold room, being beaten and in general being deliberately traumatised in a manner comparable to a tribal Rite of Initiation (54). Hank Nuwer has specifically investigated 'hazing' in Greek societies and argued that the process and the societies – many of which can be traced back to the nineteenth century – are violent and traumatic and bring out violence in neophytes. He provides a number of examples where students have died as a consequence of these initiation rituals, often due to excessive alcohol consumption (Nuwer 1999, 78). According to Leeman, potential members have to undergo various other trials such as learning information about the group off by heart and being tested on it and there are numerous internal group rituals involving dramatic costumes and so forth as would be the case in tribal initiations. Ultimately members who make it through the Rite of Passage are welcomed into the group in a ceremony. The societies – most of them single sex – have a strong social dimension and may provide accommodation, dining facilities and regular social meetings throughout the four years that a Bachelors degree generally lasts in the USA. This kind of development might be understood to reflect the degree to which these status raising, campus universities foster a strong sense of student *communitas* requiring a strong structure which itself fosters *communitas*. However, in addition to the Ivy League elite, there are numerous other comparable campus universities within the USA. The more prestigious colleges attract students from around the country while others attract students from at least across the state in which they are situated if not further afield than that.

In addition to these public universities, there are various 'private' universities. There are public Liberal Arts Colleges, which aim to offer a more rounded education and are teaching focused and also private Liberal Arts colleges. In addition to these there are Community Colleges. These do not tend to be campus institutions, are teaching only institutions and in that sense operate not unlike schools. These are generally perceived to be the least respected form of higher education in the USA and require the lowest SAT scores to gain entrance. Paralleling secular higher education in the USA is specifically 'Christian' higher education. Thus, there are 'seminaries' and universities relating to the Catholic Church and various Protestant denominations. These Christian universities include institutions such as 'Fuller Theological Seminary' or 'Bob Jones University'. Many of these institutions demand that both students and staff be active members of the denomination in question. In addition to these normally campus institutions there are Christian Liberal Arts Colleges relating, again, to various Christian denominations. Indeed, there are also numerous Bible Colleges throughout the USA again relating to specific denominations such as 'Assemblies of God (a Pentecostal denomination) Bible College, Missouri'. It is noteworthy, perhaps, that the standard and form of higher education thus varies considerably within the USA. Finnish universities, for example, simply do not recognise degrees from various American institutions – such as many Bible colleges – as being valid degrees at all. In some respects these American Christian institutions might be highly liminal as they would be campus institutions and would be likely to involve various religious rituals and so forth for their students. But, of course, in other respects they would be somewhat less so as students would be insulated in an environment where people would generally be in accord with their religious views. The environment of a university such as Yale would thus be far less insulated for evangelical students as Hammond and Hunter have pointed out in institutions which would be, to some extent at least, comparable to Yale. That said, we might expect these more liminal campus universities – precisely because they create such strong *communitas* – to produce more highly structured and even fervent student evangelical groups and this is what I think we can discern from the research that has been conducted in this area.

A Mid-Western, Campus University

In applying our theory, let us then begin with the student evangelical group about which we have the most information. This is the so called 'Students Serving Christ' group which operates at an anonymous Mid-Western, public, campus university which is medium-sized by American standards. Following our previous discussion of American higher education we might expect the degree of liminality at this anonymous institution to be relatively high for many of its students and, indeed, to be relatively high for evangelical Christians.

As we have discussed, the institution is firstly an established, public university. Though we do not know which one it is, this might imply that it would be relatively status-raising and certainly more so – in the broader national community – than education at a Community College or Bible College might be. Though the standards of American public universities may well vary considerably I would suggest that, nevertheless, attendance at such an institution would be relatively status-raising thus contributing to its degree of liminality. Secondly, we know that it is a campus university. As such it is likely that students at the university have moved at least some distance to study there which would in itself foster a kind of geographical *communitas* even if most of the students were from within the state where the university is situated. Obviously, the living arrangements would be the most significant issue in breaking-down social boundaries and these would imply a strong form of structure aimed at fostering *communitas.* We have already discussed the extent to which Oxford University's colleges might be seen to foster *communitas* and though we simply cannot know a great deal about the situation at this anonymous institution I think that it is not unreasonable to assume that the campus would bring together, to some extent at least, students from diverse religious, geographical, social and even racial backgrounds. They would be forced to live, socialise and even eat together in the halls of residence. Students from very different backgrounds may even share a 'dorm' as is customary on many American campuses. Magolda and Ebben (2006) also heavily imply that there is something comparable to a Student Union operating on this anonymous campus which organises a special week of social events for 'freshmen' as well as offering other services throughout their time at the university. As such, I would submit that this anonymous university would be likely to be relatively liminal for many of its students. Indeed, it would also be liminal for 'Christian' students as they, just like other students, would have their identity exposed to question and scrutiny in a highly intense environment. We might therefore expect this high level of *communitas* to result in the development of a highly structured and differentiated evangelical student group which preserves the faith of believers and provides the possibility of a new identity to non-believers whose own identity has become uncertain.

'Students Serving Christ'

There is a strong case for arguing that 'Students Serving Christ' reflects this kind of development which would be congruous with the theory of liminality that I am propounding. In terms of group involvement, Students Serving Christ meet relatively frequently compared to some of the other organisations examined in this volume. They meet on Friday evenings for a worship meeting and student sermon which is itself differentiated as many non-Christian students might dedicate a Friday evening to going to a bar or nightclub. In addition to the Friday meeting – which most members attend every week – there are a series of weekly Bible Studies. There is also a weekly evangelical training session. This is attended by a minority of students and teaches them how to evangelise and 'witness' to non-Christian students and for certain students there is even a Leadership Training seminar once a week. As such, the degree of student involvement in the group is high which would imply that the group is a highly significant dimension to member identity. In addition, the fact that the group meets frequently would also demonstrate that it is highly structured – as reflected in a high level of group ritual – and, indeed, significant to the identity preservation or construction of its members' identities in the highly liminal university context. Magolda and Ebben also examine the high level of outreach activity practised by Students Serving Christ. This is particularly significant during the university's Freshers' Week when the group has a table at the Freshers' Fair, distributes literature to potential members with slogans such as the 'Thee Fs' – 'Following Christ, Fellowship and Fun' – and even organises an 'Ice Cream Party' for potential recruits. This would further demonstrate the tight level of organisation in the group. The structure helps them to – in a sense – hold onto their identity in an environment where it is challenged.

Magolda and Ebben are not explicit about the religious beliefs of the group. However, their descriptions strongly imply that the evangelical group would hold beliefs that would be comparable to those of OICCU. They quote a female member as declaring, 'Satan is always firing arrows at us', implying a belief in Satan and Hell and, in addition, their detailed description of a speech by the group's leader on the subject of the Bible implies a group belief in Biblical inerrancy. It is therefore likely, though not explicitly stated, that most group members would believe in traditional Christian doctrines in a literal sense and, indeed, Creationism. In terms of lifestyle ethics we can again draw inference from Magolda and Ebben's article. They quote a student as saying that when a member slept with his girlfriend and saw nothing wrong with it they stopped treating him as a Christian. This would imply a clear differentiated boundary in terms of behaviour whereby pre-marital sex amongst Christians is completely unacceptable unless those who engage in it accept that it is wrong and repent. It is also implied that members do not drink a great deal and that it is certainly unacceptable for a member to become drunk. Thus, although we cannot be entirely sure because the relevant research into this group has not been presented, it appears likely that the ethical beliefs of Students Serving Christ would be comparable to those of groups such as IVCF in Trinidad or OICCU at Oxford University. This would again demonstrate that the group is differentiated and therefore relatively highly structured as would be expected following the level model of liminality.

Magolda and Ebben's article does not provide us with any information on how differentiated members were in terms of clothing or swearing. However, their quotations from members would appear to imply that there was a certain amount of restricted code or Christian language employed by group members. For example, they quote members of a particular 'Women Warriors for God' Bible Study chanting that they are 'warriors for God' and a leading member of this group claiming, as I have already noted, that 'Satan is always firing arrows at us'. At yet another meeting a group leader implores members to 'share your unique light that God has given you'. Though drawing upon quotes in this way is less than systematic it would still seem to indicate a certain degree of differentiated language use in 'Students Serving Christ' which is what we might expect to occur in a tightly structured organisation.

We might also expect the group to be tightly structured at an internal level. Magolda and Ebben do not examine issues such as the social class or denominational composition of the group. However, they do demonstrate that there are effectively degrees of membership within the group. Thus, members who are perceived to be suitable future Christian leaders are invited by leading members to attend Christian leadership seminars or even a month long retreat prior to the beginning of the university year in order to teach them about evangelism. As such, and as with OICCU, the group is also highly internally structured as demonstrated by the presence of levels of membership.

Following from this high degree of structure, we would expect there to be a high level of group *communitas* and thus a strong reassertion of structure within the group. It might be argued that these kinds of exclusive seminars are evidence of such a reassertion of structure whereby those who are considered, perhaps, the most committed evangelicals are invited to undergo further training. There is also a female-only Bible study. This might be interpreted as a reassertion of gender division. Though the leader of the entire group is male, the authors do not indicate the general attitude towards female leadership. Indeed, the very presence of single sex Bible studies might conceivably be seen as a reassertion of the structure whereby men and women are perceived as in some way 'different' and requiring different roles and activities. Both the Bible Study and the broader group worship meeting would appear to be highly structured. In the female Bible Study that is examined, members are expected to do 'homework' on a particular passage and present it to a kind of class of which there is a clear leader. Members are asked questions about highly personal issues during this discussion – such as when they have succumbed to the 'temptation' that the Devil has presented them with. Thus, we have, I would argue, a Bible Study that is highly structured and, moreover, structured in such a way as to incite emotion and the sharing of information. As such it would be likely to foster group bonds and a sense of *communitas.* The authors also write of the members randomly singing together that they are 'Women Warriors for Christ' – an emotional activity that would also be likely to foster a strong sense of *communitas*.

The Friday night worship meeting – the group's main meeting – is also structured in such a way as to foster a strong sense of *communitas*. The authors describe the student leader of the group delivering an impassioned and dramatic piece of oratory which would be very likely to stir the emotions of his audience. For example, at one point he reads a passage from Matthew about maintaining purity, describes how it is difficult to do this on campus, 'Sounds like hard work! So let's forget it!' he says. He then tears the relevant pages out of the Bible and throws them on the floor. He has tears in his eyes and his audience are stunned. This kind of charismatic oratory would also be likely to create *communitas*. Of course it may be that this group is influenced by the popularity of the Charismatic Movement in the USA or simply by local Charismatic churches. However, this does not explain why, as we will see, this group is so much more structured in various other respects – and fosters so much more *communitas* – than other similarly influenced student evangelical groups in the USA operating in very different structural circumstances.

'Campus Ministries' at the University of Kansas

Though it is far less detailed than Magolda and Ebben's ethnographic article, Christy Moran (2007) and Moran *et al* (2007) provide us with some useful information on American student evangelical groups. Drawing upon fieldwork at the University of Kansas (a campus, residential, public university), Moran finds that student evangelicals tend to be particularly dedicated to student 'ministry' which they even put above their college work (Moran 2007). Moran also notes examples of students who have become 'Christians' while at the university or who thought that they were Christians when they arrived and then realised that they were not (Moran 2007, 424). This would imply a high degree of liminality. Equally, Moran notes various examples of restricted code in the group such as 'For Christ's Glory' and 'Keeping Ministry First'. Though only a very superficial analysis can be made of this level of information, it would seem to be congruous with that which we have already discussed. A public, campus university of a relatively high standard – she terms it 'research intensive' – is relatively liminal, it creates *communitas* and a strong student evangelical group – with tight boundaries – can be regarded as a structural reaction to this.

Indeed, in a related article Moran *et al* (2007) go into further detail about the extent to which this anonymous group is differentiated. It is implied that the word 'Christian' is employed in a highly exclusive manner, that members do not drink much and certainly do not get drunk and that they reject premarital sex. The authors also argue that such a university – even though it is in the Bible Belt – can present a strong challenge to the identity of 'Christians' leading to their feeling under assault and needing to take refuge in what is termed a 'Christian support group'.

'Sharing the Faith Fellowship' at 'West University'

The ethnographic information presented in Bryant's article also appears to point to a highly structured and differentiated student evangelical group at a university which – for various reasons including being a campus university with Halls of Residence in line with the general model in the USA – would appear to be relatively structured and liminal for many of its students. Bryant points out that the university appears to foster *communitas* in relation to issues such as social class, geography and race and it may, therefore, be a relatively prestigious and status-raising institution. She notes: 'The university where I conducted the study attracted students from all over the US. It's a very diverse institution ...' (Int. 2007). 'Sharing the Faith Fellowship' meet not infrequently. Eighty students attend the group's weekly meeting of 'fellowship singing and Biblical instruction' and moreover one hundred students attend the group's various Bible Studies in the campus's Halls of Residence, which are also weekly. Bryant also refers to semi-formal dinners organised by the group, a 'women's dinner' (Bryant 2005, 6) and various 'Outreach events' involving topical discussions by noted evangelical speakers (10). The group which Bryant studies also appears to be highly differentiated in terms of both belief and lifestyle. In terms of belief, Bryant notes that members believed in 'Biblical inerrancy' (11) and that their identity as 'Christians' was of great significance to them (8). Bryant implies that group members do not accept evolutionary theory (18). With regard to ethical issues members are implied to be against premarital sex, homosexuality and abortion (15). In an interview Bryant further noted that the Sharing the Faith Fellowship were somewhat differentiated in terms of clothing claiming that 'expectations for modest dress amongst women were strongly expressed' and that they tended to be differentiated with regard to their attitudes towards swearing. Equally, Bryant implies that the fact that she was able to call herself a 'Christian' was not unimportant to her ability to conduct successful fieldwork which would further imply a strong sense of differentiation in relation to outsiders.

As we would expect in such a relatively liminal campus environment the main evangelical group is highly structured and differentiated, at least according to what it is possible to discern from Bryant's ethnography. We would, therefore, expect the group to foster a high degree of group *communitas* and for there to be some reassertion of structure. Obviously the relative brevity of Bryant's discussion – and the fact that her focus is not on these issues – means that, to a certain degree, we are engaging in speculation in attempting to find such a reassertion. However, there are two interesting areas in this regard. Bryant observes that Bible Studies are single-sex. I have not observed this at the universities at which I have conducted research and do not think that this can simply put down to broader traditionalist attitudes to the role of women in American society. As such, it might imply a differentiated attitude towards gender relations or a reassertion of structure in relation to gender relations. Though Bryant does not go into any detail in this regard, she does state that though the group is denominationally diverse it does not reflect the ethnic diversity of the university. She later confirmed in interview that the group were 'predominantly white and middle to upper middle class'. In a society where race might be seen as a significant issue of identity and even symbolic social status, this is an important (albeit implied) observation. It further demonstrates the degree to which the group reasserts societal structure in a context of broad *communitas*.

Hammond and Hunter's Survey

Hammond and Hunter's (1984) survey of a variety of student evangelicals at a broad range of American higher education establishments adds further credence to the idea that in a highly liminal university, *communitas* will be fostered and structure will strongly reassert itself as a result. Consequently, the more liminal university – following Hammond and Hunter – is the one where the more differentiated and fervent student evangelicals are likely to be. This is because the university – as a highly liminal environment – exposes their identity to question meaning that they can only preserve it by becoming involved in a highly structured student evangelical group. Indeed, they respond to this threat on an individual level by becoming more fervent and differentiated in their views as a kind of bulwark against the *communitas*.

Hammond and Hunter find that evangelical students on secular campuses have more difficulty holding onto their religious beliefs than those on either moderately or highly evangelical campuses. They summarise this with the words, 'The secular campus is no doubt a threat to the evangelical world-view, but it is also a trial by fire, so to speak, and thus an annealer of the world-view' (229). In other words, on the insular and relatively insular 'Christian' campuses, the world-view of student evangelicals often seems to develop in a somewhat more liberal direction than the view held when they began their studies. As Hammond and Hunter put it: 'In one sense this is exactly what we would expect from increased education' (230). There is a kind of 'falling away' from evangelicalism. In stark contrast, they observe that, 'On the secular campus, the evangelical worldview of evangelical students seems to gain solidity ... there is a consolidation of beliefs and practices' (230). Hammond and Hunter explain this reaction by arguing that the secular campus can act as a kind of assault on evangelical identity which leads to the forming of highly evangelical groups. Indeed they imply that the secular campus can be understood as a general assault on identity as their statistics suggest that many evangelical students on secular campuses may have converted while at university in disproportionately high numbers (231). Evangelical student groups are, they note, far less required on campuses where everybody is assumed to be Christian anyway (232).

I would therefore argue that the results of Hammond and Hunter's surveys are entirely congruous with the model of liminality which I have outlined. A public, secular, residential, campus university is highly structured and therefore creates *communitas* in many respects by bringing together students from various different religious backgrounds as well as cementing other social differences. This acts as an identity challenge to both Christian and non-Christian students. The apparent result appears to be that Christians protect their identity by forming tightly structured and fervent evangelical groups and, indeed, that some non-Christians – whose identity has been thrown open to question – convert and join these groups in these highly liminal circumstances. Thus, we have clear reassertion of structure in an environment of strong *communitas* and the conversions indicate a high level of liminality. By contrast, evangelicals at Christian colleges do not really have their identities challenged on a religious level. There is little need to form such highly structured groups as the degree of *communitas* and identity challenge here is considerably lower.

Conclusion

The limited ethnographic and survey research that has been conducted into evangelical student groups at American universities provides further evidence for the thesis being proposed in this book. Drawing upon Magolda and Ebben, Moran and Moran *et al* and Bryant we can see that a public, relatively status-raising, campus-based university would be likely to be structured and to create *communitas.* Drawing in particular on the more detailed discussion of Students Serving Christ, we can see that the group is highly significant to the identity of members, highly structured and highly differentiated in terms of belief and behaviour. It is also highly internally structured. As discussed, though much of the data that might be required has not been presented in these articles we can still discern some evidence of a reassertion of structure. Indeed, the highly structured group meeting also seems to lead to a high level of *communitas* as was noted in OICCU. Moran's research provides some further data in support of these interpretations.

It might be argued that the groups are simply reflecting their religious background but this can be convincingly refuted by Hammond and Hunter's research. This demonstrates – drawing upon a broad array of Christian and secular campuses – that evangelical students actually become more fervent in their beliefs on a secular campus precisely because their identity is challenged (through the *communitas* created) leading to the formation of tightly structured evangelical student groups. Indeed, such is the liminality of this context that Hammond and Hunter observe a disproportionate number of people who have converted while at university in these evangelical groups. An assessment of the situation at American universities – albeit based on relatively limited research – would appear to further evidence the model of the liminal phase that I have already outlined.

Chapter 5

The 'Christian' Ceilidh

Aberdeen University and Aberdeen University Christian Union (AUCU)

Aberdeen University is Scotland's third oldest institution of Higher Education. It is one of Scotland's four 'Ancient Universities' having been established in 1495. My research indicated that a very substantial portion of its students were Scottish and in particular from the north of Scotland, including the Highlands (Aberdeen University statistics 2002). For a large minority of students to whom I spoke Aberdeen University appeared to be a kind of second choice. Scottish students who were studying medicine there had often been rejected by Glasgow University or Edinburgh University, Northern Irish students had frequently been rejected by Queen's University, Belfast and the minority of English students had, in many cases, been rejected by universities such as Durham or, especially for less popular subjects, got in through 'Clearing' having done unexpectedly badly in their school leaving exams.[1] However, I met many students from the north of Scotland who had, in most cases, put down Aberdeen University as their first choice which reflects something in Scottish University culture which will be examined in more depth below. Aberdeen itself has a population of over 200,000 and is the third largest city in Scotland though it is geographically isolated from other large cities.

I spent two terms studying AUCU and Aberdeen University between September 2002 and September 2004. The group had around one hundred and seventy members. Unlike OICCU, the AUCU Exec in no way restricted my access to the group which would be congruous with the degree of liminality as will be discussed below. I was, in effect, made a honorary member of AUCU to the extent of being asked to stand-up and give a speech – along with other 'AUCU leavers' – at the last 'Prayer and Praise Meeting' of the term in which I completed my doctoral thesis and left Aberdeen University. I was permitted to attend any meeting that I wished to without any interference from the Exec, I was put on the group's email list and I was even allowed to attend their retreat camp which involved a two hour drive into the Scottish countryside and a two day stay in a very remote area.

In many ways, Aberdeen University was liminal for many of its students. However, it was, as I will demonstrate, considerably less so than is the case with Oxford University or the situation, for example, with many American campus universities. As such, though Aberdeen University appeared to be far more liminal than Oulu University, for example, I would submit that it is nevertheless closer to that

[1] This is an annual process whereby students who failed to do sufficiently well in their exams to take up the places offered to them by either of their two selected universities ring around different universities that have not filled all their places in various subjects.

experience than to the situation at Oxford University. However, before examining liminality at Aberdeen University I would like to look at Scotland's religious background.

Scotland's Religious Background

The religious culture in Scotland differs considerably from the English situation in terms both of organisation and traditional theology. The vast majority of the Scottish population claimed to be 'Church of Scotland' on the 2001 census though many would not be perceived as such by the Church of Scotland itself. Known as 'the Kirk', the Church of Scotland has been recognised by law as the 'national church' of Scotland since 1921 though unlike the Church of England it is disestablished and thus free from state control. Unlike England, Scotland also has a substantial native Catholic population due mainly to nineteenth century Irish immigration (though there are also some Highland islands that were never converted to Protestantism) and this numbers around 16 per cent (Census 2001). Currently, however, 42 per cent of Scots are members of the Church of Scotland with 47 per cent having been raised within the Kirk (Scottish Executive 2001). As stated, the Kirk is identified with as a default religion by considerably larger numbers of Scots. As with England, church participation in Scotland has declined as has Kirk membership and currently around 12 per cent of the Scottish population attend church once a week (Brierley 2006).

The Scottish Reformation began in around 1560 and John Knox (1510–1572) is generally perceived as its figure head. He was heavily influenced by the teachings of reformer John Calvin and thus the idea that anything that does not have specific Biblical warrant should be rejected rather than the more Lutheran view that practices that are un-Biblical should be rejected (e.g. Leith 1974). As such the Church of Scotland, like most Reformed churches, is Presbyterian. There are no bishops, 'ministers' (as they are termed in the Church of Scotland) are elected by the congregations, the Kirk is run by an elected assembly of ministers and laymen (the General Assembly of the Church of Scotland) presided over by a 'Moderator' and worship and clerical dress are traditionally plain with the focus of the service being on the sermon. The Eucharist is thus taken relatively rarely, perhaps four times a year and in the case of some congregations around once a year (Douglas 1974, 891). The theology of the Kirk has traditionally leaned towards Calvinism and therefore a belief that God pre-ordained an elect to salvation before time though many commentators stress that the Church of Scotland is relatively liberal in terms of theology and accepts a variety of viewpoints (e.g. Douglas 1974, Burleigh 1960, Part V).

Of those whom I surveyed in AUCU over the issue of religious belief, nine identified as Church of Scotland, three were from independent evangelical churches, three were from the Free Church of Scotland, three were Baptists, two were Methodists, two were Episcopalian, two were Evangelical Presbyterian and one was Free Presbyterian Church of Ulster. The latter two were indicative of the way that around one fifth of AUCU members were from Northern Ireland and during the three years that I was a researcher at Aberdeen University the AUCU president was, on two occasions, a Northern Irish female medical student. On the other occasion the president was a Scottish female medical student. The Free Presbyterian Church of Ulster, of which some were members, in particular is highly conservative in terms of both theology and practice and was founded by Rev'd Ian Paisley, a senior Northern Irish politician and conservative Christian, in 1951 (Bruce 2007, Ch. 5). Three of the sample were members of the Free Church of Scotland. This developed after a division in 1843 known as 'the Disruption' and the various subsequent divisions. The group is generally understood to be a conservative split from the Kirk though much of it subsequently was re-integrated into the Kirk (Burleigh Part V). The split is generally seen to have been part of an evangelical movement within the Church of Scotland which related to various revivals in both the late nineteenth and twentieth centuries (e.g. Brown 1997, 105). AUCU members involved in the Kirk were usually from its evangelical wing and the Church of Scotland Kirk which many attended in Aberdeen (Gilcomston South) was itself evangelical.

Two AUCU students were Episcopalian, a relatively small church which is part of the Anglican Communion and has bishops. However, in general, the religious culture in Scotland – and in particular the area of Scotland around Aberdeen – can be understood as broadly influenced by the Kirk in much the same manner that England's religious culture is broadly influenced by the Church of England.

Scottish Education and Liminality

Though part of the United Kingdom since the Act of Union of 1707, Scotland has maintained both a separate legal and education system from England and since 1999 it has had its own Parliament and devolved Government. Since the election of a minority Scottish Nationalist (and independence advocating) government in 2007 this has been called the 'Scottish Government' but it was formerly termed 'the Scottish Executive'. Its head is still termed the Scottish 'First Minister' rather than 'Prime Minister'. As with the rest of Britain, upfront tuition fees were introduced in 1998. However, by the time of my fieldwork these had been abolished and Scottish students had to pay a flat fee, of less than the English equivalent, at the end of their degree while English students at Scottish universities still had to pay tuition fees. At the time of writing, the Scottish National Party is in the process of abolishing the fees (for Scottish students) altogether. However, the Scottish University system is, to a great extent, connected to the broader British education system. As with the rest of Britain, Scottish Higher Education has expanded substantially, especially in the twentieth century, and the former division between university and polytechnic was abolished in 1992. As with rest of Britain it might be argued that there is an effective hierarchy within Scottish Higher Education and as with the rest of Britain this might be seen to relate to a combination of academic standard, extent of establishment and even social class.

Scotland's oldest university is St Andrew's University, established in 1411. This has been described as a kind of 'quasi-Oxford' by some commentators (e.g. Ainsley 1999) and attracts large numbers of English, as well as Scottish, students from relatively privileged backgrounds. It gained considerable media attention when Prince William, the grandson of the present Queen, chose go there to study for a degree in the History of Art. Interestingly, many Scottish students I spoke to in Aberdeen were rather negative about St Andrews University with some commenting, 'It's not really Scottish. I wouldn't want to go there' or 'It's full of English snobs' or 'I'm Scottish! I wanted to go to a Scottish university! At least Aberdeen's Scottish!' Edinburgh University is also seen as highly prestigious and likewise attracts many students from the independent sector from England. By contrast, both Glasgow and Aberdeen University (both established in the fifteenth century) seemed to be perceived by those whom I interviewed as more authentically 'Scottish', especially than St Andrews, and thus preferable. Though as I have said, students I interviewed who were from southern Scotland had often been rejected by Glasgow or Edinburgh (especially if they were actually from these cities) and had come to Aberdeen for that reason. This was especially true with highly competitive subjects such as medicine. As one Glaswegian female, medic and AUCU member put it, 'I didn't get into Glasgow. But I'm happy I came to Aberdeen now. I couldn't imagine being anywhere else!' Some students had been interviewed in order to be offered a place at Aberdeen University. However, most had been offered a place on the strength of their Highers (the Scottish school leaving certificate) or their A-Levels (the English equivalent). Moreover, two Scottish universities were established in the nineteenth century – Herriot-Watt in Edinburgh and Dundee University – while the remainder including Stirling University and former polytechnics like Robert Gordon's University in Aberdeen – were established or granted university status in the latter half of the twentieth century.

As with England, the Scottish education system is divided into the state and the private sector and around 20 per cent of Aberdeen University students had attended private schools. As with England there are also public schools in Scotland such as Robert Gordon's (not connected to the university) in Aberdeen. Though it should be stressed that the Scottish education system is slightly different and this brings about a situation where some students can end up starting university as young as sixteen, though I only came across this on a handful of occasions. Nevertheless, the majority appeared to start university aged seventeen. The Scottish degree lasts for four years rather than the three years that it takes at English universities. Many other tutors commented to me that the academic standard expected of first year students is, in many ways, comparable to what would be expected of English school students of the same age. The Scottish system also involves a degree classification system based around examinations which, in the case of final year exams, cannot be retaken. At Aberdeen University, it was possible, however, to repeat a year if a student failed the year. However it was not possible to repeat a module that a student passed though passed with a low grade. The degree classification in Britain is significant because some employers will demand that applicants have a '2:1' or above. A 2:1 is the second highest class of degree obtainable out of 1st, 2:1, 2:2, 3rd and Pass and, indeed, is the average received. Unlike at Oxford University, there was a system of 'credits' at Aberdeen and only when students had a certain number of credits could they receive their degrees.

Moreover, in many respects there is a case for arguing that the degree of liminality at a Scottish university would – at its broadest and for the majority of Scottish pupils – not be as pronounced as would be the case at many English universities. At least with the more respectable institutions there is a strong tradition in England of going 'away from home' in order to attend university. In my research at Oxford I never found an OICCU member who was actually from Oxford or anywhere close to Oxford. I did however find a number of OICCU members who were originally from Cambridge and they specifically said that they had not wanted to go to university in the place that they had lived all their lives and where, moreover, their parents lived. 'I wanted to actually leave home!' one such Oxford student emphasised. Many students at Oxford – and in particular at Durham – had made a point of going to university a long way from home and there is a tradition in England (e.g. Kingsbury 1974) of so doing. None of my OICCU sample lived at home during term time or went home at weekends and many did not go home during term time at all. My research indicated that this tradition does not appear to be present in Scotland. There is a tradition of attending your local or at least nearest university. Students to whom I spoke from Aberdeen, the Highlands and Islands and even from as far as Shetland argued that they looked upon Aberdeen as, as one Aberdeen native put it, 'kind of our university'. This is in marked contrast to the 'Town and Gown' divide that was observed at Oxford University. As I have said, students who were from the south of Scotland – such as from Glasgow – had normally failed to get into Glasgow University and had come to Aberdeen as a kind of second choice. As such, for many of the students at Scottish universities the university experience would be considerably less liminal because they would be likely to be at a university relatively close to where they had come from. Indeed, even if they are from Edinburgh and go to Glasgow University this is still less than an hour away by train and it would not be especially expensive or time consuming to visit home as it would be if you were from Newcastle but studying at Oxford.

Moreover, university attendance in Scotland is considerably higher than is the case in England which would be likely to mean that university attendance was less status-raising and consequently less liminal for many Scottish students than would be the case for their English counterparts. In 1997 the Dearing Report noted that, 'Participation in Higher Education is traditionally higher in Scotland than in the rest of the UK with almost fifty percent of under-21s in full time Higher Education. This is compared to a UK figure of thirty-two percent' (Dearing 1997, Ch. 2). Indeed, some years ago at least, Scotland had the highest level of participation in Higher Education in Europe (Scottish Parliament 3 August 1999). As such, it might be argued that university is far less socially significant – and thus far less status raising – than would be the case in a society such as England where far lower numbers actually go to university. But that said, Scottish universities, like those in England, do have a Student Union which operates subsidised bars and so forth. Though there are no colleges at Scottish universities, most students do live in Halls of Residence in the first year which would, I would argue, assist in fostering a certain level of *communitas*. But before looking at this issue in Aberdeen University it would be useful to examine the social background of the student body and of AUCU students.

Social Background at AUCU and Aberdeen

Only 20 per cent of Aberdeen's students attend independent schools. However, 78 per cent of their students are from the kind of background which has been understood either to be upper-class or professional. This difference was reflected in the composition of AUCU. Again I surveyed twenty-five AUCU members. Of this number far fewer than in OICCU had attended private school, three students in this case. This, once more, is slightly fewer than the percentage of private school students at Aberdeen University and, as such, these students are again under-represented in the CU. The majority of the AUCU sample were from backgrounds that were either higher or lower professional. Three students had attended private schools as stated. One student's father was simply the headmaster of the private school that he attended. The other two were an English student, whose father was a hospital consultant and a Scottish student whose father was an architect. Certainly, the latter two would be defined as higher professionals.

However, there was a large minority from Northern Ireland where the education system is different from the rest of the UK and where there are a large number of Grammar Schools and very few private schools. The four Northern Irish students in the sample noted parental professions as general practitioner, shop manager, dairy farmer and teacher. All had attended Grammar Schools. The three English students from Comprehensive schools noted parental profession as coach driver, health and safety officer and computer programmer. The Scottish students, from Comprehensives, involved the children of three ministers, five teachers, a bank clerk, a bus driver and a general practitioner. Thus, in general, those who had been to state schools were from lower professional backgrounds or, in some cases, white-collar or, as in a coach driver, a working-class background. The very small number that had been to private schools, apart from the anomalous headmaster's son, were from higher professional backgrounds. Some children of higher professionals can be seen in the state school category but, in general as with Oxford, a distinction can be noted. The majority of students were also from the country in which the university was situated but this was, again, not as overwhelming as was the apparent case amongst OICCU members. Seventeen students identified their nationality as Scottish, four as English, none as Welsh, another four as Northern Irish and none as being from any nation outside of the UK.

It might, however, be pointed out that the Scottish symbolic system of hierarchy might be perceived as somewhat different from the case in England and this would affect what little reassertion of structure we will note below. A number of experts on Scottish culture such as McCrone (1992, 18), Bruce (1993, 8) and Beveridge and Turnbull (1997, 59) have argued that Scotland, in contrast to England, is a more clearly defined and nationalist society which substantially defines itself in opposition to 'the English'. In terms of national myth, perhaps, Scotland is seen to regard itself as more 'egalitarian' and even more educated, though at the same time tougher and more masculine (e.g Bruce *et al* 2004, 148), than the English and social class, to some extent, is perceived as an English issue with the Scottish aristocracy regarded as, effectively, anglicised and therefore not authentically 'Scottish'. Consequently, Reicher and Hopkins (2001) imply that social class is a less significant aspect of identity in Scotland than it may be in England as there is a perception, which may well not be accurate, of a kind of Scots equality. However, in a strongly nationalist society the degree to which one is authentically Scottish may well be a matter of social hierarchy. Indeed, Bruce *et al* (2004, 148) suggest that the idea that Scotland is sectarian remains an important part of identity, and a kind of myth, for some Scots. I appreciate that this is a relatively short summary of this issue and lack of space precludes me from going into greater depth. But nevertheless it is germane as background to our discussion though the degree of structural reassertion will not be observed to be high.[2]

Aberdeen University as a Rite of Passage

Aberdeen University is not particularly structured, although it is more so than some universities which we will examine. We have already observed the way that university in Scotland is in general less liminal and less status-raising than is generally the case in England and that this is confounded by the tradition of attending the nearest university in many cases. But let us turn to the specifics of Aberdeen University.

Though a relatively respected institution, it is certainly not as difficult to get into as Oxford University or even other ancient Scottish Universities. For many subjects there is no interview process and students are accepted according to the results of their school leaving exams. Aberdeen University would require relatively good 'Highers' (or A-Levels) for many subjects but it would not require, at least while I researched there, a standard that was as high as Edinburgh University for example. As such, being accepted into the university does not require a relatively stressful Rite of Initiation in itself. However it may be the case that the shared experience of having been rejected, as was often the case with Aberdeen students, from a certain university assists in bonding students to some extent. Anecdotally I would suggest that there was an element of this at Durham University where the majority appeared to be 'Oxbridge rejects' – an 'Oxbridge Reject T-Shirt' was even available from the Student Union shop – and even more so at St Mary's College (Durham University) a then all-female institution where many female students were offered places having been rejected by whichever Durham University co-educational college they had originally applied to.

But in general Aberdeen University would be somewhat less status-raising and liminal for undergraduates, especially as a large minority were local and even living at home during term time in a number of cases. Perhaps as a consequence there is no formal Rite of Separation at Aberdeen University as is the case at Oxford University. There was formerly a Rite of Separation but this has now been abolished perhaps in line with increasing numbers of Scottish students attending university – and, indeed, Aberdeen University – and the experience consequently becoming less liminal. I would argue that if the experience was sufficiently liminal a formal Rite of Separation would be likely to develop. Students register, instead, through a laborious,

2 For a more detailed examination of social class notions in Scottish nationalism see, for example, Dutton (2002).

lengthy and extremely bureaucratic system of spending around half a day queuing for various forms. This did not occur at Durham for example. It may be a deliberate attempt to foster *communitas* through shared frustration about seemingly poorly organised bureaucracy but I would be surprised if what many students described as 'administrative chaos' and 'university incompetence' was deliberately thought through in this manner as a Rite of Separation. However, it should be stressed that Aberdeen University does maintain an ancient graduation ritual which takes place in Latin. A Rite of Incorporation would imply that the experience is regarded as liminal at least to some extent and something which is clearly structured.

However, in many other respects Aberdeen University was considerably less structured than Oxford University was. Students are housed in Halls of Residence. However, these are not colleges and there is nothing comparable to college formals, college Balls or College Day. Some students opt to be catered for and placed in a Hall that offers this service while many cook for themselves. Thus, the forced *communitas* of shared dining does not necessarily occur and the formal dining dimension is effectively unheard of. Each college in Oxford attempts to be a community with a college president and 'Exec', numerous college societies, a college master who administers symbolic punishments for transgressions as in a school, a college chaplain, interconnected corridors of bedrooms, college student societies and so forth. There is simply nothing comparable to this at Aberdeen and many self-catering halls involve separate cut off flats making it more difficult to socialise with the people whom you do not happen to live immediately with. Moreover, the degree of undergraduate identity is also lessoned through the living arrangements. In one case I came across two seventeen year-old freshers who had been placed in a self-catering flat with three international students who were considerably older than them. Moreover, the university – or at least this hall – seemed to have a policy of separating flats according to gender. I would submit that all of this would be likely to lessen *communitas* between first year students.

The relative lack of private school students at Aberdeen University would mean that it would be relatively unlikely that Aberdeen University students would meet students who were from very different social backgrounds and even if they did the structures to bring about *communitas* would be lacking to a certain extent. Indeed the Oxford structures that help to create trauma – such as intense exams and numerous essays – were simply absent at Aberdeen. Though, unlike with Oxford, lectures appeared to be monitored and students had to attend a certain number or risk failing the course, students appeared to write far fewer essays and certainly less than one per week. Failed exams could be retaken, the degree was not entirely contingent on the final year and there was no need to wear formal dress to university examinations. In all of these respects Aberdeen University was considerably less structured and brought about far less *communitas*.

Following our model, we would expect there to be less evidence of structural reassertion at Aberdeen University because the *communitas* would be less intense. This is, indeed, what was noted. Unlike at Oxford, there was no perceived social divide between those from state and private schools. That said, there was sometimes evidence of male students deliberately emphasising their Scottishness by wearing kilts and this was especially so when student societies, such as AUCU, had Ceilidhs

– the traditional Scottish dancing events. However, this kind of social divide was nothing other than good humoured and might be perceived as kind of 'pseudo-opposition'. I was once with a group of male AUCU members in the *de facto* student pub – 'The Bobbin' – watching a football game on the television where England was ultimately defeated. The whole pub cheered raucously every time England appeared to be about to concede a goal – and especially when they actually did – as there is a Scottish tradition of avidly supporting whichever team is playing against England. When the other team won the pub was ecstatic and one senior AUCU member put his arm around me in a mock-patronising way and said, 'Och, Edward!' and shook his head as if to imply, 'Isn't it a shame your country is so useless'. But, again, this was tongue-in-cheek. Only once in my time in Aberdeen was I told 'Ye should go back to your ain country. Your sort are nae welcome up here!' and this was by a tipsy, middle-aged local woman in a relatively rough pub who took umbrage at my accent. She had no issue with my English friend, another doctoral student, who spoke with a northern English accent.

As identity at Aberdeen University is less exposed to question we would expect fewer students to need to assert or find a strong identity by becoming heavily involved in student societies such as AUCU. This is also what occurred. AUCU had only one hundred and seventy members, in a large university, far fewer than OICCU. Also student activity at Aberdeen seemed to be far less and where it existed it appeared to be taken considerably less seriously. Thus, compared to Oxford, there were fewer student societies and those that operated appeared to be far less active. Student plays, concerts, musicals and other events far from being daily were a relatively rare occurrence. Unlike at Oxford or Durham, the student newspaper did not attempt to ape serious newspapers. It was a kind of joke newspaper and was regarded as such by many of the students at Aberdeen. When I commented on this difference I was met with responses such as, 'Oh, well I write for it for a bit of laugh really!' or 'Well ... the newspaper's bound to be better at "Oxford" isn't it!' As we will see, even the Christian Union met less frequently and was somewhat less structured than was the case in Oxford.

Moreover, there was no hostility towards AUCU amongst Aberdeen students. I once took a random sample of ten students leaving Aberdeen University library and found that only one student had even heard of the Christian Union and even then she knew little about it other than that somebody on her corridor in her first year had been in it. This relative lack of differentiation between student and 'Christian' may partly explain why the Aberdeen University Exec was so much more co-operative with me than was the case in OICCU. Indeed, during my time with AUCU, members almost never asked me about my own beliefs and the only time that this did occur was during a Bible Study based around questions such as, 'When have you felt distant from God?' Otherwise I was asked about my beliefs by an invited AUCU speaker at a particular AUCU retreat but this was most out of the ordinary and he was, moreover, not a member of AUCU. However, AUCU was structured and indeed, as with OICCU, the term 'non-Christian' would be heard in prayers for example. Let us then examine this structure or at least relative lack of it.

AUCU Belief

As a UCCF-affiliated group, AUCU, like OICCU, required that members sign its Doctrinal Basis in order to join and because of its affiliation its Doctrinal Basis is exactly the same. AUCU members appeared to be somewhat less differentiated in both their religious views and their lifestyle ethics than OICCU members. All those whom I interviewed from AUCU claimed to believe in Hell and to believe that non-Christians would go to Hell. All of those to whom I spoke claimed to believe in the Devil as an actual force in the world. Twenty three in AUCU rejected Evolutionary Theory, which was marginally fewer than OICCU. Moreover, those that did reject the theory tended to be somewhat more unsure about doing so than many OICCU members were. They might begin by saying, 'Oh, that's a difficult question' or 'I'm not quite sure about that'. All AUCU members believed in the reality of doctrines such as the Resurrection. Of the twenty-five AUCU members interviewed, five admitted that they had never had a conversion experience but had simply always been Christians meaning that somewhat fewer had undergone conversion experiences than amongst OICCU members. As will be noted below, very few AUCU members had become Christians while at Aberdeen University. I also noted conformity in terms of social belief. In AUCU all felt it was unacceptable to have sex before marriage and all said that they would not do so. All but one felt that homosexual behaviour was unacceptable. Also all felt it was unacceptable for Christians to become drunk. However, unlike in OICCU a handful – two – felt it was acceptable for Christians to smoke and two would be prepared to date a non-Christian with a few others ambiguous about this. Thus, though AUCU is differentiated in terms of belief and lifestyle ethics it is somewhat less so than is the case in OICCU.

Conversion Experience at Aberdeen

We have already examined why conversion experience can be employed as evidence of liminality in a university. It betokens a change in identity, stress that would be precipitated by identity loss and a change in a person's relationships with their friends and even parents. We have already observed the level of conversion experience at Oxford and found that it was more common amongst those from state schools (most of whom had not taken a Gap Year). Amongst my AUCU sample even fewer than in OICCU – only three – had taken a Gap Year and in all cases they had travelled abroad. None of those who converted while at Aberdeen had been on Gap Years. Eight per cent of the AUCU sample had converted while at university and, indeed, half of those were from 'Christian' backgrounds. This contrasts to 24 per cent of the OICCU sample having converted while at Oxford of which almost all were from 'non-Christian' (in OICCU's terms) backgrounds. This would seem to indicate a lower level of liminality and structure. Though AUCU made use of Charismatic speakers at certain meetings – who had often undergone conversions – I never witnessed a 'testimony' by an AUCU member and even emotive speeches were relatively rare meaning that, in this regard at least, there was less *communitas* at meetings.

AUCU Involvement

At the beginning of my research AUCU held two meetings a week. There was Wednesday Night Bible Study which would be held in one of the lecture theatres. Here there would be an evangelical speaker and normally around twenty people present. This group of twenty included what we might call a 'hardcore' of around ten, including various members of the Exec, and then another ten that would vary slightly from week to week. However, the main meeting was 'Prayer and Praise' which was on a Friday evening. Here there would be around one hundred people present and it would tend to be the same people every week that would be observed. This would imply a certain degree of commitment with AUCU being significant to the identity of those present. This would involve the singing of worship music, accompanied by electric guitars and so forth, a speech by a senior member (the precise member varied) and division into prayer groups. All of this was followed by tea, biscuits and chatting. During my first term in Aberdeen, two or three AUCU students, including the then president, would go later that night to the Student Union, set-up a stall (including banner with Bible quotes) outside the Student Union nightclub and offer coffee to drunken students in an attempt to engage with them and tell them about Jesus although this could no longer occur in the second term I was with AUCU as the Student Union had been closed. There were no other regular meetings organised by AUCU itself and this relative lack of ritual might be seen as indicative of a less than tightly structured group that is, while significant to the identity of members, less so than it might be. Somewhat informally there was also 'CU Football' on Saturday mornings, though this was attended by a number of 'non-Christians' simply because they enjoyed football. There was no overt Christian element to this weekly meeting at all.

As with OICCU, there were other 'outreach' events though in AUCU there would normally be around one a term not including the group's 'Mission Week' or Freshers' Week where AUCU would organise various events such as a 'Barbeque on the Beach'. For example, during my fieldwork AUCU hosted '*Who Wants to be a (Chocolate) Millionaire?*' in reference to the then popular television show.[3] Contestants were divided into 'Boys v Girls' and the contestants were all other AUCU members. They had to answer deliberately absurd questions and undergo amusing physical tasks such as crawling through each other's legs. The host, a senior AUCU member, even used the British version of the show's host's catchphrase, 'Is that your final answer?' However, unlike with some OICCU events this did not culminate in a speech by the group's staff worker. There were simply Biblical tracts at the back of the room in case people wanted them. Thus, the form of evangelism was somewhat less confrontational than was the case in OICCU.

As with OICCU, AUCU conducted an annual 'Mission' in which there was an evangelical speaker conducting a talk every day of the week on various relatively basic theological questions such as, 'Why does God allow suffering?' or 'Who is Jesus?' As with OICCU, there were 'Mission Week Hoodies' but only a small

---

[3] This use of chocolate – where other groups might use alcohol – is interesting in terms of balancing differentiation with the broader culture. See Chapter 8 for further discussion.

minority of AUCU actually wore them and I never observed any member to be wearing one when it was not Mission Week which I did in OICCU. We might suggest that this indicates that AUCU is less differentiated and thus less structured than is the case in OICCU. Moreover, AUCU did not engage in 'cold contact' in the same way. They did not, for example, attempt to interview students about their beliefs. They appeared more interested in 'witness evangelism'. For example, they organised a five-aside football tournament that people could watch and even take part in. Other than the subtle presence of Biblical tracts there was again no overt evangelical dimension to this other than it being clear that it was organised by the Christian Union. As we have already discussed this in itself can be evidence of a highly structured group and AUCU do indeed proselytise but not to the same extent as OICCU and not as overtly.

Another significant issue in terms of structure is that of church attendance. As in Oxford, Aberdeen students were generally in Aberdeen at weekends. There is no tradition of going home at weekends as we will see that there is amongst students in the Netherlands. OICCU members would divide themselves between two morning services on Sundays – St Ebbes (the majority church which was conservative evangelical) and St Aldates which was Charismatic. A handful of members would attend churches other than these such as another Charismatic church in Oxford. In Aberdeen, amongst AUCU, church attendance was considerably more diverse. Obviously Aberdeen was a larger city and students were more spread out than was the case in Oxford and this may have itself contributed to a less structured group but, then, I did know of some students who would ride a substantial distance in order to get to a particular church. A large minority of AUCU members (eleven of my sample) attended Gilcomston South (which was Church of Scotland), ten attended Gerard Street Baptist Church while four attended the City Church, which was Charismatic. Other members – in small numbers – attended various other independent evangelical churches. As I interviewed more AUCU members I started to find more and more members who, almost alone within AUCU, would attend a particular church. Indeed, one of the Presidents did not herself attend either of the two main AUCU churches, attending 'Hebron Evangelical Church' instead. This diversity in church attendance – and individualism – might be seen as evidence of a lower level of group structure.

AUCU, Clothes and Gender

As with OICCU, the clothing worn by some AUCU members had the effect of differentiating them from 'non-Christians'. However, I found specific 'Christian' clothing considerably less frequently amongst AUCU members than amongst OICCU members. On a few occasions I noticed two different members wearing a top with the word 'Capenry' on it – a reference to an evangelical Bible College which they had attended. I also observed one later relatively senior member to wear a shirt which said, 'I (symbol of heart) Jesus'. Occasionally I observed AUCU members to wear 'WWJD' bracelets but this was a very infrequent occurrence. Moreover, I never observed any AUCU member to wear a Mission Week Hoodie when it was not

Mission Week and relatively few of them wore these tops when it was. When I asked about this members made remarks such as, 'I just think they're a bit stupid really!' or 'I just don't like them' whereas many OICCU members would say that they wore them to show 'we're a united, witnessing community' and 'so that people know that we're Christians'.

With the exception of the minority of men that wore overtly Christian clothing, male AUCU members did not appear to dress especially differently from how we might expect any student to dress. Importantly, however, there did appear to be a slightly higher tolerance in AUCU, than in OICCU, of members dressing or presenting themselves in what we might call an eccentric manner. It is perhaps rather subjective but there did appear to be men in AUCU who, for example, wore their hair long, did not bother to shave or turned-up in scruffy clothes – thus asserting a sense of individuality – than was observed in OICCU. This might be seen as an indicator of a lower level of differentiation and control. One such somewhat eccentric AUCU member appeared, though he did not have formal office, to be relatively important within the group not least because he was evidently very popular.

But as with OICCU the most obvious difference related to the kind of dress that appeared to be acceptable amongst female members. As with OICCU, the fashion of crop-tops and hipsters, which might be seen as rather revealing, was not generally observed amongst female AUCU members. It was not observed in OICCU at all and it was observed in the case of one AUCU student who, it should be said, was not an outsider in terms of group dynamics. As with OICCU, female members I asked about this commented that the fashion was 'too sexual', 'provocative' and 'unhelpful' which might be seen to contextualise dress within 'witness evangelism' and whether or not dressing in such a manner assists this which would further imply that evangelism has the effect of monitoring and controlling the behaviour of group members. When I asked male AUCU members about whether it was acceptable for female members to adopt this fashion I was greeted, in the first instance, with humorous responses such as, 'I might be interested in that!' or 'It depends what their figures are like!' But on further discussion they mostly agreed that though they would not have a problem with a 'non-Christian' coming to a meeting and dressing in such a way they would see it as 'unhelpful' for a Christian woman to do so. Even having said this, some members felt it necessary to make jokes. One AUCU member commented that, 'I also don't think they should wear t-shirts where they've got writing across the breasts ... because I can't help but look!' In all seriousness, certain AUCU members further commented that t-shirts where there were 'hand prints on the breasts' were also 'unhelpful' and 'not appropriate'. As such the difference in clothing use and attitudes towards it amongst AUCU, when compared to OICCU, appeared to be small but there were, nevertheless, differences which would imply a lower degree of differentiation in AUCU as we would expect.

The AUCU Exec

The AUCU Exec, as a broader part of UCCF, is differentiated from other student societies, though slightly less so than OICCU. As with other CUs, it is more than simply a President, Treasurer and Secretary. It is a much larger committee that includes, for example, a Prayer Secretary, a Mission Secretary and so forth though it did have fewer members than in OICCU. AUCU, however, did not have the large series of sub-committees that were to be found in OICCU. Though as with all groups within UCCF the Exec was a theocracy and each year the outgoing Exec prayed for divine guidance over who should be on the new Exec which was then put to the AUCU membership *en masse.*

However, one significant difference was the attitude towards women which we will also discuss when examining structural reassertion. OICCU's Presidents had in recent history always been men despite the fact that there were somewhat more females in OICCU than males. During the three years I had contact with AUCU the Presidents were in fact always women. It may be that this was a way of making a political point about AUCU to 'non-Christians' and thus disingenuous and certainly it was interesting that the Deputy-President was always a man. But then the year after I left the President was a man. So it may simply reflect a less differentiated attitude towards women by AUCU. It might be expected, for example, that the female Presidents were *de jure* rather than *de facto* leaders. However, to a certain extent, they did actually appear to engage in preaching activity for example. As such, I would suggest that this less structured Exec is congruous with the predictions of the theory being propounded.

Christian Language

There was evidence of restricted code in AUCU but it was not as stark as was the case in OICCU. Most obviously AUCU members had a slightly more relaxed attitude towards swearing. As with OICCU, all AUCU members objected to blasphemous language. They justified not using blasphemous language firstly by saying it was offensive to God and the Bible forbade it and then by adding that it would offend other members. With regard to bodily swearing AUCU showed less differentiation that OICCU. Far fewer of them justified not using such language with recourse to the Bible and though all members claimed that they would not say 'fuck' or 'cunt' some male members claimed that they would sometimes use words such as 'piss' in front of other male members. Also, unlike in OICCU, more members, again mainly male, claimed that they would be prepared to say the word 'fuck' (rather than calling it 'the f-word') if they were quoting somebody else as having said it or were simply referring to it. Indeed, they had no issue with quoting the word 'shit' as long as it was being quoted but this was also generally true in OICCU and some were prepared to occasionally use it. Many male AUCU members, moreover, did not object to using the words 'git' or 'twat' though I was informed by a few members that 'These words aren't seen as being as rude in Scotland as they are in England'. However, all claimed that they would not use the word 'wanker', a term in British English which literally means 'one who masturbates'. As with OICCU I also observed far more 'disguised swearing' in AUCU than I did amongst non-Christian students. Especially obvious was the use of the word 'pants' as a kind of vaguely disguised way of saying 'crap or 'shit' as in, 'Sorry but this projector's a bit pants'. I would argue that this is very interesting in terms of differentiation in both OICCU and AUCU because it allows a kind of swearing to take-place and therefore means that frustration can be vented and that the group is not too controlled and so differentiated that it conflicts to too great an extent with the cultural background of potential converts. Reiss (2000) argues that this balance is very important is running a successful religious group.[4]

Other than swearing there were a number of other examples of restricted code. As with OICCU, the term 'non-Christian' was employed though somewhat less frequently than in OICCU. This would be seen to imply a relatively structured group with a clear 'us v them' boundary. There were many other 'Christian terms' which I observed in conversation and which were also observed in OICCU though, again, more frequently. There was 'witness' and correspondent 'bad witness'. There was 'minister' which was used in the same sense as OICCU though this perhaps less differentiated in Scotland because the term is normally used to refer to a priest whereas in England it is employed to refer to a junior member of the Government who is not in the Cabinet. Once more there was this word 'back-slide' and, as with OICCU, the word 'unhelpful' in the sense of certain behaviour being implicitly 'unhelpful' to evangelism. It was never necessary to explain why and to what it was 'unhelpful'. It was unhelpful to the task of maintaining and broadening a community of 'Christians'. For example, one AUCU member told me that his 'Christian' parents had not wanted him to study a degree in Divinity because they thought it would be 'unhelpful' to his faith.

Structural Reassertion

As we have seen, AUCU, in comparison to OICCU, is somewhat less differentiated in terms of attitudes to clothing, swearing, lifestyle, religious belief and so forth but it is nevertheless somewhat differentiated from 'non-Christian' students and is a tighter organisation than some others that we will assess. We would expect there to be less reassertion of structure than was noted in OICCU because we would expect the lower level of differentiation to foster less AUCU *communitas* because the group is less differentiated from outsiders and the university itself generally involves less *communitas*. This is indeed what was observed.

There was no clear religious or social divide with regard to who was on the Exec or who was President. The Presidents were established Christians who had not become Christian at Aberdeen but it should be emphasised that relatively few of the membership became Christian while at Aberdeen anyway. Though a large minority of the membership were Presbyterian (whether Church of Scotland, Free Church of Scotland or from one of the Ulster Presbyterian churches) there was no reassertion in this regard. Indeed, one of the Presidents while I was there was a Baptist. None of the three Presidents during my involvement had been to private school though a few other Exec members had and so there may have been an element of structural

---

4 It is also a term that I have seen on children's television in place of swearwords and this might imply that CU members – like adults setting an example to children – restricted themselves in expressing the taboo thus conveying a sense of purity. See Chapter 8 for further discussion.

reassertion considering just how few AUCU members had been to private schools but this was far less stark than in OICCU. Moreover, there was clearly no reassertion of Scottish power in a group with minorities from Northern Ireland and England. A number of CU members commented to me during my research, light-heartedly, about how, 'The CU President is always a female medic and usually Northern Irish!' But this may have reflected little more than the fact that there were a lot of Northern Irish students in AUCU and, moreover, quite a lot of medical students and specifically medical students from Northern Ireland though there could conceivably be an element of idea that 'these people will go on to do a respected job'. It may simply be that these students came across as being more intelligent than a lot of the other students and, indeed, the standards required to read medicine were clearly higher at Aberdeen University than was the case with departments that would accept students through clearing after having done poorly in their school leaving exams.[5] It may therefore have been that there was some kind of acceptance amongst Aberdeen students that medical students were likely to be 'cleverer' and some students I spoke to outside of AUCU did make this point. Indeed, when I was an undergraduate I was aware of a certain degree of sneering in relation to students of Sports Science and in particular Education (training to be a Primary school teacher) because the A-Levels required to get in were understood to be considerably lower than the 'three As' that might be needed for popular subjects such as English Literature or Law. But there was less evidence of structural reassertion when compared to some other CUs and the year after I left the CU President was a state school, English, History student.

Moreover, there was no evidence of a separate 'Charismatic' group. A few members, though not very many, would be seen to become emotional during 'Prayer and Praise'. They would look emotional, hold their arms out and dance though I never observed any of this very small minority (of around five) to speak-in-tongues for example. This minority were a mixture of Scottish, Northern Irish and English. There was a very small Speak group at Aberdeen when I was first there but this – and the Kenyan student that single-handedly ran it – was in every way part of AUCU.

Ritual and *Communitas:* 'Prayer and Praise'

'Prayer and Praise' would take place on Friday evenings in a building called 'the Mission' and there would be around one hundred present. It would begin with a few humorous opening remarks either from the President or another member of the Exec. Thereafter there would be worship songs such as 'Shine Jesus, Shine!' and after this there would normally be prayers by the whole of AUCU and a speech by an AUCU member, normally an Exec member, which would usually be quite humorous in many respects but would make an evangelical theological point. After this there might be another hymn before people divided into prayer groups which would sit in circles on the stackable plastic chairs. Senior AUCU members would stand at the front and, for example, write prayer ideas – which would be suggested by other

[5] For example, psychologist Richard Lynn (2006, 237) observes that the more intelligent in a group will generally dominate and lead the less intelligent when all else is equal.

members – on a kind of presentation board. Then each prayer group member would introduce themselves (if they did not know each other) and then there would be random prayer, often with some group members being dominant. When this finished members would resume their original seating positions. There would be a final hymn, a final prayer lead by a senior member and then members would leave to go and have tea and coffee while the band played in the background.

In many ways, this meeting was actually less structured – at least in terms of creating *communitas* – than was the case at OICCU's main meeting. For example, the hymns did not appear to build-up to a climax. They were seemingly random in style and music simply stopped between the hymns while an Exec member told people what the next hymn was going to be. This broke the climax and the dissociation that might have been created and there was, in general, far less evidence of dissociation. I do not think this is simply a matter of 'religious culture' as some might submit because one of the main churches which AUCU members (many of them Church of Scotland) attended was moderately Charismatic and AUCU had access to exactly the same instruments and facilities as OICCU but simply chose not to use them in the same way. In some respects, Prayer and Praise was more comparable to Powerhouse inasmuch as there was small group prayer which might create *communitas* and involve the sharing of personal information. However, there was certainly no spontaneous prayer or any facility in place to encourage it.

Of course, prayer would be likely to create *communitas* and we might expect some reassertion of structure in this context but this was not observed in the same way that it was in OICCU because the university did not really bring about social *communitas* to the same extent in the first place. All AUCU prayers were informal in style and attempted to sound authentic such as this prayer by a former Exec member:

> Father ... I just wanna thank you for the gift of life that you've given us through Jesus because that's ... I mean ... it's just so great. And I'd really like to thank you, Lord, for sport ... so we can just ... like ... totally de-stress and enjoy ourselves and I just wanna ... like ... thank you for the chance to study here at Aberdeen. Amen.

But certainly group prayer might be perceived to have a levelling effect and I did note some students effectively playing for status – or asserting it – in this context. Most obviously, the senior members – if they were in a particular prayer group – tended to pray the most and dominate proceedings to some extent as occurred with the member quoted above. Another senior member, in a public prayer in front of the group at the end of group prayer prayed that:

> Father God ... I thank you that you know each of us so well ... that you know everything that there is to know about us Father that you ... that you know how many hairs there are on each of our heads.

This might be seen as a play for or assertion of status as she is probably alluding to a particular Biblical passage and is therefore deliberately, publicly showing Biblical knowledge through her prayer.[6] Thus, structure reasserted itself to some extent in Prayer and Praise but clearly not to the same extent as in a more liminal group.

Wednesday Night Bible Study

As already noted, there were far fewer members at this meeting and they tended to be a kind of 'hardcore' of highly committed members as well as others who varied from week to week. The meeting would take place in a lecture theatre and would begin with a prayer lead by a particular member of the Exec who could play the guitar. There would then be two hymns accompanied by the guitar and then the invited speaker, usually a minister from around Aberdeen, would conduct his sermon. At the end of this there would be questions, a final prayer and then everybody would go home. The sermon would often be relatively lighthearted in places. However, I never observed anything comparable to the kind of 'charisma' that was frequently observed with OICCU's speakers which would, in those terms, be congruous with AUCU reflecting a lower level of crisis, perhaps, for those studying at the university.

During my broader study at Aberdeen University, Wednesday Night Bible Study was abolished ostensibly because it was not working as an 'outreach' event. Despite being advertised around the university 'non-Christians' did not generally come to it. Instead the staff worker advised members to spend that evening socialising with their 'non-Christian' friends. However, many members informed me that almost all of their friends were Christian and even mostly AUCU members in many cases.

I should also re-emphasise here that I at no point witnessed a 'testimony' at an AUCU meeting. Obviously very few AUCU members had become Christians while at university but a small minority had and they had not engaged in a public testimony. However, 'testimony' was clearly significant to AUCU because, during my research, they displayed testimonies of various members on their website, though these have been taken down at the time of writing. I have already argued that 'testimony' is highly efficient at bringing about *communitas* so we see another possibility for bringing about *communitas* not employed by the less structured AUCU.

Charisma

As already noted the speakers at AUCU meetings were not generally 'charismatic' in the same way as speakers at OICCU meetings. Speeches may have been amusing in places and emotive in others but there was not, in my experience, this sense of being taken on an emotional journey – and consequently dissociated – that I noted at OICCU meetings with a number of their invited speakers.

During one of AUCU's Mission Weeks there was certainly a relatively 'charismatic' speaker who was rather proficient in dissociating his audience –

[6] The speaker may have been alluding, for example to, 'Are not two sparrows sold for a penny? Yet not one of them will fall on the ground apart from the will of your Father. And even the very hairs of your head are all numbered. So don't be afraid; you are worth more than many sparrows' (Matthew 10: 29–31).

some of whom were non-Christians – with traditional oratorical techniques which eventually led into a serious speech about the saving power of Jesus. For example when this speaker was explaining his own conversion he made a series of jokes about turning water into wine and proceeded:

> ... it was a wonderful wine. And when you've tasted the best ... I mean ... you can't go back. You can't go back to Shiraz. You can't go back to Tesco 5 pound 99 bottles. You need something proper! *(Laughter)* I was in Paris with my wife, staying with this rich businessman who was really into wine. Passionate about it. It was such a romantic weekend. He had a wine cellar and he got me this bottle and it'd been down there for five years ... When I tasted it ... I tasted, suddenly, just how much God was good ... I'd first tasted God at seventeen but ...

I would suggest that the speaker slowly and convincingly manages to take the audience on an emotional journey here but this was the only example where this occurred during my fieldwork with AUCU. This was therefore another respect in which the structures of the meeting brought about a lower level of *communitas*. On one other occasion where I did observe an invited speaker – an American pastor and doctoral student – conduct an emotive speech a number of AUCU members I spoke to afterwards, including senior members, were rather shocked and taken aback by it. But in general I think we would expect to find charisma in a tightly structured group in crisis and as AUCU is not this to the same extent as OICCU we would not expect to find it to the same extent and, indeed, we do not.

Christian Union Ceilidhs

One of the most fascinating things about AUCU, in my experience, was the very subtle nature of much of their organised evangelism. As we have already discussed, OICCU would provide free lunch for non-Christians on Fridays but only as part of a broader event in which there was an invited evangelical speaker. They would give out coffee on May Day morning but along with Biblical tracts and even something like a Wine and Cheese Evening in a college would have an overtly 'Christian' dimension to it. AUCU organised a number of outreach events where there would be some kind of Christian speech but they also organised many events where people would have hardly known that it was a 'Christian' event at all.

We have already looked at the example of 'CU Football' which effectively developed organically and involved many students who would not be regarded as 'Christian' in AUCU's terms. Another example, which was formally organised by AUCU, was the Christian Union 'Ceilidh'. OICCU also organises the occasional Ceilidh but they are not a part of English culture in the same way that they are a part of Scottish culture. Organising a Ceilidh can therefore be seen as a direct appeal to the Scottish national identity shared by most students but, anyway, I am using this example to illustrate a further point which goes beyond the event itself. The Ceilidh is particularly popular at Scottish weddings and comes from the Scots Gaelic word for 'gathering'. It involves a series of traditional dances – such as 'The Dashing White Sergeant' and 'Strip the Willow' – which usually involve dancing in groups of at least six. For the AUCU Ceilidh, during their Mission Week, they rented out a university-owned hall – complete with very old portraits – within the fifteenth century Kings College. There were snacks and non-alcoholic drinks available and the CU simply conducted a Ceilidh along with a live band. There was no overt evangelical element to this and there was no Christian literature available at the event at all. A number of international students attended and a few did not actually realise that it was a Christian event. In this context, a handful of male members wore kilts which could be interpreted as a reassertion of structure. Another CU Ceilidh that I attended was in the Student Union and there was therefore a bar as part of the room. This also attracted large numbers of non-Christians, a few men (and women) wore various garments of Highland dress and there was no overt 'Christian' element. Unlike at Oxford, many student societies held Ceilidhs at Aberdeen University. By holding a Ceilidh with no Christian dimension to it AUCU were doing something popular and 'Scottish' which many students enjoyed and which other societies also did. This betokened, I think, a lack of differentiation especially in a Scottish context. This stands in contrast to OICCU 'Cheese and Wine Evenings', for example, where there would generally be some kind of 'Christian' and thus differentiating element.[7]

Theology and Church Politics

It might be argued that differences between OICCU and AUCU reflect differences in religious culture – and group religious belief – between England and Scotland and between OICCU and AUCU. It might be argued that Scotland is a traditionally Calvinist religious culture where the emphasis has been on glorifying God – who predestines people through Grace to go to Heaven or Hell – rather than actually converting people to Christianity. I found little evidence for this proposition. Though many members were in theoretically Calvinist churches, predestination was never preached at any AUCU meeting. The group was evangelical and it was, implicitly, an Arminian understanding that appeared to be preached even if some members, when questioned, believed in predestination. This stood in contrast to some local Aberdeen churches which openly preached that God chooses some and not others.

Though many AUCU members were from the Church of Scotland, a large group did not accept the doctrine of pre-destination or at least were not quite sure about it. Those who did saw no contradiction at all between believing the doctrine and yet being highly evangelical. Indeed, they felt that the doctrine meant that it was incumbent upon them to evangelise. There is a strong evangelical movement within the Kirk. For example, one vice-president during my research – and congregant at Gilcomston – later informed me in writing that:

> I do believe in pre-destination as it is clearly taught in the Bible not only by the Apostle Paul but also by Jesus himself, see John 6:35–40 – where far from being an anti-evangelistic doctrine the opposite is the case ... It was never a huge issue at the CU in Aberdeen (*when he was vice-president*). I realise that many people find it difficult to accept, but to deny it

[7] For further discussion of the Ceilidh and Scottish identity see, for example, Shoupe (2001).

> would be to go against the plain teaching of the Bible. My view is summed up by Charles Spurgeon who said 'I believe the doctrine of election, because I am quite sure that if God had not chosen me I should never have chosen him; and I am sure he chose me before I was born, or else he never would have chosen me afterwards'.[8]

He felt that the doctrine could make Christians, quoting the theologian J.I. Packer, 'lazy' but it could do quite the opposite and make them 'active'. As I have said, the members who were firm on the doctrine seemed to believe that it expressed the idea that everything was ultimately in God's hands and definitely did not imply that evangelism was pointless. In fact, it might even be argued that believers in this doctrine would be motivated to evangelise such that others saw them as Christians and they could therefore reassure themselves that they were and they were part of the elect.

One senior member, who was very evangelical and dedicated, told me that, 'My views are more Calvinist as I grow in my understanding of the scriptures and of God's goodness'. However, I was informed of a particular very senior member who was a Scottish evangelical and had never even heard of Calvinism until she reached her position on the Exec. Moreover, one might suggest that the fact that members had joined a constitutionally evangelical student group might mean that it was unlikely that they were particularly firm on this particular aspect of Reformed Theology at least in practice. Indeed a large portion of the members actually attended a Baptist church on Sundays and even the Church of Scotland church which some attended classed itself as 'evangelical' having become so under the stewardship of Rev'd William Still who was a considerable influence on AUCU until his death (Gilcomston 2005).

As such, I am not persuaded by the argument that the differences between OICCU and AUCU reflect the matter of Reformed religiosity. In the early 1970s, OICCU moved towards a conservative Calvinist doctrine under the Presidency of Tom Wright (1970–71) but the group became no less evangelical.[9] Indeed, as noted, many Reformed students felt that pre-destination demanded evangelicalism. As we will see, the least evangelical of the Christian groups that we will assess was a group at Oulu University that defined itself as being evangelical and was within a Lutheran (and thus not Reformed) culture and, moreover, a culture where there exists highly active evangelical revival movements as we will discuss in Chapter 7. Secondly, even if the relative lack of evangelism in AUCU can be explained by a Reformed

[8] Charles Spurgeon (1834–92) was an English Reformed preacher. Though Spurgeon was a believer in pre-destination he was highly evangelical. The student refers to the following passage: 'Then Jesus declared, "I am the bread of life. He who comes to me will never go hungry, and he who believes in me will never be thirsty. But as I told you, you have seen me and still you do not believe. All that the Father gives me will come to me, and whoever comes to me I will never drive away. For I have come down from heaven not to do my will but to do the will of him who sent me. And this is the will of him who sent me; that I shall lose none of all that he has given me, but raise them up at the last day. For my Father's will is that everyone who looks to the Son and believes in him shall have eternal life, and I will raise him up at the last day"' (John 6: 35–40).

[9] Tom Wright was consecrated Bishop of Durham in 2003.

religious culture this does not explain why the Christian Union, in so many other respects, should be so much less structured than the Christian Union at Oxford. The lack of Charismatic worship may be a matter of Scottish or Reformed culture but this does not explain other possibilities to foster *communitas* which are not taken up nor the structure/anti-structure difference that I have highlighted outside of this worship context. One might expect a highly structured group to foster *communitas* but AUCU does not achieve this in meetings to the same extent as OICCU.

It might also be suggested that AUCU is simply reflecting the church politics of Aberdeen but I really do not see how this could be the case. The majority of AUCU members attended free churches that were, in many ways, Charismatic. However, this was not reflected in AUCU meetings where only a tiny minority engaged in anything comparable to Charismatic activity and even then it appeared to be in a somewhat diluted form. As such, taking into account these potential criticisms I would argue that they are less than entirely convincing and that liminality – as an explanation for the kind of structural issues noted – is a highly persuasive model.

Conclusion

Aberdeen University is, though liminal for many students, considerably less so than would be the case with a university such as Oxford. Larger numbers of Aberdeen students lived at home or were from the area, university in Scotland is broadly less status-raising for Scottish undergraduates, Aberdeen University itself is less status raising than Oxford University as it is less prestigious and this less liminal dimension is clearly seen in the university's lack of a Ritual of Separation. Also, the university does not create social *communitas* because there is little in the way of a social divide and nor is there a clear divide between 'Town and Gown'. The university living arrangements do not create substantial *communitas* either and there is, again, little ritual. This lack of *communitas* appears to be reflected in a relative lack of student activity which, for many, is less necessary because identity is less challenged.

Within this weaker *communitas*, AUCU parallels this by being less structured than it might be in terms of issues such as ethics, swearing use, religious belief, the Exec, attitudes to women and so forth. It meets less frequently implying that it is less significant to the identity of members – or less psychologically necessary – than other groups we have assessed. AUCU is less differentiated than groups at more liminal universities and this is also noted in some of the forms of evangelism which it engages in. In general, AUCU *communitas* can be understood as somewhat lower and, as we have seen, there is much less of a reassertion of structure in relation to who is running the Christian Union. Equally, the meetings are less structured which appears to lead to a lower level of *communitas.* Of course, there is a difference in religious culture (and culture more broadly) between England and Scotland and this must be remembered in conducting such a comparative analysis. However potential criticisms in this area were noted to not undermine the model under discussion here. AUCU and Aberdeen University provide further evidence for the level model of the liminal phase. Aberdeen University is not especially liminal meaning that it is not especially structured and does not create considerable *communitas*, though it does foster it for many students. As such AUCU, within this *communitas* and reasserting societal structure by dividing 'Christians' from 'non-Christians', is less structured than CUs in different circumstances. This in turn leads to lower group *communitas* and lower reassertion of structure within the group. Group meetings also appear to reflect this difference.

Chapter 6

'We're just ordinary students who are also Christians'

Leiden University and the Christian Students Leiden (CSL)

Leiden University is the oldest institution of Higher Education in the Netherlands. By tradition it was established in 1575 as a gift to the people of Leiden from Prince William of Holland after they successfully repelled the Spanish from their city. Leiden has a population of just over 117,000 and was established by the Romans in the fourth century as a fortress. Almost all of the Dutch students whom I interviewed at Leiden University were from areas relatively close to Leiden reflecting a tradition in the Netherlands of attending your nearest university. Some lived at home or lived outside the city. According to Dutch students to whom I spoke, Dutch universities are all generally understood to be 'of a similar standard' and assuming that a student does sufficiently well in their school exams to get into university in their subject they have the right to attend any university where the subject is studied which can, and did in my experience, lead to intense competition for student housing within Leiden with some students living in The Hague or even Amsterdam. Leiden University was, many felt, 'slightly more popular' than other institutions because it was the most established and was attended by the Dutch aristocracy including the Crown Prince.

I spent one four-month semester at Leiden University between September and December 2003 and then made a follow-up visit in April 2004. During this time I had the status of Guest Researcher in the Theology Department and lived in one of the 'International Houses' where the university authorities placed international students who were studying through the medium of English.[1] Christian Students Leiden had around one hundred members. As with other groups I conducted a survey of twenty-five and interviewed a representative sample of twenty-five. It was far easier to draw up a representative sample of CSL members because they published an annual which stated sociological details about each member including their Protestant denomination, the part of the Netherlands they came from, the subject that they studied and so forth.

The Exec – or *Bestuur* – was extremely co-operative and I was able to attend any meeting I wished to. In a sense I was made a kind of honorary member in as much as I was permitted to go to all meetings, including their Annual General Meeting from which non-members were strictly excluded. The first meeting that I attended was a small prayer meeting and when I had been introduced as a fieldworker one of the

[1] For further discussion of English as a *lingua franca* amongst European students see House (2003) or Booij (2001).

Bestuur members said stony faced, 'Ok. You can of course study us. So ... normally it is customary that if you want to be in the group that we do the baptism now ...' There was an awkward pause before I realised that this was a very dryly delivered joke. At the time I spoke conversational Dutch and members were also extremely helpful with any difficulties that I experienced with the language and generally spoke English fairly fluently. In many respects, Leiden University was structured in such a way as to mean that it was not especially liminal for many of its students. Indeed, Leiden University appeared to be somewhat less liminal even than Aberdeen University though it was still liminal to some extent as we will see. But it must be borne in mind that in looking at a Dutch university we are dealing with a distinct religious and national culture. Before moving onto the issue of university structure I would like to look at this religious culture.

Religious Background in the Netherlands and around Leiden

In terms of belief, the Netherlands is one the least religious nations in Europe with 27 per cent asserting that they are atheists and only 34 per cent positively believing in God (Euro-barometer on Social Values 2005, 11). Twenty-seven per cent are deemed to be active Catholics while 12 per cent are members of mainstream Reformed Churches. However as weekly church attendance statistics are 21 per cent this would imply that a small minority in Holland are particularly religiously active. In Finland, as we will see, around 4 per cent attend church regularly but over 80 per cent are confirmed members of the Lutheran church. Attempting to understand the religious background of the Netherlands is perhaps slightly more complex than in some other countries because of the historical significance of denomination to identity.

Until around the 1970s every level of Dutch society was divided – or Pillarized – between the two 'Pillars' of Protestant and Catholic with the north mainly being Protestant and the south mainly being Catholic. Every dimension of life was separated according to denomination with Dutch Protestants and Catholics maintaining not only separate churches but separate newspapers, separate television stations, separate political parties, separate Trade Unions and separate universities (Dekker and Ester 1996). The majority of universities, including Leiden, were originally for the education of Protestant students and mainly although not exclusively for the education of Dutch Reformed students: this being the most significant Protestant denomination in the Netherlands until a merger in 2004. There was also a university established specifically for members of the *Gereformed Kerk* in 1880, a more evangelical denomination than the Reformed Church, called the Free University of Amsterdam. The University of Nijmegen was established for the education of Catholic students in 1923. Thus in the religiously sectarian society Protestants were traditionally dominant.

In relatively mixed areas, such as Utrecht which is in the north of the Netherlands, the Pillarization extended to separate schools, separate hospitals and even separate shops. During my research I spoke to one Catholic university lecturer in his sixties who recalled his mother telling him not to go to a particular shop because it was 'run by Protestants' and various other older Protestants who had similar memories of strenuously avoiding Catholic businesses. While the Dutch may not be an especially religious nation in terms of belief, the Netherlands has a relatively high level of church attendance amongst those that are religious leading to a national average of 21 per cent (Davie 2000, 9) considerably higher than England's. The Netherlands also maintains a high level of 'Christian identification'. Houtman and Mascini find that denominational identification attachment, although decreasing, is still highly significant in the Netherlands (Houtman and Mascini 2002, 455). Dekker and Ester have reached similar conclusions (Dekker and Ester 1996, 355). Many schools are still divided along denominational lines, for example. There are now 'non-denominational' schools as well and many Dutch students commented to me that parents make a point of sending their children to a denominational school 'to keep them away from Muslim immigrants' as a number of students put it. Muslim immigrants from countries such as Morocco and Turkey are perceived as the poorest people in the Netherlands. Moreover, the overwhelming majority of students at Leiden University, and in CSL, will be shown to come from the middle of the Netherlands, a Protestant area known as the 'Dutch Bible Belt' (Sobatka and Adigúzel 2002, 11) and thus a relatively religious area. Indeed, despite the apparent lack of religious belief 55 per cent of the Dutch population are affiliated to a denomination. Twenty-seven per cent are Catholic while the rest are affiliated to a variety of Protestant churches the largest being the Dutch Reformed Church (SCP Report 2004) and now its successor. Religious affiliation has declined substantially since the 1970s but, nevertheless, research indicates the salience of denomination to Dutch identity.

The area of the Netherlands where Leiden University, a traditionally Protestant university, is situated is the most Protestant area of the country as has been noted. There are many different Protestant – and specifically Reformed – denominations and restraints of space necessitate a relatively brief summary. Most of these various churches – some more theologically and socially strict than others – are Calvinist, a theological orientation that we have already discussed. The Dutch Reformed Church was established at the end of the sixteenth century and underwent a further piety movement – or 'Further Reformation' – through the seventeenth and eighteenth centuries, coming under Royal control in 1815. The decline in religious participation in the Netherlands meant that Catholicism replaced Protestantism as the largest affiliated denomination in the 1970s. However the Dutch Reformed Church – by far the largest denomination – is relatively liberal with regard to theological issues such as predestination and, indeed, merged with the 'Reformed Churches of the Netherlands' and the Evangelical Lutheran Church of the Netherlands in 2004 to form the 'Protestant Church in the Netherlands'.

The 'Christian Reformed Church' (*Christelijke Gereformeerde Kerken*) was a merger of two churches that had split from the Dutch Reformed Church in the 'Separation' (*Afscheiding*) of 1834 whereby some members who were, essentially, more revival or 'piety' oriented split away to form separate churches. The emphasis in such pietist groups was on experiencing Jesus in a manner perhaps in line with some evangelical ideas of requiring a personal conversion to God (Meiden 1988, 92). The Reformed Church's second major historical schism had been the break away of 'Reformed Churches of the Netherlands' in 1886 – the so called '*Doleantie*'. This was led by Abraham Kuyper (1837–1920) who later became the Dutch Prime

Minister. Kuyper's church was characterised by the Neo-Calvinist belief that God planned the Fall rather than merely foreseeing it. Kuyper emphasised a need for evangelism, however, claiming that God's sovereignty had to be brought all over the world through a pietist revival. A further split occurred in 1944 where the 'Reformed Church (Liberated)' split from Kuyper's church to re-emphasise Neo-Calvinist doctrine and a more conservative understanding of the Bible, other doctrines and the place of women for example (e.g. Rooden 2002). Thus while there is a Calvinist culture in parts of Holland there is also an evangelical culture and the degree of belief in doctrines such as predestination is seemingly much debated with the more conservative groups splitting due to a belief that others have rejected it along with other supposedly key doctrines.[2] Indeed, the 2004 merger led to further schisms over predestination and the ordination of women ministers. However, in general the religious background is, at least traditionally, Reformed though there are clearly numerous disagreements and nuances within this.

Dutch Education and Liminality

Unlike in England or Scotland there is no tradition in the Netherlands of wealthier parents sending their children to private schools and, as such, the school system does not entrench social divisions or at least not in this way. A number of Leiden University students to whom I spoke claimed that the state system was perceived to be 'good' and people would usually only use a private school if their child had specific problems such as learning difficulties. However other students emphasised that they felt there were considerable differences between the standards in state schools, which were all co-educational, according to the area that you lived in. As we have discussed, many students pointed out that the many schools based around a religious denomination tended to be 'better' and regarded as preferable because they generally had 'very few immigrants'. Muslim immigrants, according to those to whom I spoke, tended to attend schools which did not have a denominational affiliation. Almost all my sample of CSL had attended Protestant schools. In fact there was only one person in my sample who had attended a non-denominational school. However there is, nevertheless, an academic divide in Dutch education with some secondary schools, from the age of twelve, being 'vocational' and others focusing pupils towards university. One Dutch student told me, when discussing this, that, 'The education system here is very complicated ... well ... just like everything in Holland!'

As was the case in Britain prior to 1992 there is a clear divide within Higher Education for which, during my research, tuition fees of around 500 euros a year had to be paid. These had only been recently introduced when I was conducting my research in the autumn of 2003. In the Netherlands there are universities and there are what are known as High Schools (*Hogeschoolen*) which appeared to be comparable

---

2 Some of these churches have specific political parties connected to them which are represented in the Dutch Parliament. For example the *SGP* (*Staatkundig Gereformeered Partij*, Political Reformed Party) represents members of the most conservative Calvinist groups and has two parliamentary seats out of one hundred and fifty.

to British former Polytechnics and involved similarly vocational degrees. Students generally began their degrees at eighteen or nineteen and the degree – a Masters degree qualification if you were at university – lasted for around five years. There was no degree classification system. Students passed through accruing the required number of 'credits' and each course provided them with a certain number of credits. They had to produce a Masters Thesis which was given a Latin classification such as '*Cum Laude*'. Re-takes were permitted if a student failed a module. However, they would only have one or occasionally two chances to re-take before they would be asked to leave leading to a certain amount of academic pressure. There were also 'perks' to being a Dutch student which I did not find to the same extent in other countries. Almost all students at Leiden University appeared to 'go home' at weekends and I discovered from some South African students that was also true at Utrecht University. One of the reasons why they were able to afford to do this was because rail travel was heavily subsidised – indeed free – for Dutch students. They could even take a friend with them, who was not a student, for half price. Bus travel was also free which led to some students being prepared to live considerable distances from the university and even from the university town.

However, unlike in England, there was evidently no tradition in the Netherlands of going away from home in order to go to university. In my research, a very large portion of students would live at home – especially when they were in the first year – which was not problematic due to the public transport system. But nevertheless they were from the same part of the Netherlands as where the university that they attended was situated. A number of Leiden University students commented to me in this regard that, 'All Dutch universities are seen as being of about the same standard ... so people just go to their local university'. Others added that it was a matter of tradition that had long developed. 'You go to your local university. If you're Catholic you go to the Catholic university – which you're probably close to – or to one of the universities in the south of the country where most people are Catholic anyway.' As has been noted, students commented to me that once you had the entrance requirements for a specific subject you had the right to attend your nearest university or, indeed, any university that you wished to. In the case of Leiden, because it also attracted some students from outside the area because it was in some respects the most prestigious university, this appeared to lead to intense competition for accommodation and therefore very expensive accommodation and many students having to live some distance from the centre of what was a relatively large town. Thus I think it can be argued that the Dutch university experience is not especially liminal at least in these broad senses. No university traditions subject students to the kind of academic intensity of Oxford, students attend their nearest university and meet people from their area and the fact that most go home at weekends – and many of them live at home – would be likely to diminish the degree of liminality as well.

Social and Cultural Background

In terms of geographical composition, CSL reflected the way in which there is certainly a tendency for Dutch students to attend their nearest university because, unlike in Britain, all universities in Holland are regarded as being of the same standard. Fifty per cent of CSL members were from South Holland, the province in which Leiden is situated. Forty per cent were from other provinces that are still relatively close to Leiden. Only 10 per cent were from provinces that are distant from Leiden – Groningen or Friesland in the North and Limburg or Flanders in the south (CSL Statistics). Hence, despite the fact that Holland is a relatively small country, smaller than Scotland, there is a tendency for students to attend their nearest university and CSL appears to reflect this.

The social composition of CSL reflected Dutch universities more generally in that most were originally from what we might call professional-middle-class backgrounds, at least with regard to the profession of one of their parents. Of CSL's membership, none were from what we might term upper-class, eighteen were from higher or lower professional backgrounds, six were lower-middle-class and one, who cited her father's profession as a market-stall trader, would appear to be working-class and it is perhaps noteworthy that she alone had not been to a denominational school. While I was at Leiden University I was introduced to a number of people who were from what might be called the Dutch aristocracy through contacts I made with a particular Dutch student from a very wealthy background who happened to be involved in the International Student Society, of which I was a member. For reasons I will examine below no member of CSL was from such a background. Though the majority were women in all of the other Christian Unions that I have studied in the case of CSL this majority was very substantial indeed. Two thirds of members were female and this reflected the broader dynamics of Leiden University. It mainly focused on the humanities and medicine – which seemed to attract female students – while nearby Delft University, which concentrated on sciences, was substantially male.

In terms of religiosity, about 20 per cent of CSL were from the Reformed Churches in the Netherlands (*Gereformeerd Kerk*), 20 per cent were from the Christian Reformed Church (*Christelijk Gereformeerd Kerk*), 25 per cent were Dutch Reformed and about 25 per cent were 'evangelical'. Around 10 per cent were 'other'. This included many 'Lutherans' and also members of small Neo-Calvinist churches (CSL Statistics). With the exception of the Dutch Reformed Church all the churches which appear to compose the membership of CSL would seem to be at the conservative end of Protestantism in the Netherlands and this is particularly true with regard to the 'Reformed Churches in the Netherlands'. The Dutch Reformed Church itself is far broader and encompasses what we might term conservatives and liberals.

On Dutch Culture

Before moving on I think it would be worth examining the dynamics of Dutch culture as this will be germane to some of the findings of the research that I conducted. Though this now may be seen to be changing there was an emphasis in the Netherlands, at least when I conducted my research, on the notion of Dutch 'tolerance' though this may be perceived by outsiders as something of national myth.

A number of Holland researchers (e.g Velde 1996, Rooden 2002) have observed that the breakdown in Pillarization in the Netherlands appeared to be followed by an emphasis on tolerance and, moreover, the fact that Holland was pillarized between two very separate religious cultures has been connected to rise of the 'tolerant' Dutch idea. It might be speculated that this idea was reflected in Holland, during my fieldwork, in cultural traditions such as effectively legal marijuana which could be purchased from so called 'coffee shops' and even in tiny details which reflected a strong desire to leave other people alone and let them get on with their lives (e.g. Hooghe 2001, Watling 2001). One international student commented to me that she rang the police because of the noise of a nearby all night party that hadn't abated at three o'clock in the morning. The Dutch policeman advised, 'Well ... why can't you maybe sleep with your pillow over your head?'

These kinds of examples are used by various Dutch scholars as evidence of 'tolerance' (Ginkel 2001) and, in 2002, a Dutch supposedly 'far right' politician called Pim Fortuyn rose to prominence before being assassinated just before the General Election. He was openly homosexual and opposed Islam because he saw it as a threat to Holland's 'tolerant' society. His party – List Pim Fortuyn – came second, after he had been murdered during the election campaign, and was briefly part of the governing coalition (Gladdish 2002). As we will discuss below, this 'tolerance' was reflected in the Dutch seemingly being far more hesitant to give an opinion than was the case in Britain. Also they in general seemed to be far more concerned with their own privacy – at least with regard to discussions over sex – something which, perhaps, made me realise something about British culture that I had not previously realised having never lived abroad until that point.

Leiden University as a Rite of Passage

Though it may well be more status-raising than some universities that we have assessed – not least because it has a certain amount of prestige – Leiden University is not particularly structured and I would suggest that it is less structured than Aberdeen University at least for Dutch students. This lack of structure – and liminality – is most clearly evidenced by the way that almost all students at Leiden University would go home at weekends thus recreating the bond with their families. But let us examine the structure.

There exists no exacting ritual in order to win a place at Leiden University. As I understood it there was no interview and nor were there specific university examinations to gain entrance. If a student did sufficiently well in their school leaving examinations in the relevant subjects then they had the right to study whatever subject they wished to at whatever university happened to offer it. The only exception to this appeared to be if you wanted to do a medical degree. Dutch medical students – of which there were many in CSL – informed that so many people wanted to be medical students and achieved the required qualifications that a lottery had been developed and that they had been lucky enough to have been picked. But in general there had been no specific and structured ritual in order to get into university. That said, the first few weeks of the first term at Leiden University did appear, without meaning to be pejorative, to be chaos on a scale that I had simply never experienced at another university. One student put this to me simply, 'The university takes in far too many students every single year'. The result was a scramble for housing in the first few weeks of term. Many students would live at home for the first few weeks – or even for the first term in its entirety – before finally finding somewhere to live. Student notice boards would be crammed with hand-written notes by students trying to find accommodation. I remember one in which the student wrote about how desperate she was for somewhere to live because she had to travel two hours every day to get to university and felt excluded from university social life. This might be understood as a kind of traumatic Rite of Initiation but, unlike at Oxford University, there was no structured ritual. There was, however, a ritual of graduation for those receiving Masters Degrees. Participants wore suits and the fact of such a ritual would seem to indicate liminality. Though following Morris (1969) it is noteworthy that the ritual is not set apart through the use of deliberately bizarre clothes as occurs in a graduation ritual from Oxford or even Aberdeen.

Accommodation

There was also very few student Halls of Residence in the sense of Halls that were not separated into individual flats. These existed for International Students but not, so it appeared, for Dutch students. They were expected, even as first years, to independently find somewhere to live through various companies in Leiden that specialised in student accommodation. Unlike in Oxford or Aberdeen, the rooms that they would rent would be 'room only' meaning that they had to purchase or bring with them from home all of their own furniture. I remember on various occasions seeing students in Leiden with their parents and a trailer attached to the back of the car with book shelves and a bed on it. At Oxford, for example, even if you chose to live outside college in your second year the accommodation would be furnished and, moreover, you were permitted to live no more than seven miles from the centre of Oxford. As noted there were students at Leiden University that were living in completely different towns. I would argue that the lack of any kind of Hall of Residence would be likely to create a lower sense of *communitas*. Students are not placed together and effectively forced to socialise and even dine with many different people at the beginning of term, as in Aberdeen, and there is nothing comparable to the *communitas* and intensity that would be fostered by Oxford's college system. Many students – lucky enough to get accommodation immediately – live in separate flats and cater for themselves. There is no Student Union or College Exec to organise social events for them and thus far less structure. They are left to organise their lives for themselves, either living at home and eventually finding somewhere in Leiden or thereabouts or living in a Leiden flat from the beginning.

As already discussed the living arrangements would also be likely to create far less *communitas*. Almost all students were from the area in which the university was situated and, indeed, were from Protestant backgrounds so neither geographical nor religious *communitas* was likely to be created. As with Aberdeen, students lived all over the town which would be likely to lessen the degree of *communitas* and – aided by free public transport or the ease of cycling in the Netherlands – a large minority of students did not live in Leiden at all. They would live in villages or seaside towns some distance from the city or even in a completely different city such as The Hague. When I first arrived at Leiden University I found, to my surprise, that the International Department had housed me in The Hague some twenty minutes by train from Leiden though I did move to Leiden after around a week. I would suggest that these living arrangements and the lack of a Student Union are less than conducive to fostering a sense of Leiden University student *communitas.* The university is not particularly structured in relation to accommodation with no Halls of Residence, no related social organisation, no university level facility for cooked meals (other than a student refectory in the town centre) and no compulsion to live in Leiden. Indeed many cannot do so, at first at least, and are left to find somewhere else to live. The accommodation situation does not appear, therefore, to be conducive to *communitas* other than in the broader sense that many students have been through the shared trauma of not having anywhere to live.

Social Life

It should be stressed that Leiden University was liminal at least to an extent and this was reflected, I would suggest, in the development of university societies. That said, these societies – or at least most of them – were more comparable to a Student Union in Britain. Like the Student Union they offered cheap food and drink, helped students to find accommodation and arranged social events. However unlike the British Student Unions they did not appear to offer services such as free contraception or free counselling and they did not appear to be political in the same way. They were social clubs and students had to pay, often quite a lot of money, in order to join these 'Student Societies' most of which had their own building in Leiden and even employed student staff such as barmen and waiters. However, it should be stressed that there was no Rite of Passage to join these societies as there is in American Greek fraternities.

Within these mixed-gender societies were further sub-groups known as *Dispuuten* as they traditionally involved discussing various subjects. In many societies students elected to join a specific *dispuut* and each *dispuut* had its own executive committee with a chairman, treasurer and secretary. There was a general view at Leiden University amongst all students to whom I spoke that members of the Dutch aristocracy tended to join a particular student society called *Minerva.* Though anybody could join the society, you had to be invited to join the most prestigious *dispuuten* and students felt that only 'aristocrats' would be invited to join these *dispuuten.* There may be an element of exaggeration but if this is true then it would have a significant effect on *communitas* at Leiden University. Students to whom I spoke agreed that they tended to make most of their friends through their student society and in particular through their *dispuut*, though naturally through lectures and so forth as well. Students would often find people with whom to live through their student society. The societies might be seen to imply a certain degree of student structure at Leiden University though this is still evidently not as structured as at the British universities that we have discussed. This structure would, I think, foster *communitas* amongst members of individual societies though it should be stressed that this varied between societies.

With some student societies you could go and dine and drink there very cheaply every day and a few members did. With others this facility was only available once a week. As such, these class-based *dispuuten* – to the extent that they were – might be seen as a reassertion of structure to the *communitas* brought about by the student society. However, as I have already pointed out, these groups were, in some ways, more in line with British Student Unions than British student societies and, moreover, were in many ways less structured than British Student Unions. They were simply there for the purposes of socialising and so, in reality, were the *dispuuten.* They did not provide assistance or pastoral care in the same way that the Student Unions did. And though they were a matter of identity they did not provide a highly particular social identity in the manner that many British student societies – and especially the Christian Union – might be seen to. Some highly structured societies at Durham University created a very particular and strong identity such as DICCU but also Treasure Trap (the Medieval Role Playing Society). These Leiden groups reflect a certain degree of structure – and thus a certain degree of student *communitas* – but it does not appear to be high degree.

Moreover, unlike at Oxford and as with Aberdeen, students would not restrict themselves to socialising mainly in student pubs. Alcohol in the Netherlands was relatively cheap – far cheaper than in Britain – and students would make use of the local bars and participate in local events. There was no evidence of animosity between locals and students and most of the students were themselves locals to a certain extent. The only exception to this was that Leiden's annual celebration of its liberation from Spanish rule was perceived as a 'local' event. 'Drie van Oktober' (celebrated on the night of 2 October) was a public carnival in Leiden's main square which continued along its canals and lasted all night. I was told that students tended to 'keep their heads down' during this or they might get 'thrown in the canal' as it was a 'local' celebration for Leiden people. Many CSL members to whom I spoke made a point of keeping out of the city centre during this celebration which happened to be on the same night as one of their meetings, which was a half hour walk from the city centre.

Another area where *communitas* was limited at Leiden University was in relation to International Students. One way in which Oxford University, for example, may be liminal for English students is the fact that there are international students – whether as undergraduates or, more often, as exchange students – and they are housed on corridors and dine with all the other students. They are not separated, at least not by the college, because they are expected to be able to speak English like everybody else. The result may well be their developing friendships and sexual relationships with English students further exposing the identity and worldview of these students to question. I would argue that this would be considerably less likely to occur at Leiden University. There are no international undergraduates because the courses are run in Dutch. There are 'international' undergraduates as exchange students but their courses are in English and are quite separate from the courses attended by Dutch students. Some departmental lecturers were not Dutch and conducted undergraduate lectures in English but these were to Dutch students. There were also international post-graduates, again studying through English. The university separated these exchange students and post-graduates into 'international houses' where the expectation was that everybody spoke English. Naturally, this and the shared experience of amazement at Dutch culture along with various structures such as an active international society seemed to foster a strong sense of 'international student' *communitas*. However, it also meant that Dutch students were somewhat cut off from international students. For example, on my corridor in my international house in Leiden I was the only person that knew any Dutch people socially – through my fieldwork – and the only person in the building of sixty residents that spoke any Dutch despite some students having been in Leiden for over a year.

However, there was, I think, a certain degree of *communitas* amongst Leiden students and this was reflected in the development of these different student societies. Though they were little more than Gentleman's Clubs that also accepted women there was an element of identity to membership. Those especially in 'Minerva' were perceived to be of a certain social type, perhaps comparable to 'Rahs' at Oxford. A number of these student societies were traditionally based around a Protestant denomination or Protestantism more broadly and CSL was the largest example, though it was different by virtue of being 'evangelical'. It was a registered Student Society and operated like one except that it was far smaller and had relatively limited facilities. In some ways it was sub-cultural – even amongst student societies – because it was 'Christian' and, indeed, 'evangelical' Christian. But in many other respects it paralleled the student societies and one senior member commented to me, 'We want to be a proper student society'. Thus whereas some Oxford University students to whom I spoke reacted to OICCU in a very hostile manner and accused it of 'brainwashing', the main outsider reaction to CSL that I heard was summed up in the response, 'Oh! You're studying them. I hear they have some cool parties!' Equally, no member of CSL ever attempted to 'witness to me' and there was no difficulty conducting my fieldwork.

CSL Joining Ritual

We have already observed that OICCU had a kind of joining ritual for lapsed Christians in the form of testimony. CSL's Rite of Initiation was somewhat more light-hearted. It occurred at the group's AGM which was deliberately formal and mockingly ritualistic. It would start at around 7pm and go on until the early hours of the morning. One member informed me that the previous year the meeting had gone on until 6am. There was, for example, a prominent picture of Queen Beatrix on the wall behind the *Bestuur*'s table and the table was draped in a special CSL banner. Members had to wear smart clothes, the *Bestuur* wore medals to indicate their status and former *Bestuur* members had walking sticks to show they were 'old'. Much of the meeting was very light-hearted – and deliberately archaic in language – though a few took it seriously and one member was unhappy that I, as a non-member, was present at all. I had to introduce myself and justify why I should be allowed to be there and fortunately my presence was ultimately approved by those assembled.

As part of this meeting the new members had to go to the front and each of them had to justify why they should be allowed to join by giving some kind of comical reason. One female student said that she should be allowed to join because she was very good at sewing. A male member stood up and said, 'Okay, will you sew up my trousers then!' One of the new students, who perhaps had some social difficulties, gave serious religious reasons as to why he should be allowed to join and it was evident that he had completely misunderstood what was socially expected of him. The new members were allowed to join with general shouting and applause and accordingly given archaic and official-looking certificates. But this was nothing more than a deliberate comic formality. Those who had joined were members as long as they subscribed to CSL's views and paid their membership fee. There was no question of members being rejected at the meeting. It could be understood, therefore, as a kind of group bonding ritual. It was a Rite of Initiation but it was, in a way, satirising Rites of Initiation at the same time.

CSL Belief

In many ways, CSL were not particularly differentiated in terms of belief. They were a Protestant group in a country where Protestant-affiliation is almost 50 per cent and where historically people strongly identify as either Protestant or Catholic. They were differentiated, perhaps, in the sense that they brought together evangelicals from the various different Reformed (and other Protestant) denominations and we have already observed the high degree of schism apparent amongst Dutch Calvinists in particular. However, constitutionally one of their most important aims was to 'make disciples of the people especially through a relational network'. Their aim was to evangelise to Leiden students.

Following the model being presented, we would expect CSL to be somewhat less structured than AUCU and this is indeed what was observed. CSL's doctrinal basis is less specific than UCCF's and more appears to be assumed. The aims of CSL are to evangelise for Jesus in His Kingdom and to let people come to know Jesus and be His disciples. Members must assent to a number of core beliefs including the desire to be like Jesus. They must assent to the view that the Bible is true and is a guide by which to live, they must believe in the changing power of evangelism and prayer and the leading presence of the Holy Spirit, they must act according to God's will, have love for all people and make people disciples of Jesus. Their mission is summarised as: 'Witnessing, Fellowship, Prayer and the Word'. Of a sample of twenty-five, all believed fundamental Christian doctrines to be literally true. However, other results were slightly more diverse. Five believed in Evolution, five were not sure and fifteen rejected it. Twenty-four believed that non-Christians would go to Hell but many found this very difficult to express. They emphasised that it was up to God, that it was not their place to say or even that they did not like the word 'Hell' and would prefer to call it something else. Of twenty-five CSL members, three were prepared to firmly express their views and to assert as fact, that, for example, Christians should *not* engage in premarital sex, that Evolution *is* an unacceptable belief for a Christian and that non-Christians *will* go to Hell. But even so, two of this minority said that they would express such opinions very differently in front of a Dutch person for fear of causing offence. In general, the reaction to my questions was not as strong as was the case with this small minority. With regard to questions of theology, most members were firm in their answers. It was universally felt, for example, that you could not be a Christian if you did not believe in the reality of the Resurrection. There were, however, questions where this firmness was not so. As noted, members were asked if they felt that non-Christians would go to Hell. All but one member did think this but a straight answer could not be obtained. Most began by saying that this was 'up to God' and they were in no position to judge. When I asked them *their* opinion on this, members might say, 'It's only my opinion', 'Does my view matter that much for you?' and so on. When eventually they would express their view many would actually caveat it, 'I don't want to seem intolerant but ...' or 'You might not believe this but I personally ...' or 'The Bible says ... and I believe in the Bible' or 'I don't want to call it Hell but ...' They reacted similarly when expressing their view that homosexuality was unacceptable.[3] This may have been in line with the Dutch desire to appear as 'tolerant' which we have already discussed. Many others claimed they had difficulty believing the doctrine in question. Almost all eventually assented to it but only after much discussion. Most members did not believe in predestination. Those that did emphasised that what it meant was that God was ultimately sovereign and in charge and salvation was purely by His Grace rather than through human effort. In a sense, they were very unclear about whether they believed it or not, though many members would end prayers, 'By Grace alone'. However members that did believe in Hell emphasised that people would go there if they did not become Christians and there, therefore, appeared to be an implicit belief that becoming a Christian was a matter of personal choice. Like some AUCU members, they saw no contradiction between being Reformed and being an evangelical and pointed me towards Abraham Kuyper as evidence for this. Indeed, quite a few members who had been raised as Dutch Reformed attended this church with their families when they were home for weekends but upon leaving home moved over to evangelical churches if they were ever in Leiden at the weekend for example. I would therefore dispute the idea that the relative lack of evangelism that we will note in CSL is simply a reflection of a Calvinist belief in predestination.

In relation to social belief, there was also more diversity. All felt it was acceptable for Christians to drink though generally not to get drunk. In my experience, though, many CSL members who claimed it was unacceptable to get drunk did become what I would term tipsy. Twenty-three felt it was acceptable for Christians to smoke, in fact most were amazed that the question was asked at all. (This seemed to reflect a cultural difference which will be observed in Finland. In Britain smoking appears to be socially unacceptable – and especially so amongst many evangelical Christians – in a way that it is not in many other countries.) None would date a non-Christian, however. Though it should be stressed that members seemed to define the term 'Christian' far more loosely than other groups that I studied. Also, six felt that sex before marriage was acceptable, though this was expressed very diplomatically and in a very nuanced form such as, 'Maybe it's better to wait but if people really can't wait I'm not going to judge them as not being Christian because of it'. Indeed, a small minority of male members who claimed it was not acceptable admitted to having had premarital sex which was never admitted to in OICCU or AUCU.

3 For further discussion of this specific area see Dutton (2004).

Interestingly, amongst a small minority of female CSL members there seemed to be an attitude, at least at first, that this question was rather impertinent and really was none of my business although everybody eventually answered. By contrast, some members of AUCU (both male and female) were perfectly happy to discuss Christian attitudes to masturbation with me and inform me that, aged twenty, they had never masturbated and that they regarded it as 'un-Biblical' to do so. It seemed that talking about sex was less acceptable in Holland than it was in Britain and since my research in Holland a number of Finns – and Americans – have commented to me that the English are somehow 'obsessed with sex'.[4] CSL would appear to be generally more liberal except with regard to dating non-Christians which all felt was unacceptable and unwise. (However, the term was defined less exclusively.) Thus, CSL would appear to evidence an even lower degree of differentiation and control than AUCU. Certainly, in terms of social belief we can see that CSL's views are slightly more in line with most students or at least a larger minority were.

Conversion

None of my sample from CSL had become Christians while at Leiden University in a context where only one person in my sample had taken a Gap Year (in America) where, interestingly, he had had a conversion experience. It would be more accurate, however, to state that none of the members had undergone conversion experiences as the term 'Christian' was not defined exclusively which would in itself imply a low level of differentiation. The minority that had had conversion experiences had usually had them while they were teenagers on some kind of Bible camp. I only found one person – a female student – in CSL who had had a conversion experience and become a 'saved' Christian while at Leiden University. She did not frequently attend meetings. She was not herself from a family affiliated with any church which makes her circumstances all the more unique as almost all the members had been to Protestant schools. This would imply a relatively low level of liminality and identity change at Leiden University and CSL's levels of conversion appear to reflect this. Following on from this, there were never any testimonies at CSL meetings and, as we will discuss below, in comparison to some other groups that I studied there were not a large number of meetings anyway.

CSL Involvement

With regard to commitment, CSL were in some respects as structured as AUCU. At CSL's main meeting there might be around seventy present and I would always observe the same people week after week. However, the group did not meet as frequently as AUCU and this might be seen to imply that it is less significant to identity and that the circumstances mean that a stronger degree of structure is not required. CSL members would meet once a week in alternate forms of meeting.

[4] This may be as a reaction to the traditional stereotype of 'No sex please, we're British'. Further research in this regard would be very interesting.

One week the entire group would meet in a particular church hall which they had to rent for the occasion. This meeting was known as '*Lezing*' ('Reading'). Members would arrive on their bicycles, socialise and purchase coffee from a kind of bar. They would then sit at long tables while there would be announcements from *Bestuur* members and prayers led by them. There would also be silent prayer. When this was finished members would queue to get their dinner and sometimes a bottle of beer to go with it. When they had finished eating, the tables would be put away and the chairs would be turned to face a projection of a hymn. They would sing a few hymns and after this they would continue socialising and the men, more than the women, would be observed to drink beer.

The alternate meeting was the *Dispuut* meeting. There were four *disputen*. The one that I attended occurred in a particular student flat a twenty minute walk from central Leiden where there were many blocks of flats in which students lived. Members would arrive and chat and eventually there would be prayer and then a meal which was normally pasta based. Afterwards there was always a dessert. After this, there would be a group discussion over some issue related to Christianity and usually to the issue around which the *dispuut* was based. The *dispuut* that I attended was interested in music – there were three other *disputen* – and on one occasion members discussed whether or not it was appropriate for Christians to listen to heavy metal music. This would be followed by some hymn singing and a final prayer. At this meeting, again, I would always observe the same people each fortnight. Though it may not have been strictly enforced these meetings, unlike OICCU's meetings for example, were closed. They were for members only though I was informed that there would not be a problem bringing along a friend if you wished. What perhaps might be more of a problem would be a student who was not in CSL simply turning up at a *Dispuut* meeting. But in general it can be clearly argued that CSL were relatively low in terms of ritual.

Whereas AUCU had meetings for non-members to attend twice a week, CSL had such meetings around twice a term and their terms ('semesters') were considerably longer than terms at Aberdeen. The first such meeting was simply a pub night after a particular *dispuut* meeting. This had been advertised and the idea was the CSL members invited their non-member friends along. The second occasion during my fieldwork was 'Mr. and Miss Leiden'. As discussed, each year Leiden celebrates its liberation from the Spanish in 1575 with a large street party. In order to lampoon this, CSL held an event in a Leiden bar a few days before called 'Mr and Miss Leiden' (it was named in the English) in which members were invited to come dressed as *pauperen* – working-class, Leiden local people. Almost all of those who attended obliged with the female members, particularly, adopting the fashions that they perceived to denote *pauper vrouwen.* I even noted women who generally wore relatively conservative clothing take part in this contest – for a man and a woman would be crowned 'Mr and Miss Leiden'. As such, most of the women wore ostentatiously revealing clothing: hipsters, crop tops, trousers deliberately worn low, low cut tops, mini-skirts, fish-net stockings and huge amounts of make-up. Of course, by adopting such styles the members were making a satirical point and were doing so on a particular occasion.[5] At the end of the evening a senior CSL member in a shell suit and a suitably attired female member were crowned 'Mr and Miss Leiden' and they danced on a table, swigging from beer bottles and pretending to be very drunk.

A handful of CSL members were also involved in a group called 'Contrast' which was aimed at international students. The group met once a month for 'Cultural Evenings' and a meal and they also offered – once a fortnight – free Dutch conversation classes. Contrast was co-run by a particular CSL member and members of other non-evangelical Reformed student groups relating to specific churches. The first event, in September 2003, was a Dutch evening in which there was typical Dutch food, the Contrast members dressed in Dutch national costume and there was a quiz about Holland. They had advertised this, in our building at least, by sending everybody a flyer and a daffodil – giving flowers was very common in Holland – to welcome them to the Netherlands and invite them to the party. The following month's evening was an 'Arty Party' in which one of the many artists working in Leiden showed us how to paint and we were then asked to paint our feelings about Leiden or Holland. Many of the pictures produced involved bicycles. The evening the following month was a 'British Evening' which I was asked to organise along with a Northern Irish member of OICCU who was at Leiden as an exchange student such that he could add 'European Studies' to his Law degree. We taught them some Ulster Scots and some Scots Gaelic and also Ceilidh dancing. For the meal we had Shepherd's Pie with tea. The tea had milk in it which was something that the Contrast members were totally unaware that anybody did. In a sense, Contrast was an example of CSL evangelism inasmuch as it was co-run by CSL members.

CSL Clothes and Gender

Apart from a very small minority of female members who had rather old fashioned hair-cuts and literally one or two CSL members who might wear 'WWJD' bracelets, there was no observable difference in the kind of dress or style adopted by CSL members when compared to the kind of clothes worn by people who were not members. I did ask some male members about what they thought about the then fashion of wearing crop-tops with hipsters as a small number of female members did. Nobody I spoke to had any problem with this at all. One point that I did notice was that one member dressed in Goth type clothing, thus expressing a certain degree of individualism certainly within Christian circles. Again none of the CSL members had any problem with this at all and subsequent to my research this female student went on to be a very senior member of the organisation.

There was also no issue with regard to the position of women. During my research the President was a man but the previous year it had been a woman and after I left it was also a woman. A few members to whom I spoke about premarital sex told me that they did not like the idea of having sex with a woman who had had

[5] This is interesting in terms of structure because I doubt that many female OICCU members would dress in such a manner even to make a satirical point.

sex with another man. One actually said to me, 'Don't you find the idea disgusting?' This might be seen, on the part of some male members at least, to betoken a slightly differentiated attitude towards female purity. Certainly, as discussed, most members did not approve of pre-marital sex.

The CSL *Bestuur* and General Structure

This aspect of CSL, according to one senior member, was deliberately undifferentiated. 'We want to be like a proper student society', he emphasised to me. Indeed, when I asked members why they did not openly evangelise at their outreach events one member commented, 'We don't want people to think we're weird. We're ordinary students who are also Christians'. This was in very stark contrast even to what certain senior AUCU members said about how, for example, 'God is King so this makes us all Princes and Princesses which is great!' or about being, with regard to the university, 'in the world but not of the world' evidenced, for example, in refusing to do essays on a Sunday in the case of various AUCU students. CSL's *Bestuur* paralleled exactly the situation with student societies such as *Minerva*. Indeed the rest of CSL was also run in the same manner with a series of *Dispuuten* each with three officers. In all cases these officers had archaic Latin titles as was the case in groups such as *Minerva*. Thus, in structural terms CSL was not differentiated and it was only as structured as other secular student societies. Indeed, it had a lengthy annual meeting much of which was dedicated to lampooning this very structure.

Christian Language

The language employed by CSL members was also somewhat less differentiated than in some of the other groups we have discussed. CSL did not use terms such as 'non-Christian' in their prayers which would imply strong boundaries. Members ended their prayers with the phrase 'Thank you very much therefore' and 'By your grace alone' but there was, according to other Dutch people to whom I spoke, nothing particularly odd about this. It was simply the language of the Dutch churches. Members would also use phrases when praying such as – addressed to God – 'Thank you for being here tonight with us' which some Dutch students I spoke to claimed was not the kind of phrase they had ever heard in their experience of attending Dutch Reformed Churches. As such, this kind of language in prayer might be regarded as slightly differentiated.

Swearing, perhaps unsurprisingly, was an area in which CSL members tended to be slightly differentiated though not to the same extent as OICCU and AUCU members. Differentiation was clear but it was complicated by the fact that the orientation of Dutch swearing is very different from that of English. Male members did not have any difficulty using swearwords that they knew to be sexual and even the female members had no problem using English swearwords (which was common in Holland) which they knew to be sexual.[6] One female member was amazed when I informed her of just how rude some English people thought that the word 'fuck' was. Members commented that they would use these various sexual and bodily Dutch swearwords if they were angry but tried not to. This included terms such as 'shit' and '*klootzak*' (scrotum) and I would suggest that OICCU members in particular tended to reject equivalent English swearwords which were middle-ranking in terms of their perceived offensiveness such as 'shit'. However, all CSL members did reject the strongest Dutch swearword – *Godverdomme* (Old Dutch for 'God damn it'). They argued that this word was 'insulting', 'disrespectful' and even 'forbidden by the Bible'. All but two were not even prepared to use its disguised version '*Godverdikemme*'. A non-religious Dutch student – who tried to explain Dutch swearing to me in a bar – found *Godverdomme* so offensive that he was not prepared to say it and, to the mirth of his friends, insisted on writing it down on a beer mat for me. However, in a sense it is difficult to compare the issue of swearing. As discussed, both OICCU and AUCU members mainly rejected profanity which is generally perceived as mild swearing in England and Scotland. However CSL members were rejecting only the strongest forms of swearing. This could reflect a low level of differentiation but it is made more complex because the reasons for the rejection may be different. On the surface, at least, the level of differentiation with regard to swearing appears to be low. Certainly religious Netherlanders found 'God damn it' very offensive. On one occasion I recall saying 'damn' in front of two Dutch evangelical Christians because they had neglected to buy any milk to go with the tea for the British evening, not knowing that the British had milk in tea. For comic effect I said, 'damn' – the mildest swear-word I could think of in the context of an English-language conversation, in British English at least. They evidently could not believe what they were hearing and one of them just gasped, 'Excuse me? Can you not say that?!'

Communitas and Structural Reassertion: The *Bestuur*

As we have observed there were some social differences within CSL but there was no clear evidence of structural reassertion which is what we would expect if the level of *communitas* is low. I would argue that precisely because CSL is not especially highly structured the level of *communitas* is not especially high making such a structural reassertion somewhat less necessary.

The only point that I observed in this regard, and I have noted the same phenomenon in AUCU, was the prominence of people who were training to be doctors. The President during my research was training to be doctor as were many other people in senior positions in CSL. Sociologically this may possibly have the same kinds of explanations as those suggested with regard to AUCU. Equally there was no evidence of a pattern with regard to the kind of church that *Bestuur* members were from. They were representative of the broader CSL membership. As discussed, in a relatively loosely structured group we would expect a relatively low level of

6 Stapleton (2004) argues that women swear just as much as men but they use different swearwords and find different words offensive.

communitas and a relatively low level of structural reassertion and, in general, this is what we appear to find.

The only difference that was observed was that a small minority of members were more enthusiastic about outreach activity than other members. They would, therefore, come to the outreach pub night and a small handful of female members – literally three – involved themselves in the international group 'Contrast' which was in some ways more evangelical than CSL itself. For example, I once went on a Contrast trip, one Sunday, to a nearby seaside town. Present were three Contrast members, a male French student who spoke no Dutch, was doing a work placement in Leiden and lived on my corridor and then myself. When we got back to Leiden it was strongly implied that we might consider accompanying the Contrast members to an English language, independent evangelical church that was meeting in about half an hour. I went with them and the French student went home. Indeed, it was members of this 'English church' that cooked the Shepherd's Pie for Contrast. (There was a noticeable British minority in Leiden which congregated around an Irish theme pub and a shop which sold imported British food that it was otherwise impossible to buy in Leiden.) That aside though, the trip might be seen as following a very basic proselytising method of providing an enjoyable experience and then presenting the possibility of further group involvement.

Ritual and *Communitas:* '*Lezing*'

The *Lezing* meeting, which involved the entire group and occurred fortnightly, was structured on a certain level but did not appear to be as structured as a meeting such as 'Prayer and Praise' which, as we have discussed, might be seen as more deliberately designed to create *communitas*.

The meeting began with prayers and I would suggest that the silent praying in particular would have assisted in fostering *communitas*. Obviously eating and drinking together would, likewise, have helped to foster *communitas* and, in fact, this was something that neither OICCU nor AUCU did as a group. After the meal there was hymn-singing and to a certain degree, as with hymn-singing in any church, this shared experience is likely to create a certain degree of *communitas*. However, the facilities were in existence to create far more *communitas* through the use of a band, creating a climax and so forth. This did not occur and, instead, a particular female student simply played the piano while members stood and sang worship songs, in general, translated into Dutch such as 'Shine Jesus, Shine!' Sometimes members sang in the original English. While this was happening some members could be observed to hang around at the back drinking coffee or sometimes beer and these were, it should be said, sometimes quite senior members. There was a piano at this meeting but during singing at the *Dispuut* a guitar and drums were used.

It might be argued that this lack of *communitas* simply reflects something in Dutch Reformed culture. Members are imitating the churches that they have been raised in, it might be argued, and the Charismatic Movement – or comparable activity such as dancing in church and the use of music that provokes this – is not particularly popular amongst Dutch Reformed Churches. I would counter that CSL are using exactly the kind of songs that are popular in evangelical and Charismatic churches. The meeting cannot be seen to be imitating some kind of traditional, Dutch Reformed meeting. Indeed, some of the songs used were deliberate jokey songs such as 'We Thank you CSL' to the tune of a '*Sinterklaasje*' song. It should be pointed out that there is a Dutch celebration on 5 December called *Sinterklaas* where the said character, who is a kind of cross between Father Christmas and a Bishop, travels round Holland giving sweets to children along with his black slave *Zwarte Piet.* There are many children's songs relating to this event and in a particular Reformed student group a whole evening was dedicated to this with female students dressed as *Zwarte Piet* throwing biscuits at people and *Sinterklaasje* having a female student on his knee and asking her innuendo-based questions about whether or not she had been a 'good girl' before having a pretend fight with somebody dressed as Father Christmas. This kind of comic song would likewise not reflect imitation of the church. Moreover, it is not imitating the kinds of churches that CSL students attended at weekends and members informed me of this.

I accept, though, that it may be the case that members are reflecting a culture in which lively worship is rare. However it, again, raises the question of why a person would wish to engage in lively worship including charismata. We have noted that there is a case for arguing that this reflects a highly structured religious group which itself reflects identity challenge. It would therefore follow that a group in an environment that was not liminal would not reflect this and we have noted that Leiden is not especially liminal and CSL is not especially structured. Of course it would not necessarily follow that people in a highly structured group would necessarily be 'charismatic'. Obviously, *communitas* can be expressed and created in other ways. But this does not undermine the point that the meeting is not especially highly structured and does not create a high level of *communitas.* I would suggest that one further piece of evidence for that is that some people were singing while others were drinking beer. In this sense CSL were not even engaging in a shared activity as a group – a structure which might foster *communitas.* So we can see here a lack of structure resulting in a relative lack of *communitas.* I would argue that this lack of structure in meetings – at least on a certain level – is congruous with the broader lack of structure that we observed in CSL as a group.

Ichthus

Even before I began my fieldwork in Leiden I came across another evangelical group at the university called Ichthus. This was a 'group' as opposed to a registered 'Student Society' and it had around thirty members at the time. I travelled to Holland to talk to the leaders about the possibility of doing fieldwork with the group. They put the idea to the group and it was decided that they did not want me to. They felt that my presence in such a small group would interfere in their ability to carry on as they normally did.

I was unable to conduct fieldwork with this group and was only permitted to attend a joint meeting between them and CSL if I promised not to make any fieldwork notes or use any of the activities that I observed their members engage in as part of my doctoral thesis. As such, any information I could garner about the group was either second-hand or anecdotal. But that said, the group did seem – anecdotally – to be considerably stricter in terms of belief and lifestyle than CSL and indeed some CSL members specifically told me that they had not joined Ichthus for this very reason. Following the theory under discussion, the Dutch evangelical students would be attracted to the more loosely structured CSL than the highly structured Ichthus and this is precisely what was observed. Indeed we would expect people whose identity was under threat – for whatever reason – to be attracted to a group of this kind. This is anecdote but it may well be noteworthy that the OICCU student who I met through Contrast regularly attended Ichthus meetings as he could speak very good Dutch. He personally told me that he found out about Ichthus because they, like OICCU, were in IFES (the International Federation of Evangelical Students). Moreover, he found that they were the most similar to OICCU of the Christian groups at Leiden. And we have noted that the liminal circumstances in Oxford are very different from Leiden's at least for many Dutch students.

Conclusion

Leiden University is less liminal for Dutch students than is Aberdeen University. There is no ritual in order to get into the university and no Rite of Separation. Students are mainly from the area around Leiden and are thus mainly Protestant and relatively local, many live at home for at least part of their studies or live outside of Leiden and there are no Halls of Residence for first years and nothing organised for them to create *communitas* at a university level other than lectures. Even the way that international students are housed can be seen to lessen the degree to which Leiden University is liminal for its Dutch students. However there is some liminality and this is reflected in the creation of student structures known as Student Societies. These, however, are relatively weakly structured and simply add a slightly greater degree of structure to student socialising, a little bit like the Student Union at British Universities. It is noteworthy, as well, that there were very few clubs at Leiden University offering a strong identity whereas these were ubiquitous at Aberdeen University and even more so at Oxford. CSL is offering an identity both to Evangelical Christian students and, to some extent, non-Christians to whom it evangelises occasionally. The group is differentiated in terms of religious belief and ethics but much less so than AUCU and its structure – other than the need to assent to its principles – is hardly differentiated at all. Indeed, membership of all Leiden University societies involved assenting to certain principles. Clothing is also hardly differentiated and CSL meets far less frequently than other groups implying a lower level of structure and a lower level of importance to identity but CSL is structured to the extent that the same people are frequently noted to attend meetings. Even its outreach meetings are not especially differentiated from those of other student societies where non-members are encouraged to join.

In consequence it has been demonstrated that the level of *communitas* and thus the level of structural reassertion is lower in CSL than in other groups. We have looked at, and refuted, the potential criticisms in relation to Calvinism and Church culture and we have observed that a group more comparable to OICCU in terms of structure and belief has not managed to become a significant force at Leiden University which would imply that it is not offering what is needed structurally in such circumstances.

Chapter 7

Trying to Find the Core

OKO at Oulu University in Finland

Oulu University was established in 1958 and currently has around 17,000 students. It is located a few miles from Oulu city centre. Oulu is the largest settlement in northern Finland with a population of around 120,000. The city has a growing technology industry and the largest employers are the mobile phone company Nokia and also the city's paper-making factory. For all of the students to whom I spoke, Oulu was their first choice of university. There are a relatively small number of universities in Finland – which is larger than Britain but has a population of around five million – and as such many students are limited as to where they can study. For example, there are only three universities in Finland where students can study Law: Helsinki University, Turku University and Lapland University, based in Rovaniemi which is some distance north of Oulu and positioned on the Arctic Circle.

I spent a term studying OKO and also a number of other Christian student groups operating at Oulu University between September and December 2007. More broadly I was able to speak to many different students during this period and found that a large minority were originally from relatively close to Oulu. In the case of OKO, however, it was very difficult, for reasons that I will discuss in more detail below, to produce any kind of meaningful sample of group opinion. As such, this method had to be abandoned and, as I will argue below, the very fact that this was so difficult allowed me to understand a great deal about the nature of the organisation. During my time with OKO there appeared to be around three or four regulars who attended all of the meetings. I was not made an honorary member or anything of the kind. Indeed, most of the students to whom I spoke at the meetings were often not actually paid up members of the group themselves. All that the group asked of those present was that they wrote down their name in the group's book. They could also be placed on the group's email list if they so desired.

In many ways, Oulu University appeared to be the least liminal experience for most of its students. Indeed, I would go so far as to question whether university in Finland can be understood as a Rite of Passage at all. If it can, there is certainly considerable evidence that it is a very loosely organised Rite of Passage and it appears to be even less liminal than the situation at Leiden University. However before further examining this liminality – or relative lack of it – I would like to examine the religious background in Finland.

Finland's Religious Background

Over 80 per cent of Finns are paid-up members of the Evangelical Lutheran Church of Finland and even higher numbers have been through its rituals and have subsequently elected to leave (ELF Statistics 2007). The church is highly influential and its rituals remain significant to the lives of many Finns – even if only for reasons of culture and tradition – in a way that is not the case at all in countries such as England or the Netherlands. In order to be classified as Lutheran, Finns must elect to be members of the church. In order to do this they must be baptised and they must pay a modest 'church tax' as a percentage of their income. If they wish to stop being members of the church then they can 'divorce the church'.

The overwhelming majority of Finns – over 80 per cent – are baptised, confirmed and married within the Lutheran Church. Indeed, they must be confirmed – and paid up members of the church – in order to be married in the church. Strictly speaking they must be church members in order to be buried by a Lutheran priest though many priests waive this obligation. So significant is baptism as a tradition in Finland that I have come across a number of cases in my own research into Finnish religiosity whereby a couple living abroad where one of the partners is a Finn return to Finland to have their child baptised by a Finnish Lutheran priest even though it could just as easily have been baptised a Lutheran in Denmark or Germany, to give just two examples of the country of the non-Finnish parent where the couple were living and intended to continue living (Dutton 2007a). Confirmation is also an important Rite of Passage and 90 per cent of teenagers – aged around fifteen – are confirmed after which there is usually a family party at which they receive presents. Normally, the process of confirmation involves going away into the countryside on a week-long retreat camp at a special retreat centre, which is perceived to be very popular amongst Finnish teenagers. They are officially confirmed in a church ceremony attended by their parents when they return from this camp (Nimelä 2006).

Regular church attendance in Finland is very low with only around 4 per cent of Finns going to church at least once a fortnight (Davie 2000, 9). However, on special occasions church attendance – and other religious rituals – remain relatively popular with churches being very full at Christmas and Easter but also at various other occasions such as All Saints Day and Finnish Independence Day. On All Saints Day, many Finns still go to their local graveyard and lay down candles in memory of the dead. As such, in terms of church involvement in life, Finland might be understood as a somewhat more religious culture than some even if the involvement is only for reasons of tradition such that life changes can be mediated through ritual. This is reflected in the way that the overwhelming majority of Finnish people – 90 per cent – have been confirmed into the Lutheran church and have, as a consequence, been educated about its beliefs and practices and taken at least one communion in order to be confirmed (Winter *et al* 2002).

In terms of theology and organisation, the church is obviously Lutheran. It retains, therefore, bishops, apostolic succession and various rituals that can be related to its original Catholic heritage. In terms of theology – and this may be simplifying the issue – there appears a strong emphasis on God's Grace and the idea that people are in no position to judge issues of faith as only God can do that and this idea has been widely discussed (e.g. Gregersen 2004). However there is a strong evangelical movement within the Finnish Lutheran Church as we will discuss. Unlike the parish system in the Church of England, a diocese is divided into a number of congregations. Normally a distinct town is one 'congregation' and it will have, depending on its size, possibly ten priests and then one head-priest (*Kirkkoherra* – '*Church Lord*') who is elected by the members of the congregation. Indeed, Bishops are also elected. Whereas the Church of England has numerous small parishes each with one or maybe two priests, some of which are strongly evangelical, some of which are strongly Anglo-Catholic, some of which are liberal and so forth; in Finland priests from various opposing traditions must work together and, indeed, conduct masses together. Since the ordination of women priests in Finland in 1986, this has led to a number of priests refusing to work with their female colleagues because they are opposed to their ordination. It has also led to some new priests refusing to be ordained alongside women. This issue is particularly controversial in Oulu and in the broader Oulu Diocese. Until the year 2000, the Bishop of Oulu was Rt Rev'd Olavi Rimpeläinen. He refused to ordain women who obtained jobs as priests in the Oulu Diocese meaning that they had to be ordained elsewhere. A female priest in the diocese (working in Oulu itself) produced a widely disseminated doctoral thesis at Lapland University purporting to prove that female priests in the diocese had been discriminated against and generally ill treated under his leadership (Saarinen 2005). In 2007, the Archbishop of Finland instructed that male priests had to work with their female colleagues. One priest in the Oulu congregation of Karjasilta – Rev'd Vesa Pöyhtäri – brought this to a climax in April 2007 by failing to turn up at a mass with his colleague Rev'd Satu Saarinen, the writer of the doctoral thesis about discrimination against female priests. The press were present at the mass and it was reported in the national newspapers (*Kaleva* 30 April 2007). He then refused to confirm teenagers alongside her and refused to conduct a mass with another female priest. A church court sentenced him to two months' suspension and he is appealing at the time of writing (*Keskisuomalainen* 3 October 2007). Elsewhere in Finland, a male priest has a criminal record as he was fined after having been successfully prosecuted in the criminal courts for breaking Finland's anti-discrimination laws by refusing to work with a female priest (*One News* 11 December 2007).

Awakening Movements

Though Finnish church services do not express theological and worship style differences these are found in the church's various 'Awakening Movements' – some of which are highly conservative and evangelical. It would useful, before moving on, to examine some of these awakening movements.

There are four main revival movements in Finland, some with various sub-groups or schisms but all are within the Lutheran Church. Each movement has its own central organisation, a newspaper or magazine and even a summer convention which can attract thousands of attendees. Active members also attend weekly group meetings in addition, perhaps, to attendance at a Lutheran service. The original 'Pietist Movement' was founded by a 'peasant' called Paavo Ruotsalainen (1777–1852). The core emphasis of this group was on humanity's insignificance compared to God and the group also emphasises human sinfulness. The Evangelical Movement was founded by Frederik Hedberg (1811–1893). It split from the Pietists and tends to stress the importance of gaining salvation, most crucially through baptism. Henrik Renqvist (1789–1866) was a leading figure in the 'Praying Movement'. Members of this small group, mainly found in the south west, may pray up to twenty times a day and some prayers may last for hours. They also emphasise private confession (Stoddard 1973: 77–8). The largest revival movement in Finland is the Laestadians which was founded in Lapland by Swedish priest Rev'd Lars Laestadius (1800–1861). His was a highly conservative interpretation of Lutheranism, returning to traditional belief and rejecting liberal strains of thought. Many of these movements – and most notably the Laestadians – tend towards teetotalism. In general, Laestadians do not drink, women do not wear make-up or ear-rings and they shun contraception leading to very large families. It has been estimated that up to a quarter of the population of Oulu are from Laestadian backgrounds and the diocese is generally understood to be Oulu's most religiously conservative. Laestadians are not particularly evangelical. However the Laestadian break away *Rauhan Sana*, which is slightly less conservative, is more evangelical. In addition, National Mission – which is evangelical and, to some extent, Charismatic – was founded in the 1960s. It should be emphasised that all of these groups are part of the Finnish Lutheran Church. In the case of Laestadians, members would be likely to attend weekly Laestadian meetings as well as a broader Lutheran service, though usually conducted by a Laestadian priest.

Finnish Culture and Social Stratification

Obviously it is difficult to summarise some of the most relevant and distinctive dimensions to Finnish culture with brevity. However, Finland, I think it can be argued, has in common with many nations that have been colonies a kind of self-perception of national equality, even if this may actually be a national myth. For example, Finnish folklorist Pertti Anttonen (2005, 150) points out that Finland is a strongly ethno-nationalist culture whereby to be Finnish involves the racial idea of being an 'ethnic Finn' and, to a great extent, the necessity of speaking Finnish as a native language. Thus, he argues, Finns tend to have a relatively nationalistic or patriotic culture.

Equally significant, he suggests, is the 'national myth' in Finland that all Finns are essentially equal. Until 1809, Finland was ruled by Sweden. This meant that by the nineteenth century – when it fell under Russian rule until independence in 1917 – the middle and certainly the upper class were Swedish-speaking Finns and at the time of writing Swedish-speaking Finns make-up around 5 per cent of the population. Anttonen observes that Swedish speakers have an ambiguous position within the Finnish nation. On the one hand they are accepted as Finnish citizens. However many Finnish-speakers will refer to themselves as 'Finns' in contrast to those who speak Swedish who are termed 'Swedes' and therefore are implicitly not 'ordinary Finns' who by definition must speak Finnish as a native language. Anttonen further notes that social differences are played up between the language groups but played down within them. Thus, there is a common perception amongst Finns that Finns are equal and that there is, or was until recently, little social distinction between them. Thus, 'Swedes' (and not 'Finns') constitute the upper-middle and indeed 'upper class'. As such, the language that a person speaks in Finland is symbolically important to social stratification. Swedish is Finland's second official language and if a town has a Swedish-speaking population of over 6 per cent it is officially bilingual and Swedish-speakers have the legal right to all public services – including schooling – in Swedish.

Otherwise, I would submit that education appears to be a particularly important means of social stratification amongst Finnish-speaking Finns and the perceived importance of education in Finland has been widely discussed (e.g. Lander 1976, 97, Järvinen and Vanttaja 2001). Indeed, in place of titles Finns will tend to write their academic qualifications before their names in equally formal circumstances. There are many ways in which the significance of education can be noted. For example, there is a public holiday to mark 1 May known as 'Vappu'. During this festival, many Finns traditionally eat and drink in the open air and thus Finns come together as part of national event. Finns who have attended 'Academic School' emphasise this by wearing the sailors' caps that they receive on graduation while students who graduate from these schools have a special photo taken which is sent to family and friends and a party in the local town wearing their new caps. This would imply that it is, to some extent at least, status raising and the use of the caps at Vappu might be understood as a kind of reassertion of structure (Dutton 2006b).

General attitudes to alcohol in Finland also appear to be quite different from some of the other cultures that we have examined, especially amongst those who would call themselves 'religious' or 'believers'. Traditionally at least members of certain awakening groups would be teetotal and would not enter bars or even restaurants in some cases. This remains the case in relation to bars with groups such as the Laestadians. According to many Finns to whom I spoke over the course of my research, the attitude was that you either drink in order to become drunk or you do not drink at all. It has been argued that part of the reason for the historical popularity of the Laestadians is that the group effectively stops Finnish members from drinking, at least openly and there is seemingly evidence that it does this (e.g. Winter *et al* 2002). There is a general perception amongst Finns that they have a profound problem with alcohol which their neighbours do not (see Dutton 2008a). At the time of writing, Finland has the highest level of binge-drinking in Europe and is the only country in Europe where the leading cause of death is alcoholism (BBC 1 June 2006, BBC 1 November 2006). This difference must be taken into account in looking at the attitudes to alcohol amongst evangelical students though it should be said that none of those I spoke to were against all alcohol use. Finland, like England and the USA, has been classified as a 'Temperance Culture' whereby alcohol is seen somehow as special and as a kind of temporal marker rather than something quotidian. However, it has been suggested that Finland is a very extreme example of a Temperance Culture compared to other such cultures (Levine 1993).

We must also take into account the idea that Finland is not a 'speaking culture' and that sitting in silence is relatively acceptable socially (e.g. Tulviste *et al* 2003, Torkki 2006). Being loud and excitable in a public place does appear, according to various researchers in this area, to very much go against Finnish cultural tradition and these factors must also be taken into account when examining the behaviour of evangelical students and their invited speakers. Indeed, in this regard and in other areas Finnish culture has been compared to that of Japan due its speaking patterns and language structure (e.g. Lewis 2005) or its 'Shame Culture' (Laine 2006) whereby people and the culture more broadly is particularly concerned about how it is perceived by others. Finland's culture has also been compared to that of the Greenlandic Inuit in relation to its pre-Christian religion and the contemporary influence of this (Dutton 2007a) as well as with regard to the general structure of social phenomena such as alcoholism, suicide, revivalism and an apparent nostalgia for a past way of life (Dutton 2008a). Indeed, until around the 1940s, Finns were commonly understood to be a racially 'mongoloid' people – partly because their non-Indo-European language was assumed to be related to Mongolian – and this self-perception of being at least partly 'eastern' still holds even amongst various geneticists and certainly amongst many ordinary Finns even if the idea that Finns are 'European' is currently being promoted (Anttonen 2005, 132).

This is of course a very brief analysis of Finnish culture – a culture which is commonly termed as 'unique' or uniquely 'between east and west' (e.g. *Visit Finland* 2007) – and I appreciate that. However, for the purposes of this broader discussion I think that we need to be equipped with, perhaps, the most salient points in relation to Finnish cultural distinctiveness.

Finnish Education and Liminality

There are almost no private schools in Finland. A very small minority of Finnish parents might send their children to an English language 'International School' or even a private Swedish language school, which would be private in an area where there are very few Swedish-speakers such as Oulu. However, the overwhelming majority of Finnish students of all social backgrounds attend state-funded, co-educational day schools. Though there may be differences in standard, Finns generally perceive their schools to be of a relatively high standard and well funded. Compulsory education begins at seven prior to which there are publicly funded 'Day Care' centres. Finnish secondary school, however, is divided on a number of levels. Most obviously, it is divided by language. In general, Finnish-speakers will attend Finnish language schools – though, since around 1970, they must learn Swedish throughout secondary school and pass it in order to graduate from upper secondary school. The Swedish-speaking minority attends schools where instruction is in Swedish and Finnish is learned as a second language. This language division continues throughout the education system as there is an exclusively Swedish-speaking university in Turku (which was Finland's capital under Swedish rule) known as 'Åbo Academy'.

However, we will concentrate here on the Finnish language schools as Oulu University is a Finnish-language university and all of the students I have met during my research have been Finnish-speakers. At aged fifteen, Finnish secondary education divides into two tiers. According to students' examination results, they can either attend *Lukio* (Academic School) or what can be roughly translated as Trade School, which might train a student to be a chef or a car mechanic. The former kind of school, by contrast, directs students towards polytechnic or university and they must pass an examination in order to enter. This phase generally lasts around three years so students leave school aged around nineteen though some are older than that. As already noted, the overwhelming majority of teenage Finns – though a decreasing number – are confirmed when they are roughly fifteen. This involves going away on a 'Confirmation Camp' for a week, which would, I submit, be likely to have a strongly liminal dimension. Indeed, the few members of OKO who claimed to have had conversion experiences had generally undergone them while on Confirmation Camp which would, to some extent at least, be a testimony to the ritual's liminality. Leaving what we might call 'lower secondary school' is also marked with a ritual whereby students dress in comical costumes and are driven on special decorated floats through the centre of their town. Graduating from Academic school – which is attended by the majority of the population – also remains a noticeable cultural ritual. School graduates receive a special 'sailors' cap' and, in the case of females, a rose in addition. On the day of graduation, the tradition is to go to bars and so forth wearing this cap. Entering university was perceived by the many Finns – though not a large number of students – to whom I spoke to be an arduous and even traumatic task. It involved taking highly competitive exams – set by the university department to which they were applying – for very limited places in certain subjects. A small number of Finnish students to whom I spoke had failed to 'get in' the first time and therefore took a year out and worked before trying to pass the exam again. They tended, unsurprisingly, to emphasise its difficulty. Though this research was not structured I did meet, during my time at Aberdeen University, a number of Finnish students studying there because they had been unable to get on to their desired course at any Finnish university offering it.

In a sense, we might suggest that this difficult entrance ritual might imply that the Finnish university system was highly liminal but in many other respects it is not so and it might even be argued that the Finnish university entrance exam is perhaps comparable to leaving exams at a university such as Oxford, though, of course, the Finnish university entrance exams can be infinitely re-taken if so desired. Most strikingly, I would suggest that one factor that would make university somewhat less liminal – at least for male students – is National Military Service. Some kind of 'national service' is compulsory amongst young Finnish men and, though they can opt for 'Civil Service', the overwhelming majority still opt for the tradition of military service. It lasts a year and is clearly a highly liminal phase which brings together young Finns from different backgrounds and areas, involves inculcation with an ideology, induced trauma in the form of arduous military conditions, submission to authority and so forth. Indeed, there has been detailed research arguing that maintaining injury remains a significant problem amongst Finnish conscripts (Mattila *et al* 2006). Though the conscripts can sometimes go home at weekends, unless they are in the Navy, they must still wear their military uniform while travelling.[1] I would therefore submit that this would likely be a highly transformative phase which would

1 Some students (and former conscripts) also stressed that military service varied according to where it took place and that doing it in Lapland – where it usually becomes very cold in winter – was far more arduous than other postings.

render university considerably less so for the majority of male students who would already have undertaken national service before they began. In addition, it would render them somewhat older than in England and it is very rare to find a male, Finnish student who is under twenty-one.

This issue of age is also significant. Finnish students are, in general, older when they begin university than British students by at least a year and usually more. Whereas Oxford students might be perceived to be liminal between childhood and adulthood – and often financially reliant on their parents – Finnish students appeared to be regarded as adults and, indeed, it is not uncommon to find undergraduates who have taken eight years or more to do their degrees and work part time while doing them. Until recently, at least, Finnish students received state funding for as long as they required it and even now they can take ten years to do their Masters Degree (the normative qualification) if they wish. Finnish university degrees are modular and failed modules can be re-taken as many times as is necessary to pass them. This length of degree, however, may be part of the reason why Finnish students appeared to be regarded as adults. Due to the age issue, perhaps, it is not unheard of to find married couples with a child where both partners are full-time students. The Finnish social security system means that this is financially possible because there are no tuition fees and students receive a grant. Thus, I would suggest that Finnish students are not seen, at least not clearly so, to be 'betwixt and between' in terms of their status and this relative lack of liminality is reflected in many other areas of Finnish university life such as the living arrangements and the lack of formal rituals or obligations that we note at universities such as Oxford. In general in Finland, university is also like a job in the sense that students go there during the day – on weekdays – and go home, often some distance, at night with the university facilities completely shut at weekends and late at night. This is in contrast to some American campuses where there is 24-hour access to the library. Drawing upon Oulu at least there appears to be relatively little student identity – though there is some – and many student societies do not appear to be particularly active or distinctive from the broader groups operating within the towns in which the universities are situated as will be discussed in more detail below.

Moreover, Finnish university degrees tend to push students towards a specific job which stands in contrast to the idea at a university such as Oxford – or simply the British system more broadly – where many graduate jobs will simply demand 'a degree'. By contrast, in Finland students must essentially make up their minds about a job relatively early in their degree and follow the relevant courses. Thus, if you read Theology you are either directed towards being a priest or a teacher of the subject. In this sense the element of students discovering what they want in life – at least with regard to basic career choice – while at university is less possible. To a certain extent, students must be relatively clear before they start their degrees. It is, I think, symbolically significant that there is no graduation ritual at Finnish universities at all which again implies a lack of liminality and structure. This may be partly because, for many students, university life is so extended that it may, in a sense, lose its intensity and allow time for adjustment to adult status making a ritual less necessary.

One of the few clearly transformative issues is that, like in England, many Finns must go to a new town in order to attend university. However, this is because of the nature of the departmental distribution rather than a broader tradition. The Finnish language Theology Departments in Finland are in Helsinki (in the far south) and Joensuu (in the east) meaning that many Theology students must go to university far from home. Law can only be studied in Helsinki, Lapland and Turku.

In this sense, university is liminal as some students must live quite far from home, though many of the male students will already have done so. Many students in OKO were originally from an area of Finland that is two to three hours from Oulu though I should emphasise that Finns to whom I spoke often regarded a city that was two hours away as 'near'. However, as will be discussed in relation to Oulu, the further internal structures are not conducive to a highly liminal Rite of Passage and, indeed, it would appear to be less liminal than Leiden. Also Finnish universities do not lessen symbolic social differences – as Oxford does – as they are linguistically divided with Swedish-speaking Finns generally attending the Swedish-language university 'Åbo Academy' in Turku which offers most subjects, including Theology. I would argue that, in many respects, the Finnish university system is the least liminal of those examined so far.

Oulu University as a Rite of Passage

To a great extent, Oulu University can be seen to parallel our broader description of the Finnish university system in terms of liminality. *Communitas* may be fostered, to some extent, by the way that new students have all passed a highly competitive examination to get into the university but, that said, most students I spoke to were convinced that the examinations were not difficult. As one student put it, 'If you've done okay at school you should have no problem getting into the university ... as long as you actually do a bit of work and revise for the exams'. This kind of comment was representative of the views of Oulu University students to whom I spoke about this. A similar attitude was not found towards Oxford University college interviews amongst students I spoke to there. Also once you are studying Theology at Joensuu, for example, there is little problem transferring to Helsinki at some later point and I spoke to a number of students who had started at a certain university and later changed to another one during the course of their degree.

Rites and Accommodation

There is no Rite of Separation or Rite of Incorporation at Oulu University run by the university itself. There is, however, a less structured Rite of Incorporation organised by the students from individual departments for the new students, though it is completely voluntary. New students wear their sailors' caps and 'student overalls' which might be seen to foster a sense of *communitas*. These overalls are different colours according to the department in which they are studying. The students are then taken drinking and so forth. According to many students to whom I spoke this tradition is upheld mostly by 'technology' and 'engineering' students. At Vappu new Engineering students are 'baptised' in Oulu's river for which they traditionally dress up in amusing costumes before sliding into the river in front of a large student crowd (Dutton 2006b). However, these rituals are voluntary, not attended by all students and not a matter of university structure but rather something organised by Oulu University's student-run departmental societies. Perhaps they can be compared in many ways to Leiden's 'Student Societies'. There is, in a sense then, no symbolic ceremony at either end of the often lengthy experience in order to foster *communitas*.

Equally, there are no Halls of Residence along the lines of the British or American model. Students either find their own housing with other students through advertising or, when they begin their degrees, the university might assist them in finding self-catering flats owned by the university. According to students to whom I spoke such accommodation is almost always single sex which might also be seen, to a certain degree at least, to lessen the emotional intensity and therefore *communitas* and liminality of the experience for some students. Also some accommodation may be at least a twenty minute bus ride from the university and may not necessarily be with other Oulu University students. Many students to whom I spoke had lived at various points with students at Oulu Polytechnic for example. As such, the accommodation system clearly lacks any of the structure of a college. There are no rules to abide by and, to a certain extent, university is a kind of place of work to which students travel to lectures before returning home at the end of the day. As the lengthy degree progresses, I spoke to many students who had independently found flats in Oulu with friends and others, though a minority, who had married and even had children but nevertheless were still studying. As such, the accommodation system at Oulu University cannot really be seen to foster a strong sense of 'Oulu University' *communitas* or even of student *communitas* as only the student accommodation near the university would be likely to achieve that. As already discussed, the length of the degree may also be significant in fostering a sense of student *communitas*. At Oulu, just like in Finland more broadly, an undergraduate student might be any age between twenty and thirty. This not only means, I would submit, that the university experience is less intense but also that the very idea of 'student' is simply 'a person who is studying'. The implications of the word 'student' in the UK – that the student is in their late teens to early twenties and is effectively 'becoming an adult' – is not really there at Oulu University. This would also be likely, I think, to lessen the sense of student identity.

Trauma

There is very little within the other structures of the university which would assist in fostering *communitas*. There are no student bars, for example, meaning that students generally socialise in the centre of Oulu along with people who are not students. The university system is also not particularly intense or structured which would mean that the opportunity for creating bonds through shared trauma is not drawn upon. As with other universities in Finland, Oulu University students can re-take modules that they fail as many times as they need to in order to pass. This is unproblematic partly because there are no tuition fees and the Finnish government will provide ten years of funding to complete a degree which, in theory, could be completed in five years or fewer. The only aspect of the degree that cannot be re-taken is the Masters Thesis (*Pro-Gradu*) which is given a specific mark. However, all students commented to me that unless you wish to be an academic no employer even asks what mark you received for your *Pro-Gradu.*[2] They simply want to know that you passed your degree. As such, there is very little in the way of university-induced pressure on the students. Once they are in the university, there is little pressure in terms of the need to pass a course on the first or even second attempt.

Student Identity

That said, there is some evidence of student identity at Oulu University. In purely ritual terms, there is the baptising of the new engineering students which occurs on the morning of Vappu Eve. Following tradition, a particular statue in Oulu is 'capped' – a student sailors' cap is placed on its head. There is then a student march – in which many participants wear their departmental overalls and caps – through Oulu to a certain park. In this park, students drink and picnic while the new engineering students are 'baptised' in the river. This would be likely to foster a sense of student *communitas* and there is even evidence of some structural reassertion with the departments having different coloured overalls, some groups of students having their overalls graffitied and engineering students attaching a black tassel to their sailors' caps. But other than this annual ritual – in which only a minority of students take part – there is a kind of Student Union which organises social events and has an elected student council. As a member of this group, Finnish students receive certain benefits such as half price rail travel. It is also in ultimate charge of all official student societies – such as sports societies – and is in charge of their funding. As already noted, many departments have departmental student societies which organise social events for departmental members. There is also a student newspaper at Oulu University but, though run mainly by Oulu University students, this is aimed at all students in Oulu and is available throughout the city. Though it would appear that Oulu University is not particularly liminal it can still be regarded as such to a certain degree consequently fostering some sense of student identity and *communitas.* Evidently, this can be seen in the reassertions of structure found in departmental societies and other organisations which themselves foster an internal student *communitas* through student dress, for example. However those societies that do exist are, in the main, not exclusive to Oulu University students and they do not meet frequently as many at Oxford did. For example, the Sports Societies or the university's branch of 'Amnesty International' also welcome those who are not Oulu University students. (Though there was, for example, a specific 'Oulu University Role Play' society.) In this sense, the groups might be regarded as relatively loosely structured. Despite their rituals, the departmental societies are, in effect, only drinking societies for departmental members and in that sense are far less structured than the

[2] Though, interestingly, some male students commented that they did put military service and the rank attained during it on their CVs. Some were convinced that many potential employers might even judge them according to this.

kind of student societies that we have discussed at Leiden University. Meetings of these societies are also not particularly frequent. This lack of structure would be what we would expect in a context where I think it can be argued that a high level of *communitas* has not been fostered by the overall university Rite of Passage and where the degree of liminality for many students might not be considerable when we consider their likely previous experiences and age. In many ways, this lack of structure is also reflected in Oulu University's main student evangelical group OKO as we will see below.

Relatively few students to whom I spoke had even heard of OKO and the only advertising that the group did within the university was on the university's 'societies notice board' under the university Chaplaincy's section. Their advertisement for their Saturday night meeting was alongside the advertisements for the youth and student divisions of a number of the Finnish Lutheran Church's 'Awakening Movements' such as 'National Mission'. OKO, by contrast, was broadly Lutheran and in that sense kind of aimed at all 'believers' within the Lutheran church. The students who were not involved who had heard of OKO, whom I spoke to, were a very small group (three) of relatively liberal Lutheran science students who organised a weekly Bible study in the chapel attached to the university. This group felt that OKO were relatively strict and conservative and did not accord with their interpretation of Christian belief or practice. Most students to whom I spoke, however, had never heard of OKO.

The Structure of OKO

In previous chapters I have begun with a representative sample relating to the group's religious and ethical beliefs. However, it was far more difficult to do this in the case of OKO for reasons that I will examine below.

I attended many of the group's weekly meetings over the period of a term in the autumn of 2007 and spoke to many other Christian students who had attended their meetings. The group was considerably smaller than at other universities with between twenty to thirty students attending the weekly meeting on Saturday evenings in a Lutheran church hall in the city centre. The first point we might observe is the relative infrequency of group meetings. The group met once a week for a sermon by an invited speaker, sandwiches and coffee, hymn-singing and, on some occasions, games and group prayer. In addition there was the occasional Bible study but otherwise the group met once a week only. This might be seen to imply that it was not hugely significant to maintaining the Christian identity of members which would be in line with the relative lack of *communitas* fostered by Oulu's university structure. Equally OKO, though theoretically an evangelical group, organised no outreach events themselves other than their meetings which non-Christians were welcome to attend.

The second point which would further evidence the lack of identity significance for OKO amongst those involved in it would be the patterns of attendance. Essentially, almost nobody attended an OKO meeting every week. Over a period of four weeks, for example, I observed only three people who had attended all four of these meetings. Students might attend every fortnight or even less frequently than that. Even the members of the group's Executive Committee – who were running the group – would not attend frequently. In general it appeared that they would only attend on the evenings when they were actually running the meetings. As such, a particular Exec member might attend once a month or less. The Exec was mixed between men and women though the majority of students who attended OKO's meetings were women. This relatively sporadic attendance by students would appear to further indicate that the group was not highly significant to the maintenance of identity for many involved. This in itself might imply that Christian students did not require a group to maintain their 'Christian' identity in this way. This finding would be congruous with the way in which the structure of Oulu University – and the relatively limited *communitas* which it fosters – does not expose a Christian student's (or any other student's) identity to question in a way that the structures of Oxford University might be seen to. During my fieldwork, I spoke to Christian students who might attend OKO once a month or even less frequently than that. 'It depends on how busy I am' said one student. This was a not unrepresentative remark and would again betoken OKO's lack of identity significance to many of the students involved in it.

The structure of OKO was also far looser than any of the other groups that we have looked at. Precisely because the attendance at OKO's meetings was so fluid it was very difficult to determine who was 'representative' – though I did interview the very small number that attended meetings essentially weekly. Most of those whom I interviewed were not actually paid up members of OKO. They simply attended the meetings and this was in no way problematic. Those to whom I spoke who were on the Exec were members but other students were given positions of responsibility without any test of membership or faith. For example, one female student played the piano at a number of meetings, yet she was not a member of OKO. She was simply one of the few 'regulars' and she attended around once a fortnight. The only official structural act which the person running the meeting would do would be to pass around a book. There would be a page with the title and date of the meeting and those present would be invited to write their names in it. Another sheet would sometimes be passed round so that members could be put on the group's email list if they so desired. Obviously, this stands in stark contrast to a group such as OICCU whereby joining involves signing a Declaration of Faith and whereby there is a relatively complex internal structure. Though the majority of students to whom I spoke at the meetings were opposed to the ordination of female clergy, there was no issue with female leadership as there appeared to be in a group such as OICCU which would further demonstrate a lack of differentiation and structure on the part of OKO.

Not only did most students who were at the meetings attend relatively rarely but there was no restriction on who could attend. Meetings of OICCU are open to all members of the university while meetings of OICCU College groups are open to all members of the college. By contrast, anybody could attend an OKO meeting. Some of the students were from the university, some from Oulu Polytechnic and some were just interested passers by who were Christians working in Oulu and who had been involved in a similar group when they were at university. As such, the structure of OKO was very loose. There were no rituals of membership, formal membership was a rarity anyway and, though the group was constitutionally Lutheran, all were ultimately invited to attend and become involved. Equally, there was relatively little evangelical activity despite the fact that the group was theoretically evangelical. Other than a joint event with two other groups I am not aware of any other outreach. I do not think that this is a cultural issue because, as we have already discussed, there are some highly evangelical 'Awakening Movements' within the Finnish Lutheran Church of which many of those at the meetings were actually members. In a sense, the group appeared to be the most obviously 'introversionist' of those discussed in that outreach was not a significant feature. The group was effectively a means by which Christian students and Christian young people in Oulu could meet like-minded people. The fact that many attended relatively infrequently might imply that this need to preserve identity was not high in the university context – hence the relatively loose structure of the group.

Religious and Ethical Views in OKO

As already discussed, it was very difficult to create a representative sample of opinion because of the seemingly irregular nature of attendance at meetings. I will therefore focus here on those who attended the most frequently – weekly and fortnightly. After that I will examine the less frequent attendees, including senior members.

In general, those who attended around once a fortnight were a handful of relatively young female students, in their very early twenties and late teens. These issues are important because, broadly speaking, we might expect Oulu University to be more liminal for young female students. They would not have undergone National Service, they had not taken a year out for any reason and they were, perhaps, more ambiguous with regard to their adult status than some of the older students would be likely to be. Interestingly, these regulars were all single as well and the lack of a serious relationship – which did seem to be the case – might contribute to this sense of ambiguity. It was also noteworthy that these young female students tended to be far more strident in their views on pre-marital sex and other issues than were older Christian students and especially married ones. These younger female students were usually from awakening movement backgrounds, normally from the group National Mission. Let us examine this core, female sub-group. Interviews were conducted in a combination of Finnish and English.

Suvi was a twenty-one-year-old Maths student. She was from a Lutheran background on the Finnish west coast, claimed that her parents were not 'believers' and had become a Christian on her Confirmation Camp when she was sixteen. She believed in all of the supposedly key Christian doctrines – including Hell for non-believers and the idea that the Bible is the inerrant Word of God – in the traditional sense. However, she was not sure about whether or not she accepted Evolutionary Theory. With regard to ethical views, she felt, for example, that alcohol was acceptable 'but only in a very small amount' and 'I wouldn't have it at my wedding', that Christians should dress 'modestly', that swearing was a 'bad habit' that she tried to avoid it as a Christian and that 'the Bible makes clear that sex before marriage is not acceptable'. Equally, she felt that having a non-Christian boyfriend was unacceptable. She was single and opposed to women priests, which is generally perceived to be a sign of religious conservatism in Finland. She was not a member of OKO and would attend around once a fortnight. She was from some way south of Oulu.

Elina was sitting with Suvi and attended around once a week. She was nineteen, single and also from some distance south of Oulu in the Bible Belt area, a term that we later discuss. Elina was also studying Maths at Oulu University. She had been raised in the 'National Mission' Awakening Group and was from a 'believing' background. Her views were exactly the same as those of Suvi except that she was firmly of the view that Evolution is incompatible with the Bible and she did not believe in it. Despite her relatively regular attendance she was also not a member. She had attended every week for four weeks.

Satu also attended relatively frequently. She was twenty, single and also studying Maths. She was from a Christian background and had been raised in the 'National Mission'. She was also not a member of OKO and her views were in line with those of Elina. She was one of those who had attended every week for four weeks.

The final member of this female subgroup – who attended about once a fortnight – was Kati. She was also not a member. She was a twenty-one-year-old student from Oulu Polytechnic and had been raised around two hours south of Oulu (again in the west coast, Bible Belt area) in the 'National Mission' and was therefore from a 'believing' background. Again, her views were the same as Elina's.

The other student who attended every week in four weeks was a single twenty-four-year-old male student – Pekka - who had been raised in the far south of the country in the small 'Praying Movement'. He was also studying Maths and his views were the same as those of Elina. However, he emphasised that he felt that not every member would be as strongly opposed to the ordination of women priests as he was. The only other regular during my time with the group was a Canadian international student – also studying science – who spoke no Finnish but attended the meetings and was from a 'conservative Christian' back at her university in Canada.

Thus, with the exception of this male member, the core OKO attendees were young female students. This might imply, as we would expect, that Oulu University is more liminal when a student starts it meaning that a group such as OKO might be significant to their preservation as Christians. As they spend longer at the university it may be that the experience is less liminal as they become more secure in their status and situation and attendance at such a group is less important. The older students to whom I spoke, in general, all attended relatively infrequently but some admitted that they used to attend more frequently when they first became involved. Very few of these older students, however, had ever actually been full members of the group. I tended to find that these members – in their mid to late twenties – were engaged or even married. They tended to have relatively similar views to the younger students although they were often slightly more liberal about issues such as Hell for non-believers, for example and in some cases even dating non-Christians. One such male member aged twenty-seven told me that he used to believe in Hell but now he was not quite sure while another quite senior member said that he believed that Hindus went to Hell because they are Pagans but it is possible for Muslims and Jews to go to Heaven. Older members also had slightly different views with regard to premarital sex. Here they were more inclined to answer the question in a very vague manner or simply refuse to tell me their opinion on the matter at all. It might possibly be inferred from this that they were aware of the traditional evangelical 'Christian' taboo – in Finland at least – on pre-marital sex but had nevertheless had pre-marital sex and did not wish to admit this or lie to me. However, one engaged couple to whom I spoke in their late twenties were open in telling me that they had never had sex and would not do so until they were married. This kind of change in religious opinion would be in line with the research in America by Hammond and Hunter (1984) which we have already discussed. Christian students in a not particularly liminal environment appear to become more liberal as they get older and become more educated. By contrast, they found that the opposite occurs amongst Christians at a highly liminal university. They deal with the identity challenge by becoming more stridently 'Christian'.

The majority of students who attended with any regularity were also from an area of Finland known as the 'Bible Belt' which extends south of Oulu and along the west coast towards Turku. This area tends to have a relatively large number of Finland-Swedes – though I did not meet any Swedish-speakers in OKO – and tends to be relatively religiously conservative. The high proportion of students from such areas might be seen to further demonstrate the way in which the group helps to preserve the 'believing' faith of those who are already 'believers'. In terms of the group's theology and ethical belief – therefore – the group was relatively conservative though members seemed to become more liberal as they got older. As such, the regulars tended to be younger and more conservative. However, this broad religious conservatism was reflected, for example, in the speakers whom the Exec chose to invite to meetings. These included Rev'd Vesa Pöyhtäri, the *Rauhan Sana* priest who had – at the time – just been suspended from his post and also a priest in the Oulu branch of an ultra-conservative group on the borders of the Finnish Lutheran Church called the 'Lutheran Society'. Unlike Awakening Groups, this group has its own separate churches and these do not allow women priests. However, the structure of OKO was clearly weak and this would imply, following the theory that I am propounding, that Oulu University does not provide a considerable challenge to the 'Christian' religiosity of students because it does not foster a high level of *communitas* and is not highly liminal.

Communitas at OKO Meetings

Compared to the weekly meeting of OICCU, for example, OKO meetings were not particularly structured and were perhaps the most comparable to CSL's *Dispuut Meetings*, except without the 'dispute'. Meetings would begin with a prayer led by whoever was leading the group that week. There would then be a hymn and members would go and get sandwiches and coffee. When this was over there would normally be the sermon by whichever invited Lutheran priest was speaking that week. Though this may simply be a cultural issue, as we have discussed, these sermons were never in any sense 'charismatic' or emotion-inducing. They generally appeared to be more like academic presentations of the relevant Biblical information.

After this there would be questions, then another hymn and, sometimes though not always, there would be group prayer following this. As such, there was very little opportunity – other than through the occasional group prayer – for the fostering of *communitas* in OKO meetings.

I would suggest, therefore, that OKO is congruous with what we would expect of a group in circumstances where the university level of *communitas* is not particularly high. As we would expect, the core of the group is overwhelmingly young female students for whom this part of the university experience may be a challenge to their conservative Christian faith. Otherwise, though the students that attend are relatively conservative Christians, they do not attend regularly implying that the Rite of Passage, to the extent that Oulu University is this, is not a major challenge to the faith. Interestingly, no student to whom I spoke had 'become a Christian' while at university. Almost all were from 'believing' backgrounds and those few who were not had converted at confirmation camps and were, anyway, from some form of Lutheran background. Moreover, the core attendees were those Christians for whom we might expect Oulu University to be the most liminal – young, female students from Finland's 'Bible Belt'.

'National Outreach Students'

It should be pointed out that another evangelical student group operated at Oulu University and met on Monday evenings for a Bible study at which there would be, in my experience, around twenty people of whom a large majority were female students. The group was the Oulu student division of a particular Awakening Group. We will give it the name 'National Outreach Students' as it was very small and I do not want to identify individuals. As with OKO, those who attended the Bible study varied on a weekly basis. However, the attendance was more regular than was the case with OKO – perhaps because it was not on a Saturday – with around a third of students attending regularly. The regular National Outreach attendees were exactly the same group of female students who were the regular OKO attendees. In addition to these, there was another young female student who occasionally went to OKO and was, during my research, in charge of the National Outreach student group. There were a few other National Outreach regulars in addition to this while other attendees came only every few weeks or even less frequently. The group's Bible Study took place in the front room of a particular flat in the city centre.

In many ways, this group was even more loosely structured than OKO. It had no formal membership but, as with OKO, a piece of paper would be passed around such that attendees could register that they had been there. The group also had no formal Exec, as OKO does, and no paid staff worker which OKO also had. A former leader of the group informed me that she would regularly ask people if they wanted to 'help out' in various respects and that she would happily accept the help of anybody who wished to assist. As such, the structure of the group was highly informal and many of those involved were simply Christians who were not members of National Outreach and had no background in it. She commented that they possibly preferred her group to OKO because it was smaller and more intimate, though, of course, many of

National Outreach's regulars were also members of OKO. Hence, it might be argued that attendance at National Outreach helped some students at least to meet not just other 'Christians' but other people who had been raised in the same Awakening Movement within the Finnish Lutheran Church. As such, this might be regarded as a kind of reassertion of structure. It would imply that for a certain core of Christian students Oulu University is more liminal – at least than it is for many other students – meaning that groups such as OKO and National Outreach are helpful in preserving their faith. As the former President, a female from the 'Bible Belt', informed me:

> When I lived at home I was living in a kind of bird's nest of Christianity but now I'm here at university I'm in the real cruel world and my faith has had to strengthen because for the first time I've had to debate my faith with atheists. I think God has kind of brought me to them.

As with OKO, National Outreach engaged in relatively little evangelical activity other than paying – as a group – to sponsor an Ethiopian child and organising a Christmas event at the university with free food along with the Oulu Pentecostal Youth Group and OKO.

As such, National Outreach, like OKO, is a very loosely structured student group with a small handful of regular members who we might speculate are – considering their sociological background – finding that, as Christians, Oulu is relatively liminal for them meaning that groups such as OKO and National Outreach are psychologically helpful. This would again be congruous with our theory of levels of liminality. And it is again noteworthy that as with OKO the group does not attract people who are not Christians which would imply that the university environment is not highly liminal.

Conclusion

The above analysis of Oulu University and OKO appears to add further credence to the model of liminality already outlined. For many students, Oulu University is not a particularly liminal experience. Most students are at least twenty when they begin their studies and the majority of men have undertaken the highly liminal Rite of Passage of military service. There is some evidence of student identity and structure as seen in the Student Union and departmental societies. However, in general, Oulu University does not appear to be particularly structured or traumatic and does not appear, therefore, to foster a high level of *communitas.* Moreover, it is debateable whether university in Finland is really understood as a Rite of Passage. There is at least a case for arguing that it is more like a kind of job and it is often so extended and the age range of undergraduates so wide that it becomes difficult to perceive 'students' as one group undergoing a movement from childhood to adulthood. This might be slightly easier – though still generalising – at a university such as Aberdeen or even Leiden where students effectively must finish their degree in a much shorter period of time. As with Leiden and to a lesser extent Aberdeen, student accommodation in Oulu is also not conducive to fostering a high level of *communitas* for the reasons that we have already outlined. The only area which might render Oulu more liminal than Leiden is that many students there had been raised two hours or more from

Oulu by car. In saying that, I should emphasise that the Finnish understanding of distance appeared to be somewhat different from that found in England or Holland and there was no tradition of Finnish students going home at weekends. But the other structures of the university were clearly less liminal.

As Oulu University is not highly liminal we might expect OKO to be relatively unstructured and undifferentiated in terms of belief and broader structure. To a great extent, this is what we have found. No member whom I interviewed had become a 'Christian' while at university. OKO is very weakly structured with few regulars being formal members, no tests of faith and it meets only once a week. Most students attended only occasionally and this includes, in the case of irregular attendance, even those in relatively senior positions. However, it was possible to discern a core group of 'regulars' who were generally female, relatively young, Maths students, from the 'Bible Belt' and highly religiously and socially conservative in their backgrounds – in most cases – and current belief and lifestyle. As we have seen, there is a strong case for arguing that Oulu University would be more liminal in relative terms – and thus more of an identity challenge – for such students. In line with previous research in this area, older students appeared to be slightly more liberal – often having been less so when they were younger – and attended less and, as discussed, the group was not especially evangelical or structured. This is, indeed, what we would expect in an environment that is not especially liminal and does not, therefore, pose a major challenge to Christian identity. The core of the group – in terms of attendance – are those who find university most liminal but as this change is negotiated they appear to become slightly more liberal and there is no need to stridently preserve their faith from outside attack. Oulu University and OKO is, therefore, in line with Hammond and Hunter's research and the theory of liminality which we are examining.

Chapter 8

Why Jesus Chose *that* Corridor

I began this book by looking at some of my own experiences with a student evangelical group at the highly transitional university which I attended as an undergraduate. To a certain degree, the corridor on which I lived could be understood as a kind of microcosm of Durham University at that time or, at least, as a microcosm of certain colleges within the university. Speaking to other students anecdotally it appeared that large numbers knew at least one person who had undergone a conversion experience to evangelical Christianity while studying at Durham or who had found that their original Christian beliefs had intensified.

I drew upon the example of the corridor because of the extent to which it appeared to illustrate the model of the liminal phase for which I have been arguing. As we have already observed, there are two main models of the Rite of Passage. Victor Turner's model – developed drawing upon his fieldwork in Zambia – has become known as the *Communitas Model.* He argues that during the Rite of Passage social differences between neophytes are broken down and a sense of togetherness is fostered in a phenomenon that he terms *communitas.* However in examining the variously liminal phase of pilgrimage Eade and Sallnow criticise this model and argue that there is evidence of *Contestation*; of some pilgrims deliberately marking themselves out as different from each other and even exaggerating social differences. As such pilgrimage involves a complex series of different responses and this calls into doubt Turner's assessment of pilgrimage as an example of *communitas*.

Reconciliation

The experiences on that corridor that I have already described appear to provide evidence for both models. On the one hand, there was a sense of *communitas.* This was deliberately fostered by the broader 'Durham University Rite of Passage' instructors through students living in college and thus sharing accommodation and everyday activities with people from diverse backgrounds. It was further fostered through various other rituals which involved, for example, everybody wearing similar clothes at a semi-formal dinner on the first day at university before attending a 'bop' and being encouraged to drink heavily together. Though it is relatively subjective, I would submit that compelling evidence for this *communitas* can be found in the impromptu party that developed on the first night in a particular corridor student's room. It fostered and expressed this sense of *communitas* and it was the very structure of the university – as with the very structure of the tribal initiation – that had helped to bring this *communitas* about. As we have already noted, a pilgrimage might not foster this forced *communitas* in such a way. It might well be, depending on various sociological factors, considerably less liminal and *communitas*-fostering for its participants than the kind of intense tribal initiation rituals examined by Turner.

However, fairly quickly, reassertions of the structures from outside of the Rite of Passage began to develop on the corridor and beyond. Turner, in assessing the Ndembu of Zambia, has termed these 'pseudo-oppositions' but I find this unconvincing when we think of the animosity that the Christian Union aroused at Oxford University and, indeed, Durham University. These structural reassertions related most obviously to social class differences and, in an even more pronounced form, to religious differences with a very clear and strongly differentiated Christian clique developing on the corridor. As discussed in Chapter 1, I also find the idea that the *communitas* is only 'partially realised' to be unconvincing in relation to many Rites of Passage. Our more detailed assessment of Oxford University demonstrates that the structure of the university would create – compared to other universities that we have discussed – a very high degree of *communitas*. As such evidence of structure in this context can be regarded as due to something more than just a lack of *communitas* and Hammond and Hunter's (1984) article would appear to implicitly substantiate this. The Christian Union, as a reassertion of structure, contained a high proportion of students for whom we would expect Oxford University to be the most liminal and *communitas*-inducing which would imply that we are not seeing a lack of *communitas* but something more complex. We are witnessing structure (the university), *communitas* and then a reassertion of structure within this.

As such, I would argue that the *Communitas Model* and the *Contestation Model* can be reconciled if the Rite of Passage is understood in terms of levels of structure and this, I would submit, is borne out in our examinations of the different student evangelical groups and the universities in which they operate. Focusing on Oxford University, there is a not unconvincing case for arguing, as Desmond Morris does, that England (or Britain) is a kind of highly complex version of a tribe. Of course anthropologists such as Sandall (2001, 6–8) have examined the considerable differences between a 'tribe' and a 'civilization' but pushing the analysis to its broadest I think that Morris's comparison is reasonable. Following this 'super-tribe' comparison, the English education system becomes a highly extended Rite of Initiation. The university system is a further extension of this Rite of Initiation for those who specialise to an event greater extent than others. Oxford University, as arguably England's most prestigious university, therefore might be seen to train those who are the most likely to be in highly significant positions within the tribe.

From Oxford University to Oulu University

Like the Rites of Passage which Turner examines, Oxford University is highly structured as a Rite of Passage and it is also highly transitional, marking the change into full adulthood as with tribal Rites of Initiation. For many students, it might also be seen as transitional in terms of social class. But these very structures help to foster a strong sense of *communitas* on another level as noted in the trauma-inducing examinations and the way in which the accommodation system is seemingly designed to break down social boundaries in many cases. Consequently, in this strong *communitas,* there is a lack of structure and the structure of the super-tribe reasserts itself in the form of exaggerated social differences and, indeed, highly pronounced religious differences. The latter has been observed in OICCU. As such, the group helps to preserve students as Christians in an environment which challenges their identity and it also challenges the identity of non-Christians. This highly structured group, however, is within the Rite of Initiation and thus follows the same system. Its structures foster a strong sense of 'Christian *communitas*' and, as such, there is evidence of a further reassertion of structure in relation to social class, Christian background and Christian denomination or style. Thus, we have seen structure on one level bringing about *communitas* but this very *communitas*, because of its unstructured nature and the consequent psychological difficulties that it brings about, leads to the development of a further structural reassertion and so forth. Though we have had to rely on second-hand research in relation to the situation at other highly liminal universities, the published research in relation both to transformative campus universities in the United States and St Augustine Campus in Trinidad, and the student evangelical groups operating there, evidences a similar pattern. In terms of understanding the degree to which these universities are transformative, the extent of students 'becoming Christian' while at university is noteworthy because it indicates transformation and, in some cases, a stark change in identity and a change in the students' relationship with their 'non-Christian' parents. In OICCU, students who had converted while at Oxford University – whether from 'Christian' backgrounds or not – were a large minority.

By contrast, at a far less liminal university – such as Oulu University – we see something very different. Oulu University appears to be considerably less liminal, the status of students appears to be less ambiguous, the university experience is less transformative and far less clearly a Rite of Initiation. Oulu University, in this regard, is not particularly highly structured though it is structured and liminal to some extent. Thus we see the development of OKO which, like the university, is relatively loosely structured both in terms of belief and lifestyle and in particular with regard to issues such as group boundaries and meeting attendance. It is not especially significant to the identity of students as the university system offers no significant challenge to identity for most students. Perhaps unsurprisingly, we do not find any university converts in this group. Though Leiden University and even more so Aberdeen University might be regarded as more liminal than Oulu, they are nevertheless relatively unstructured – at least compared to Oxford University – and this is reflected in a less structured student evangelical group and less structural reassertion within it. In making this analysis we have, of course, accounted for religious and social differences in the various environments. As such, assessing the university as a Rite of Passage in a variety of different cultures allows us to observe a pattern. The more structured and liminal the university is, the more *communitas* it will create meaning that the greater will be a structural reassertion on another level. Through examining the Rite of Passage in terms of levels of structure, the two models of liminality can therefore be reconciled and usefully employed.

Anthropology of Religion and Religious Studies

I think that that this model has potential for further research. Obviously there has been a school within the Anthropology of Religion which has for some time been rather sceptical of Turner's *Communitas Model* and with this research I would hope to resurrect the model, albeit in a nuanced form and combined with some of the insights provided by Eade and Sallnow. I would term the revised model the *Level Model.* Obviously, the research here examines a specific Rite of Passage – university – and focuses on a specific kind of religious organisation operating in this context. It has focused on student evangelicals because they are, in theory at least, offering a new identity in a context where student identity can be effectively under assault. However it would obviously be interesting to apply the model to other Rites of Passage – with religious dimensions – and see if it is useful in this context. University is a highly extended Rite of Passage but it would be possible to look at other Rites of Passage – such as weddings for example – employing this model. Equally, it would be possible to apply the model to the increasing study of non-religious Rites of Passage, where these are in a group context. I have already applied the model to the Finnish spring rite 'Vappu' (Dutton 2006b) and found that it is workable and leads to some fruitful results but there are many other comparable Rites of Passage to which it could be applied.

However, in suggesting that the model can be moved outside of the purely Religious Studies discipline and into Anthropology more broadly I appreciate that the model raises certain questions that I have not examined so far because the main orientation of this book is Religious Studies and Anthropology of Religion. The model assumes the usefulness of categories such as 'religion' and 'culture' and implicitly makes various other assumptions that have been questioned in Post-Modern anthropology but often go unquestioned when scholars of Theology or Religious Studies discuss Rites of Passage as part of the Anthropology of Religion within Religious Studies. Indeed, Turner's *Communitas* model is often presented or drawn upon quite uncritically in Religious Studies literature and especially that aimed at students[1] while this is not the case in Anthropology. Equally, to a certain extent at least, I am advocating a form of structural model and this perspective has also been widely criticised amongst anthropologists and especially Post-Modernists. It is, I think, beyond the scope of this book to delve into these debates within contemporary Anthropology though I would submit that the Post-Modern perspective is highly unconvincing not least because Post-Modernism (and cultural relativism) itself reflects a kind of ideology just as it criticises modernist perspectives for so doing. Also Bruce (2002, 231) notes the inconsistency of Post-Modernism in using supposedly logical argument rooted in a certain worldview to persuade people of the veracity of Post-Modernism which questions the 'rightness' of this empirical-based, 'western', 'modern' world view. This is germane to my research because some Post-Modernists might suggest that my use of the anthropological method is merely 'another world view' that is no more

[1] For example, in a book aimed primarily at Religious Studies students Douglas Davies (2002) examines Turner's discussion of Rites of Passage in depth without looking at Eade and Sallnow's critique.

valid than that of the evangelicals that I have examined. I would counter, following Sandall (2001), that my method is superior because it has empirically testable results and that even the evangelicals that I have studied at least partially accept the empirical method unless its results conflict with a belief that they regard as especially important such as, in some cases, the Genesis creation account. However, for a debate over the usefulness of 'culture' as a category in anthropology – which might also be applied to 'religion' – readers might refer to Fox and King (2002). Equally, for some persuasive critiques of Post-Modernism and Cultural Relativism readers might refer to Roger Sandall (2001) or Bruce (2002, Ch. 12). Both Cultural Relativism and Post-Modernism have a following in contemporary anthropology and anthropologists are on occasion expected to orient themselves with these debates.

Also, the model aside, I think that the above examination of student evangelism raises some points that I have been unable to explore here that would be interesting in terms of further Religious Studies research. For example, it was noticeable that while the groups tended not to engage in any considerable alcohol-use – as many student societies did – three of them organised parties relating to sweet things: there was a Chocolate Party at my college, *Who Wants to be a (Chocolate) Millionaire?* at Aberdeen University and an 'Ice-cream Party' at an American University. It would be interesting to see how common the use of chocolate and the like is in such groups. It may be that, because they forbid themselves from using alcohol and thus differentiate themselves, many student evangelicals present themselves as 'normal students' through conveying the idea – in a light-hearted way – that they also have some kind of vice. We have also seen various ways in which student evangelicals allow themselves to be childish such as by doing homework or using child-like swearwords such as 'pants' and the use of chocolate might be seen to reflect this. I think some very interesting research both into the use of things like chocolate in student evangelical groups and into the issue of childishness and purity would potentially be of great interest

Higher Education Research

Many of the ethnographies drawn upon for the discussion of American university evangelical groups had been conducted by scholars whose field of expertise was education and, in one case, 'higher education research'. I think that my own research contributes to this field by demonstrating that the structure of the university – and the degree to which it can be perceived as liminal – has a highly significant effect on the way in which students organise themselves and thus on practical issues such as student psychology.

Put simply, my research would appear to indicate that a highly liminal university such as Oxford University exposes the identity of students – to varying degrees depending on the liminality – to question and this can be psychologically difficult. As such, evangelical Christian students deal with this problem by forming a kind of clique. However, this strongly structured group would be attractive to non-Christians whose identity was under question. This is evidenced by the levels of conversion at Oxford University whether amongst students from churched backgrounds or those, in a small number of cases, with no religious background. The conversion experience itself might demonstrate not just a change of thinking but also, as we have seen, a kind of psychological breakdown which is more likely to occur at times of stress brought on by a person's identity being challenged. Indeed, the evidence would seem to imply that, in many ways, the more prestigious the university is the more likely it is to foster *communitas* leading, in England or the USA at least, to highly evangelical student groups and, indeed, conversion experience. To put it in very basic terms, one of the consequences of a working-class state school pupil excelling and getting into Oxford University may therefore be that they are more likely to become an evangelical than had they attended a less respected institution.

Within the field of higher education research, it would be interesting to examine student organisations other than student evangelicals and see if they parallel the degree of structure and *communitas* found in the broader university context and in the student evangelical group. For example, a number of British universities host a Medieval Role Play Society. At Durham University this group – known there as 'Treasure Trap' – appeared to be highly differentiated in much the same way as the Christian Union. Members would walk through town and even attend lectures dressed in Medieval clothes. They would go to forests outside Durham to engage in battles at weekends, organise Medieval banquets in full Medieval dress (where potatoes were not allowed as they had not been yet been discovered) and attend a weekly, full-costume meeting where some would speak in Middle English. Superficially at least Treasure Trap appeared to be related to the university's Pagan Society. Further research into such groups, in this context, would be highly informative. Moreover, from a purely practical perspective the model that I have outlined might assist higher education experts in predicting the kind of difficulties that students will encounter in the university environment by examining the structure of the university and, though taking into account the potential for individual differences, the problems that an individual might encounter and how liminal and problematic in terms of identity the given university might be for such a student.

Cultural Studies

Obviously my own fieldwork for this study has been effectively based around four cultures – England, Scotland, the Netherlands and Finland. In a sense this study might be seen as a contribution to the study of each culture because it demonstrates – in comparative terms – the nature of the university environment in that culture or at least of a specific university environment in that culture.

However, in general, 'university' as a broad Rite of Passage appears to be the most liminal in England and the least so in Finland. I have suggested, in my discussion of the Finnish university system, why this might be but I think that further research in this area within Finnish studies would be very interesting, though it is perhaps beyond the scope of this volume. It would be fascinating, for example, to examine whether there is structural evidence that the Finnish university experience – at Helsinki University for example – was more liminal prior to the introduction of Military Service for all young Finnish men. Historically, Helsinki University was divided between Finnish-speakers and Swedish-speakers because Helsinki University was the only university in Finland until 1918. Historical research on the effect of these structural differences on Helsinki University as a liminal phase would therefore be of considerable interest.

Equally, it might be argued that Aberdeen University itself was historically more liminal because until relatively recently there were only four major universities in Scotland, of which it was one and it was the only university in the north of the country. Indeed, the university formerly had a Rite of Incorporation which might in itself indicate that it was more liminal. The nature of the Christian Union in this more liminal historical context in relation to non-Christian students at Aberdeen at the time would, I think, be a very interesting piece of research which would further test the model that I have propounded.

Practical Evangelism

There is a discipline within anthropology known as 'Applied Anthropology'. Put simply, the basic idea is that the anthropologist should not simply observe the tribal group and attempt to make sense of it within the anthropological method. In a sense, this is regarded as kind of using the tribe without giving anything back. The idea behind Applied Anthropology is that the research should be employed in some way so as to assist the tribe that is being studied. In a sense, the research should be employed to assist in the development of the tribe. As we might expect, this viewpoint has been criticised by relativists as culturally imperialist and it has been argued that each culture is unique and should be, in effect, left alone as such. To assist the tribe in any way at all, it might be argued, is to alter the 'unique' culture (Gardner and Lewis Ch. 1). But, of course, to discover a tribe in the first place, let alone spend years studying it is, on some level at least, to interfere with the 'unique' culture. That said, working on the assumption that the social anthropologist should, in some way, compensate the group that he or she has studied I think it is possible to argue that this research achieves this in relation to student evangelicals and possibly evangelical Christians more broadly.

As discussed, each British Christian Union has a 'staff worker'. The staff worker is a full time employee of UCCF and, in my experience, a university graduate who was involved in the Christian Union at their own undergraduate university. The staff worker works with a particular university Christian Union, or a number of them, and helps to direct them. I spoke to a number of CU staff workers during my research and one of them commented on my research that, 'I think it'd actually be quite useful to Christian students ... because it kind of brings in a new factor that they can take into account.' He meant that my research was a factor to be considered when planning evangelism or evangelical activity. In that narrow sense the research might be understood to give something back, on their own terms, to the groups which have been studied.

From the Evangelical View-point

Obviously, many evangelicals might dismiss the idea that university structure is related, in some way, to conversion to Christianity or the nature of the evangelical student groups. Students become Christian, some might argue, because the Holy Spirit guides them to, God reveals Himself and they make the choice about whether or not to commit to God through Christ. I suppose it could be countered that God has chosen to somehow work through the structures of the university just as God, perhaps, chooses to reveal Himself to people when their identity is under threat. In terms of practical evangelism, the research might be seen to present a factor to be taken into account as the staff worker suggested. There is a view amongst many evangelicals that Christians, like Jesus, are 'incarnated' into a particular cultural environment. As such they must, to some extent, take into account their surrounding culture – or 'contextualise' their activities – in order to successfully evangelise. Often, St Paul is used as evidence for this perspective when he writes, 'To Jews I became a Jew to win the Jews'.[2] Following this viewpoint, it might be argued that, in order to be effective, a student evangelical group must reflect the culture of the university in which it operates and this might include the issue of the university's structure. That is to say, the nature of the university will have a significant effect on the kind of Christian Union that will be required to preserve students as Christians and to persuade non-Christian students (or help God persuade them) to become Christians. At Oxford University, a tightly structured Christian Union will be necessary and this same tightly structured group, while it may upset many students, will be appealing, by virtue of this structure, to students whose identity has come under question due to the very nature of Oxford University. Precisely because Oxford University performs this function, OICCU is in an auspicious position to engage in evangelism because of the degree to which Oxford University is liminal. As we have discussed, it is particularly liminal – in broad terms it should be stressed – for certain groups within the university, such as those from state schools who have not taken a Gap Year and who, perhaps, have little family history of attending Oxford University or other prestigious institutions. If a particular college has a large CU and is quite socially mixed then it might be regarded as especially liminal for such students so students at such a college should be especially targeted through witnessing activity.

However, by contrast, such a group would not work as well at a university such as Aberdeen. As Aberdeen University is less structured it requires a group that is, in every respect, less structured than OICCU. This is what I found at Aberdeen University. One might go further and submit that were AUCU to be like OICCU it would be considerably less successful because a group like OICCU would not be

[2] 'To the Jews I became like a Jew, to win the Jews. To those under the law I became like one under the law (though I myself am not under the law), so as to win those under the law. To those not having the law I became like one not having the law (though I am not free from God's law but am under Christ's law), so as to win those not having the law. To the weak I became weak, to win the weak. I have become all things to all men so that by all possible means I might save some. I do all this for the sake of the gospel, that I may share in its blessings (I Corinthians 9: 20–23).

what most 'Christian' students – let alone 'non-Christian' students – would require in such moderately liminal circumstances. This is more clearly evidenced at Leiden University. As we have discussed, this is even less liminal for many students than Aberdeen University and the largest evangelical group – CSL – is somewhat less structured than AUCU. Fascinatingly, there was a group at Leiden University that appeared, at least, to be comparable to OICCU and even had an OICCU member amongst its number. However, the group was very small and many members of CSL claimed that they had not joined it because it was 'too strict'. It was, in other words, 'too structured' and 'too differentiated' for these evangelical students to wish to be involved with it. CSL was far more attractive to them.

Obviously further research would be required by evangelical practical theologians to really make use of these findings and it is certainly not for me to present them in the discourse of evangelical theologians. My interest, as a social anthropologist of religion, is in testing the possibility that my research may have contributed something to the groups that I have researched in their own terms, following the presuppositions of Applied Anthropology. In a sense, it is an ethical interest. I would suggest that, to some extent at least, this research has done this by providing a 'factor' – and a means of assessing such a factor – which could be taken into account in conducting future student evangelism.

Meeting Jesus

As we have seen, there has been relatively little research conducted on student evangelical groups. In many ways this is surprising because at many universities – and particularly at highly liminal and structured universities such as Oxford and similar institutions in the USA – student evangelicals are in an ideal position to evangelise. They are surrounded by many students whose identity is effectively under a form of assault and they are able to offer a new identity to them or a stronger version of their Christian identity such that the assault can be successfully withstood.

University is, to varying degrees, a modern Rite of Initiation and a status-raising ritual. At some universities the degree to which the university operates as a liminal phase is not considerable and in these contexts we do not find a particularly large, differentiated or active student evangelical group. Instead, we find groups such as OKO at Oulu University and CSL at Leiden University. By contrast, at a university which, as a consequence of its structure, is highly liminal we find a very different kind of student evangelical group. Oxford University, and universities like it, are structured in such a way as to present a strong challenge to student identity and a group such as OICCU reacts by strongly preserving Christian identity but also by offering it to non-Christian students at a time in their lives when they are highly susceptible to it.

As such, an English school pupil from a modest background may do far more while at Oxford University than simply raise their social status in the broader society and meet students from very different backgrounds from their own. The structural nature of Oxford University means that such a student is far more likely than at many other universities to meet Jesus there and to become, perhaps, a very different person from the one they were before they began.

Bibliography

Ainsley, Robert (1999), *The Bluffer's Guide to University*, London: Oval.

Allen, Michael (1988), *The Goals of Universities*, Buckingham: Open University Press.

Anttonen, Pertti (2005), *Tradition through Modernity: Postmodernism and the Nation State in Folklore Scholarship*, Helsinki: Finnish Literature Society.

Argyle, Michael (1994), *The Psychology of Social Class*, London: Routledge.

Armstrong, Karen (2001), *The Battle for God: Fundamentalism in Judaism, Christianity and Islam*, London: HarperCollins.

Arthur, Linda (1999), 'Introduction', in Arthur, Linda (ed.), *Religion, Dress and the Body*, Oxford: Berg.

Baker, David (October 1999), 'A radical ministry of principled pragmatism: an interview with Vaughan Roberts – the rector of St Ebbes Church in Oxford', in *Evangelicals Now*._

Barbieri, Annalisa (15 November 2004), 'A Brief History of Bare Midriffs' in *The New Statesman.*

Barclay, Oliver (1997), *Evangelicalism in Britain 1935–1995*, London: Intervarsity Press.

Barclay, Oliver (1977), *Whatever Happened to the Jesus Lane Lot?*, London: Intervarsity Press.

Barclay, Oliver and Horn, Robert (2002), *From Cambridge to the World: 124 Years of Student Witness*, Leicester: Intervarsity Press.

Barr, James (1981), *Fundamentalism*, London: SCM Press.

Bauman, Kurt (2001), 'Home Schooling in the United States: Trends and Characteristics', *Population Division*, Working Paper: Series 53 http://www.census.gov/population/documentation/twps0053/twps0053.pdf.

BBC (1 November 2006), 'Alcohol now Finland's Top Killer', http://news.bbc.co.uk/1/hi/world/europe/6106570.stm.

BBC (1 June 2006), 'UK amongst worst binge drinkers', http://news.bbc.co.uk/1/hi/health/5031624.stm.

BBC (14 January 2003), '"Irresponsible" Hodge under fire', http://news.bbc.co.uk/1/hi/education/2655127.stm.

BBC (25 March 1998), 'Corporal punishment banned for all', http://news.bbc.co.uk/1/hi/uk/politics/69478.stm.

Bebbington, D.W. (1989), *Evangelicalism in Modern Britain: A History from the 1730s to the 1980s*, London: George Allen and Unwin Ltd.

Bellah, Robert (1967), 'Civil Religion in America' in *Daedalus*, 96:1.

Berger, Peter (1997), *Redeeming Laughter: The Comic Dimension of Human Experience*, New York: Walter de Gruyter.

Berman, William and Sperling, Michael (1991), 'Parental Attachment and Emotional Distress in the Transition to College', in *Journal of Youth and Adolescence*, 20:4.

Best, Amy (2000), *Prom Night: Youth, School and Popular Culture*, New York: Routledge.

Beveridge, Craig and Turnbull, Ronald (1997), *Scotland after the Enlightenment: Image and Tradition in Modern Scottish Culture*, Edinburgh: Polygon.

Bloch, Maurice (1992), *Prey into Hunter: The Politics of Religious Experience*, Cambridge: Cambridge University Press.

Booij, Geert (2001), 'English as the *Lingua Franca* of Europe: A Dutch Perspective', in *Lingua e Stile*, 36.

Bowman, Glenn (1985), 'Theoretical itineraries towards an anthropology of pilgrimage' in Makhan, Jha (ed.), *Dimensions of Pilgrimage: An Anthropological Appraisal*, New Delhi: Inter-India Publications.

Bramadat, Paul, (2000), *The Church on the World's Turf: An Evangelical Christian Group at a Secular University*, New York: Oxford University Press.

Brierley, Peter (2006), *Religious Trends 2005/6*, London: Christian Research Association.

Brown, Callum (2001), *The Death of Christian Britain: Understanding Secularisation 1800–2000*, London: Routledge.

Brown, Callum (1997), *Religion and Society in Scotland since 1707*, Edinburgh: Edinburgh University Press.

Bruce, Steve (2007), *Paisley: Religion and Politics in Northern Ireland*, Oxford: Oxford University Press.

Bruce, Steve (2002), *God is Dead: Secularization in the West*, Oxford: Blackwell.

Bruce, Steve (1995), *Religion in Modern Britain*, Oxford: Oxford University Press.

Bruce, Steve (1993), 'A Failure of the Imagination: Ethnicity and Nationalism in Scotland's History' in *Scotia*, 17.

Bruce, Steve (1984), *Firm in the Faith*, Aldershot: Gower Press.

Bruce, Steve (1978), 'A Witness to the Faith: Dialogues of Evangelicalism as Rhetoric and Reality' in *Scottish Journal of Sociology*, 2:2.

Bruce, Steve, Glendinning, Tony, Paterson, Iain and Rosie, Michael (2004), *Sectarianism in Scotland*, Edinburgh: Edinburgh University Press.

Burleigh, J.H.S. (1960), *A History of the Church of Scotland*, London: Oxford: Oxford University Press.

Bryant, Alyssa (2005), 'Evangelicals on Campus: An Exploration of Culture, Faith and College Life' in *Religion and Education*, 32:2.

Census 2001 (2001), http://www.statistics.gov.uk (British National Census).

Coggan, Donald (1934), *Christ and the Colleges: A History of the Intervarsity Fellowship of Evangelical Unions*, London: Intervarsity Press.

Conn, Walter (1986), *Christian Conversion: A Developmental Interpretation of Autonomy and Surrender*, New York: Paulist Press.

Davie, Grace (2000), *Religion in Modern Europe: A Memory Mutates*, Oxford: Oxford University Press.

Davies, Douglas (2002), *Anthropology and Theology*, Oxford: Berg.

Davies, Douglas (1984), 'The Charismatic Ethic and the Spirit of Post-Industrialism' in Martin, David and Mullen, Peter (eds), *Strange Gifts: A Guide to Charismatic Renewal*, Oxford: Blackwell.

Dearing, Sir Ron (1997), 'Report of the Scottish Committee', Chapter 2, www.leeds.ac.uk/educol.

Dekker, Paul and Ester, Peter (1996), 'Depillarisation, Deconfessionalisation and Deideologisation: Empirical Trends in Dutch Society, 1958–1992', in *Review of Religious Research*, 39:4.

Douglas, J.D. (1974), 'The Church of Scotland' in Douglas, J.D. (ed.), *The New International Dictionary of the Christian Church*, Exeter: Paternoster Press.

Douglas, Mary (1996), *Natural Symbols: Explorations in Cosmology*, London: Routledge.

Drane, John (2006), 'The Emerging Church' in *International Journal for the Study of the Christian Church*, 6:1.

Durkheim, Emile (1995), *The Elementary Forms of Religious Life*, New York: Free Press.

Dutton, Edward (2008a), 'A 'Unique Culture'? Migration, Nostalgia, Alcoholism, Suicide and Religious Revival in Finland' in *Siirtolaisuus/Migration*, 35:1.

Dutton, Edward (2008b), '*Communitas* and Contestation in a University Evangelical Group: The Liminal Phase and Levels of Structure' in *Acta Ethnographica Hungarica*, 53:1.

Dutton, Edward (2007a), 'A Shared Pre-Christian Past? Contemporary Finnish Baptism in Light of Greenlandic Naming Rituals' in *Anpere: Internet Journal of the Anthropology of Religion.*

Dutton, Edward (2007b), '"Bog off Dog Breath! You're Talking Pants!" Swearing as Witness Evangelism in Student Evangelical Groups' in *Journal of Religion and Popular Culture*, XVI.

Dutton, Edward (2006a), 'Political Correctness, Evangelicalism and Student Rebellion at British Universities' in *Journal of Social, Political and Economic Studies*, 31:4.

Dutton, Edward (2006b), 'University Students, Drunks and the Old Gods: The Finnish "Vapunaatto" Sacrifice and Liminality' in *Journal of Finnish Studies*, 10:1.

Dutton, Edward (2005a), 'Crop-tops, Hipsters and Liminality: Fashion and Differentiation in Two Evangelical Student Groups' in *The Journal of Religion and Popular Culture*, IX.

Dutton, Edward (2005b), 'Higher Status Behaviour and Status Ambiguity: A Discussion of Exaggerated Higher Status Identity at Oxford University' in *Durham Anthropology Journal*, 13.

Dutton, Edward (2004), 'Tolerant Evangelism: A Student Evangelical Group in a Tolerant Culture', in *Dutch Crossing*, 28.

Dutton, Edward (2002), 'Nationalist Socialism? The Position of the Scottish Socialist Party in Contemporary Discourse on Scottish Nationalism' in *Scotia*, 26.

Eade, John (2000), 'Introduction to the Illinois Paperback' in Eade, John and Sallnow, Michael (eds), *Contesting the Sacred: The Anthropology of Christian Pilgrimage*, University of Illinois Press.

Eade, John and Sallnow, Michael (1991), 'Introduction' in Eade, John and Sallnow, Michael (eds), *Contesting the Sacred: The Anthropology of Christian Pilgrimage*, London: Routledge.

Eidheim, Harald (1966), 'Lappish Guest Relationships under Conditions of Cultural Change' in *American Anthropologist*, 68:1.

Eisinga, Rob, Felling, Albert and Lammers, Jan (1996), 'Deconfessionalisation in the Netherlands: 1964–1992' in *Journal of Contemporary Religion*, 11:1.

Eurobarometer of Social Values (2005), 'The Netherlands', EU.

Evangelical Lutheran Church Statistics (2007), http://evl.fi/EVLUutiset.nsf/Documents/F322C5D68B64DB62C225728700454792?OpenDocument&lang=FI.

Fetterson, David (1988), *Ethnography: Step by Step*, California: Sage.

Fielder, Geraint (1988), *Lord of the Years: Sixty Years of Student Witness*, Leicester: Intervarsity Press.

Fisher, Shirley (1994), *Stress in Academic Life: The Mental Assembly Line*, Buckingham: Open University Press.

Fox, Kate, (2004) *Watching the English: The Hidden Rules of English Behaviour*, London: Hodder and Stoughton.

Fox, Richard and King, Barbara (2002), 'Introduction: Beyond Culture Worry' in Fox, Richard and King, Barbara (eds), *Anthropology Beyond Culture*, Oxford: Berg.

Francis, Leslie (1992) 'The Personality Characteristics of Student Members of the Cambridge Inter-Collegiate Christian Union' in *College Student Journal*, 26:3.

Francis, Leslie, Gilpin, Gillian and Robbins, Mandy (1999), 'The reliability of the Francis Scale of attitudes towards alcohol among student members of the Christian Union in Northern Ireland and Scotland' in *Irish Journal of Psychology*, 20:1.

Furseth, Inger (1999), 'The Study of a Reconstructed Present and Reinterpreted Past' in Helander, Eila (ed.), *Religious and Social Transition*, University of Helsinki.

Galanter, Marc (1999), *Cults: Faith, Healing and Coercion*, New York: Oxford University Press.

Gardner, Katy and Lewis, David (1996), *Anthropology, Development and the Post-modern Challenge*, London: Pluto Press.

Gennep, Arnold van (1960), *Rites of Passage*, London: Routledge.

Gibson, Ian (1978), *The English Vice: Beating, Sex and Shame in Victorian England and After*, London: Duckworth.

Gilcomston South (2005), 'William Still' www.gilcomston.org.

Gilhus, Ingvild (1997), *Laughing Gods and Weeping Virgins: Laughter in the History of Religion*, London: Routledge.

Ginkel, Rob van (2001), 'Discourses on Dutchness' in *The Low Countries*, 9.

Gladdish, Ken (2002), 'The 2002 Dutch Election' in *Dutch Crossing*, 26:1.

Goodhew, David (2003), 'The Rise of the Cambridge Inter-Collegiate Christian Union, 1910–1971' in *Journal of Ecclesiastical History*, 54:1.

Graduate Centre (2007), 'American Religious Identification Survey', http://www.gc.cuny.edu/faculty/research_briefs/aris/key_findings.htm.

Gregersen, Niels Henrik (2004), *The Gift of Grace: The Future of Lutheran Theology*, Fortress Press.

Hammond, Philip and Hunter, James (1984), 'On Maintaining Plausibility: The Worldview of Evangelical College Students' in *Journal for the Scientific Study of Religion*, 23:3.

Harris Interactive (2007), 'Poll on American Religious Belief', Harris.

Heath, Iona (21 August 2004), 'Editorial: Women in Medicine' in *British Medical Journal*, 329: 412–13.

Hebdige, Dick (1979), *Subculture: The Meaning of Style*, London: Routledge.

Helander, Eila (1986), *To Change and to Preserve: A Study of the Religiosity of Evangelical University Students and Graduates in Trinidad*, Helsinki: The Finnish Society for Missiology and Ecumenics (Helsinki University Doctoral Thesis).

Hooghe, Marc (2001), 'Borders of Hospitality: The Difficult Birth of a Multicultural Society' in *The Low Countries*, 9.

House, Julianne (2003), 'English as a *Lingua Franca*: A Threat to Multilingualism?' in *Journal of Sociolinguistics*, 7:4.

Houtman, Dick and Mascini, Peter (2002), 'Why do Churches become Empty while the New Age Grows? Secularisation and Religious Change in the Netherlands' in *Journal for the Scientific Study of Religion*, 41:3.

Hudson, R.A. (1996), *Sociolinguistics*, Cambridge: Cambridge University Press.

Hughes, Geoffrey (1991), *Swearing: A Social History of Foul Language, Oaths and Profanity*, Oxford: Blackwell.

James, William (1952), *The Varieties of Religious Experience*, London: Longmans, Green and Co.

Jones, Andrew (2004), *Review of Gap Year Provision*, London: Department of Education.

Järvinen, Tero and Vanttaja, Markku (2001), 'Young People, Education and Work: Trends and Change in Finland in the 1990s' in *Journal of Youth Studies*, 4:2.

Kaleva (30 April 2007), 'Kirkkoherra avustu Pöyhtärin sijaan'.

Keskisuomalainen (3 October 2007), 'Naispappeutta vastustavalle pastorille rangaistus', http://www.ksml.fi/uutiset/kotimaa/naispappeutta-vastustavalle-pastorille-rangaistus(13895).ece.

Kingsbury, Richard (1974), *The Realities of University Life*, London: University Tutorial Press.

Laine, Tarja (2006), 'Shame on us: Shame, National Identity and the Finnish Doping Scandal' in *International Journal of the History of Sport*, 23:1.

Lander, Patricia (1976), *In the Shadow of the Factory: Social Change in a Finnish Community*, New York: Schenkman Publishing.

Leach, Edmund (1964), 'Anthropological Aspects of Language: Animal Categories and Verbal Abuse' in Lennenberg, Eric (ed.), *New Directions in the Study of Language*, Cambridge (Mass): The MIT Press.

Leeman, Thomas (1972), *Rites of Passage in a Student Culture: A Study of the Dynamics of Transition*, New York: Teachers' College Press.

Leith, John (1987), 'Presbyterianism' in Eliade, Mircea, (ed.), *The Encyclopedia of Religion*, New York: MacMillan.

Levine, Harry (1993), 'Temperance Cultures: Concern about Alcohol Problems in Nordic and English-speaking Cultures' in Lader, Malcom, Edwards, Griffith and Drummon, D. Colin (eds), *The Nature of Alcohol and Drug Related Problems*, New York: Oxford University Press.

Lewis, I.M. (1989), *Ecstatic Religion: A Study of Shamanism and Spirit Possession*, London: Routledge.

Lewis, Richard D., (2005), *Finland: Cultural Lone Wolf*, London: Intercultural Press.

Lowman, Peter (1983), *The Day of His Power: A History of the International Fellowship of Evangelical Students*, Leicester: Intervarsity Press.

Lurie, Alison (1992), *The Language of Clothes*, London: Bloomsbury.

Lynn, Richard (2006), *Race Differences in Intelligence: An Evolutionary Analysis*, Augusta GA: Washington Summit Publishers.

Magolda, Peter and Ebben, Kelsey (2006), 'College Student Involvement and Mobilization: An Ethnographic Study of a Christian Organization' in *Journal of College Student Development*, 47:3.

Margolis, Jonathon (22 September 1999), 'Party for Jesus: How God Got Cool on the Campus' in *The Guardian.*

Mattila, Ville, Parkkari, Jari, Korpela, Heikki and Pihlajamaki, Harri (2006), 'Hospitalisation for injuries among Finnish conscripts in 1990–1999' in *Accident Analysis and Prevention*, 38:1.

McCrone, David (1992), *Understanding Scotland: The Sociology of a Stateless Nation*, London: Routledge.

McDonagh, Frank (1997), 'Class and Politics', in Storry, Mike and Childs, Peter (eds), *British Cultural Identities*, London: Routledge.

McEnery, Anthony (2006), *Swearing in English: Blasphemy, Purity and Power from 1586 to the Present*, London: Routledge.

Meiden, Anne van der (1988), 'Puritanism and the Second Reformation in the Netherlands' in Beek, Walter van der (ed.), *The Quest for Purity: Dynamics of Puritan Movements*, Amsterdam: Mouten de Gruyter.

Moran, Christy (2007), 'Public Identity Work of Evangelical Christian Students' in *Journal of College Student Development*, 48:4.

Moran, Christy, Lang, Denis and Oliver, Jenea (2007), 'Cultural Incongruity and Social Status Ambiguity: The Experiences of Evangelical Christian Student Leaders at Two Mid-Western Public Universities' in *Journal of College Student Development*, 48:1.

Morris, Desmond (1992), *Christmas Watching*, London: Jonathan Cape.

Morris, Desmond (1969), *The Human Zoo: A Zoologist's Study of the Urban Animal*, New York: Book Company.

Nash, Walter (1989), *Rhetoric: The Wit of Persuasion,* Oxford: Blackwell.

Newberg, Andrew, D'Aquila, Eugene and Rause, Vince (2002), *Why God Won't Go Away: Brain Science and the Biology of Belief*, New York: Ballantine.

Nimelä, Kati (2006), 'The quality and effectiveness of confirmation classes in Finland' in *Journal of Beliefs and Values*, 27:2.

Noakes, Ron (1984), 'The Instinct of the Herd' in Martin, David and Mullen, Peter (eds), *Strange Gifts: A Guide to Charismatic Renewal*, Oxford: Blackwell.

Nuttall, A.D. (1996), *Why Does Tragedy Give Pleasure?*, Oxford: Clarendon Press.

Nuwer, Hank (1999), *Wrongs of Passage*, Bloomington: Indiana University Press.

One News (11 December 2007), 'Three church staff fined for gender discrimination', http://tvnz.co.nz/view/page/411366/1498767.

Orans, Martin (1965), *The Santal: In Search of a Great Tradition*, Detroit: Wayne University Press.

Percy, Martyn (1996), *Words, Wonders and Power: Understanding Contemporary Christian Fundamentalism*, London: SPCK.

Rambo, Lewis (1993), *Understanding Religious Conversion*, New Haven: Yale University Press.

Randall, Kelvin (2005), *Evangelicals Etcetera: Conflict and Conviction in the Church of England's Parties*, Aldershot: Ashgate.

Rasmussen, Hans-Erik (1986), 'Some Aspects of the Reproduction of the West Greenlandic Upper Social Stratum – 1750–1950' in *Arctic Anthropology*, 23:1/2.

Reed, Bruce (1978), *The Dynamics of Religion: Process and Movement in Christian Churches*, London; Darton, Longmann and Todd.

Reicher, Steve and Hopkins, Nick (2001), *Self and Nation: Categorization, Contestation and Mobilization*, London: Sage.

Reiss, Steven (2000), 'Why People Turn to Religion: A Motivational Analysis' in *Journal for the Scientific Study of Religion*, 39:1.

Rooden, Peter van (2002), 'Long-term Religious Developments in the Netherlands: 1750–2000' in McLeod, Hugh and Ustorf, William (eds), *The Decline of Christendom in Western Europe: 1750–2000*, Cambridge University Press.

Saarinen, Satu (2005), '*My Yoke is Easy and My Burden is Light*': *Women pastors' experiences on* (sic) *their pastorhood in the diocese of Oulu from the late 1980s to the beginning of the 21st century*, Inari: Puntsi. (This is a commercially published Lapland University doctoral thesis written in Finnish and including an English language summary.)

Sandall, Roger (2001), *The Culture Cult: Designer Tribalism and Other Essays*, Oxford: Westview.

Sargant, William (1997), *Battle for the Mind: A Physiology of Conversion and Brainwashing*, Cambridge, MA: International Society for Human Knowledge.

Scottish Executive (2001), 'Analysis of Religion in the 2001 Census', http://www.scotland.gov.uk/Publications/2005/02/20757/53570.

Scottish Parliament (1999), 'Further and Higher Education in Scotland', www.scottish.parliament.uk.

SCP (Social and Cultural Planning Office of the Netherlands) (2004), 'Religious Changes in the Netherlands', Amsterdam.

Sevaldsen, Jørgen and Vadmand, Ole (1993), *Contemporary British Society*, Copenhagen: Academic Press.

Shepherd, Massey (1987), 'Anglicanism' in Eliade, Mircea, (ed.), *The Encyclopedia of Religion*, New York: MacMillan.

Shoupe, Catherine (2001), 'Scottish Social Dancing and the Formation of Community' in *Western Folklore,* 60:2/3.

Sobatka, Tomáš and Adigúzel, Feray (2002), 'Religion and Spatial Differences in the Netherlands', published by University of Groningen, www.ub.rug.nl.

Stapleton, Karyn (2004), 'Gender and Swearing: A Community Practice' in *Women and Language*, 26:2.

Stark, Rodney (1996), 'Why Religious Movements Succeed or Fail: A Revised General Model' in *Journal of Contemporary Religion*, 11:2.

Stevens, Anthony (1982), *Archetype: A Natural History of the Self*, London: Routledge.

Stoddard, Theodore (1973), *Finland: A Country Study*, Washington DC: US Government.

Stoffels, H.C. (1982), 'De Navigators: werving en training bij een evangelische beweging' in *Religieuze Bewegingen in Nederland*, 4.

Stromberg, Peter (1993), *Language and Self-Transformation: A Study of Christian Conversion Narrative*, Cambridge University Press.

Tomlinson, Dave (1998), *Post Evangelical*, London: SPCK.

Torkki, Juhana (2006), *Puhevalta*, Helsinki: Otava.

Tulviste, Tiia, Mizera, Luule, Geer, Boel de and Trygvassan, Marja-Terttu (2003), 'A silent Finn, a silent Finno-Ugric or a silent Nordic? A comparative study of Estonian, Finnish and Swedish mother-adolescent interaction techniques' in *Applied Psycholinguistics*, 24.

Turner, John (2008), *The Mainstreaming of American Evangelicalism: The History of Bill Bright's Campus Crusade for Christ*, Chapel Hill: University of North Carolina Press.

Turner, Victor (1992), 'Variations on a Theme of Liminality' in Turner, Edith, (ed.), *Blazing the Trail*, Tuscon: University of Arizona Press.

Turner, Victor (1982), *From Ritual to Theatre: The Human Seriousness of Play*, Baltimore: PAJ Publications.

Turner, Victor (1969), *The Ritual Process: Structure and Anti-Structure*, New York: Aldine Publishers.

Turner, Victor and Turner, Edith (1978), *Image and Pilgrimage in Christian Culture: Anthropological Perspectives*, New York: Columbia University Press.

Velde, Henk Te (1996), 'The Debate on Dutch National Identity' in *Dutch Crossing*, 20:2.

Visit Finland.com (Acc. 2007), www.visitfinland.com.

Walker, Andrew (1998), *Restoring the Kingdom: The Radical Christianity of the House Church Movement*, Guildford: Eagle Press.

Ward, Pete (2003), 'The Production and Consumption of Contemporary Charismatic Worship as Investment and Affective Alliance' in *Journal of Religion and Popular Culture*, V.

Watling, Tony (2001), 'The Continuing Reformation? Religious Processes and National Identity in the Netherlands' in *Dutch Crossing*, 25:1.

Weber, Max (1991), 'The Sociology of Charismatic Authority' in Gerth, H.H. and Mills, C. Wright (eds), *From Max Weber: Essays in Sociology*, London: Routledge.

Wilson, Bryan (1970), *Religious Sects*, London: Weidenfeld and Nicolson.

Winter, Torsten, Karvonen, Satrari and Rose, Richard (2002), 'Does religiousness explain regional differences in alcohol use in Finland?' in *Alcohol and Alcoholism*, 37:4.

Interviews

Dr Alyssa Bryant, Higher Education Institute, University of California (Los Angeles) (3 December 2007). By email.

Prof. Eila Helander, Department of Practical Theology, Helsinki University (16 November 2007). By telephone.

Biblical Quotations

All Biblical quotations in this book are taken from the New International Version. This was generally the version that was used by the British Christian Unions that I studied.

Index

Printed in Great Britain
by Amazon

87016628R00102